MOSES MAIMONIDES AND HIS TIME

STUDIES IN PHILOSOPHY AND THE HISTORY OF PHILOSOPHY

General Editor: Jude P. Dougherty

Studies in Philosophy
and the History of Philosophy Volume 19

Moses Maimonides and His Time

edited by Eric L. Ormsby

THE CATHOLIC UNIVERSITY OF AMERICA PRESS
Washington, D.C.

LIBRARY OF CONGRESS CATALOGING-IN-PUBLICATION DATA
Moses Maimonides and his time / edited by Eric L. Ormsby.
p. cm.—(Studies in philosophy and the history of philosophy : v. 19)
Bibliography: p.
Includes index.
1. Maimonides, Moses, 1135–1204. 2. Philosophy, Jewish. 3. Philosophy, Medieval. I. Ormsby, Eric L. (Eric Linn), 1941– . II. Series.
B21.S78 vol. 19
[B759.M34]
100 s—dc19
[181'.06] 88–18910
ISBN 978-0-8132-3078-8

Contents

Foreword vii

1. NORMAN ROTH, The Jews in Spain at the Time of Maimonides 1
2. MARK R. COHEN, Maimonides' Egypt 21
3. ARTHUR HYMAN, Demonstrative, Dialectical and Sophistic Arguments in the Philosophy of Moses Maimonides 35
4. JOEL L. KRAEMER, Maimonides on Aristotle and Scientific Method 53
5. DANIEL H. FRANK, Humility as a Virtue: A Maimonidean Critique of Aristotle's Ethics 89
6. IDIT DOBBS-WEINSTEIN, Medieval Biblical Commentary and Philosophical Inquiry as Exemplified in the Thought of Moses Maimonides and St. Thomas Aquinas 101
7. BARRY S. KOGAN, "What Can We Know and When Can We Know It?" Maimonides on the Active Intelligence and Human Cognition 121
8. JEROME GELLMAN, Freedom and Determinism in Maimonides' Philosophy 139
9. WILLIAM DUNPHY, Maimonides' Not-So-Secret Position on Creation 151

Select Bibliography 173
Index 175

Foreword

The present volume had its origin in a conference held at The Catholic University of America on October 13–14, 1985, under the dual auspices of the School of Philosophy and the Embassy of Spain, to celebrate the 850th anniversary of the birth of Maimonides. The papers by Professors Roth, Cohen, Kraemer and Kogan appear here, with some revision, largely as they were presented; Professor Hyman, who also participated, has contributed a new and different paper for this volume. Professors Dobbs-Weinstein, Dunphy, Frank and Gellman were invited to contribute original essays on various aspects of Maimonides' thought and graciously complied.

It is a pleasant duty to acknowledge the constant encouragement and support of Professor Jude P. Dougherty, my friend and former colleague at The Catholic University of America, who invited me to edit this volume. I also wish to thank Professor Antonio Ramos-Gascón, general coordinator of the Program for Cultural Cooperation between Spain's Ministry of Culture and North American Universities, for a generous subvention to assist with the publication of the volume.

Finally, I am grateful to Donna Hedge-Cormier and Elizabeth Thomson of the McGill University Library for their exemplary care and skill in the preparation of the manuscript.

1 The Jews in Spain at the Time of Maimonides

NORMAN ROTH

From one point of view, the importance of Spain in the history of Jewish civilization is apparent when we consider that Jews lived there almost as long as they had lived in ancient Israel, from the conquest of Canaan (usually dated around 1300 B.C.E.) to the destruction of the Temple by the Romans in 70 C.E. The Jews lived in Spain, as we know from both documentary and epigraphical sources, already at least in the year 300 C.E., and perhaps as early as the time of St. Paul, and remained there until the expulsion in 1492. No other country in the world has had a Jewish population anywhere near that length of time. But it is scarcely this alone which makes Spain so important for the Jews. Rather, it is the undeniable fact that every aspect of Jewish culture and civilization flourished at the highest level, and often uniquely, in Spain: the revival of the Hebrew language, poetry, literature, science, philosophy, Biblical commentary, Talmudic study and commentary, art and even music; nowhere in Jewish life, including the modern period, do we find such an explosion of culture.[1] It is for this reason that I do not like to talk about a particular "golden age" of Jewish culture in medieval Spain, for the whole history of that civilization was a golden age for the Jews.

1. For the revival of the Hebrew language, see my article "Jewish Reactions to the *ʿArabiyya* and the Renaissance of Hebrew in Spain," *Journal of Semitic Studies* 28 (1983): 63–84, and in Spanish, Carlos del Valle Rodriguez, *La escuela hebrea de Córdoba* (Madrid, 1981). On secular Hebrew poetry in Spain, my "The Lyric Tradition in Hebrew Secular Poetry of Medieval Spain," *Hispanic Journal* 2 (1981): 7–26, gives a kind of survey; for science and other cultural aspects of Jewish life in Spain, see Edwyn Bevan and Charles Singer, eds., *The Legacy of Israel* (Oxford, 1928), the excellent chapter on "The Jewish Factor in Medieval Thought," and the detailed essays in George Sarton, *Introduction to the History of Science* (Carnegie Institute, 1927), especially vols. I and II. Abraham Neuman, *The Jews in Spain* (Philadelphia, 1942; two vols.) gives a basic introduction to Jewish culture, while Fritz (Yitzhak) Baer, *A History of the Jews in Christian Spain* (Philadelphia, 1966; two vols; abridged translation from the Hebrew), with a Spanish translation, *Historia de los judíos en la Espana cristiana* (Madrid, 1981; two vols.), provides some insight into the general history of the Jews in Spain.

Nevertheless, we know that it was not all sweetness and light. In that long expanse of time during which the Jews lived in Spain, there were three relatively brief periods of persecution. One was the Visigothic period, from the sixth century until the Muslim conquest of Spain in 711.[2] The second was the invasion of the fanatical Muslim Almohads from North Africa at the end of the twelfth century; the third was the fifteenth century, which witnessed the persecution of Jewish converts to Christianity and culminated with the expulsion of the minority of the Jewish population who chose to leave Spain in 1492. The distortion of the actual situation of the Jews, and the attitude of the Christians and especially of their Catholic Majesties (Ferdinand and Isabella) toward them, needs to be corrected and is hardly properly understood by Jewish historians. One has only to read the plaintive writings of great Jewish scholars who went into exile from Spain to realize how little they "blamed" their native country, and how much they still considered themselves Spaniards. No less has the Almohad situation in Spain been distorted by most writers with respect to the extent of persecution of the Jews and the supposed destruction of Jewish life.

However, the purpose of this presentation is not yet to reconstruct Jewish history in Spain, but to attempt to draw a picture of something of the life in Muslim Spain in the period before and during the time of Maimonides.

In a recently published book on Maimonides, I noted that were he to have been born in another land, France or Germany, for instance, he would at most have become another one of those almost anonymous rabbis who wrote endless commentaries on commentaries on the Talmud. In that case, he would be of interest to no more than a small handful of Jewish scholars who specialize in such matters. Instead, this man became the greatest genius ever produced by the Jewish people. His productivity and creativity were prodigious. Merely to name the titles of all his books would take several pages. He wrote in the areas of logic and philosophy, astronomy, a complete commentary on the Mishnah, commentary on the Talmud (perhaps on both the Babylonian and the Palestinian), Biblical exegesis, language and grammar, an important multilingual dictionary of drugs, numerous medical treatises, hundreds of legal *responsa,* ethical and theological treatises, and the complete code of Jewish law (*Mishneh Torah*) in four-

2. See Solomon Katz, *The Jews in the Visigothic and Frankish Kingdoms of Spain and Gaul* (Cambridge, Mass., 1937; photo rpt. N.Y., 1970), and in Hebrew, Alfredo Mordecai Rabello, *ha-Yehudim bi-Sefarad lifney ha-kibbush ha-ʿaraviy* (Jerusalem, 1983).

teen volumes.[3] No wonder one of his Hebrew translators, Judah al-Ḥarizi of Spain, coined the expression about him, "From Moses to Moses, none arose like Moses."

Such an accomplishment could only have been possible for a Jew born and educated in al-Andalus (Muslim Spain).[4] While Maimonides certainly rose above all other Jewish scholars, he was not entirely unique. In the eleventh century, Samuel Ibn Naghrillah became prime minister and commander-in-chief of the army of the Muslim kingdom of Granada. Surrounded by other Muslim *taifas,* or city-kingdoms, which were its bitter enemies, Granada waged constant battles with her enemies every year for eighteen years. Samuel led his Muslim troops in these battles, never losing a single campaign. In the midst of this, he found the time to compose three massive volumes of Hebrew poetry and proverbs, and also to become an acknowledged authority on Jewish law and even Biblical exegesis.

One of Ibn Naghrillah's protégés, Solomon Ibn Gabirol, was writing very fine poetry at the age of sixteen. He not only became one of the four greatest Hebrew secular and sacred poets (Ibn Naghrillah, Ibn Gabirol, Moses Ibn Ezra, Judah ha-Levy), but also composed several ethical and philosophical works. His most important, an immensely difficult Neoplatonic work, became very popular among medieval Christian Scholastics in Latin translation as *Fons Vitae,* "Fountain of Life."[5]

3. Bibliographical information on the major editions and translations of Maimonides' work may be found in my *Maimonides: Essays and Texts* (Madison, Wisc., 1986).

4. It is not necessary to go into extensive detail as to the origin and meaning of the Arabic term *al-Andalus,* except that there are apparently some who are confused about it and believe that it refers to both Spain and North Africa (and perhaps even Egypt). This is not correct, for the Arabic term which did include both Spain and North Africa (but never Egypt) is *al-Maghrib,* meaning simply "the West." The term *al-Andalus* was applied only to Spain. Some derived it from the (fictitious) name *Andalus,* son of Tubal, son of Yafet (in Genesis) who supposedly settled in Spain and gave it his name, while the majority of the Muslim sources relate it to the *Andalush* or Vandals who settled there (cf. the details conveniently assembled in al-Maqqarī, *History of the Mohammedan Dynasties of Spain,* tr. Pascual de Gayangos [London, 1840] I, 17, and p. 315, n. 5. The statement by Antonio Arjona Castro, *Andalucía musulmana* [Córdoba, 1980], p. 12, n. 1, that the derivation from *Vandals* is not attested in early sources and does not appear until thirteenth-century Christian chronicles is incorrect; nor is it true that Dozy was the first modern scholar to note this etymology.) It has even been suggested that the term itself may be of Jewish origin; cf. the journal *Al-Andalus* 4 (1936): 213.

5. Ibn Gabirol's secular and religious poetry has been completely edited by Dov Jarden in several volumes, and the secular poetry also edited on the basis of another manuscript by Ḥayyim Schirmann. There is an English translation of a small sample of some of his religious poetry, *Selected Religious Poems* (Philadelphia, 1923). Some of his poems may be found in translation in various of my articles; see especially my "Panegyric Poetry of Ibn Gabirol: Translations and Analysis," *Hebrew Studies* 25 (1984): 62–

The next generation of poets included two other great masters, Moses Ibn Ezra and Judah ha-Levy. By this time, the quantity and quality of Hebrew secular and religious poetry had reached such a level that Moses Ibn Ezra was able to compose a book on the history and nature of this poetry, with particular attention to the secular verse.[6]

When we consider that well over a hundred names of Hebrew poets of Spain, only a small portion of whose work has actually survived, are known to us, and when we consider also that this was the period of the revival of the Hebrew language and the first scientific investigation into Hebrew grammar and lexicography, which profited greatly from comparative analysis with Arabic, we must ask the questions, Why now, and Why in Spain? Not long ago, I attempted to answer that question and demonstrated that this was not mere coincidence. Rather, it was a reaction to the religio-nationalist claims of the supposed superiority of the Arabic language and culture over all others.[7] The Jews themselves have very much succumbed to that theory. Until this time, all Jewish writing in the Muslim world had been in Arabic. The spoken language of the Jews was Arabic and in parts of Spain, such as Toledo, remained so through the fourteenth century.

Now, the combined efforts of linguists and philologists and poets and story writers were brought to focus on an attempt to demonstrate that Hebrew was at least the equal of Arabic as a tool of cultural creativity. In this, they succeeded admirably. The results were not merely to be seen in the tremendous growth of Hebrew poetry, but also in a body of secular literature of Hebrew fiction which drew upon some of the themes found in popular Arabic writing (called, in both languages, *maqāmāt*). There is no denying that the Hebrew stories, as

81. Ibn Gabirol's *Fons Vitae* has been published in both Latin and Hebrew translations, and there are some English and other translations of uneven quality. His *Improvement of the Moral Qualities* was edited (Arabic, rather than original Judeo-Arabic) with an English translation by Stephen Wise (New York, 1901). That there were errors in the edition became obvious as soon as it was published, and there is a real need for a corrected edition of the Judeo-Arabic text, with a new translation. There is still no significant study of Ibn Gabirol in Hebrew or in English, but see José M. Millás Vallicrosa, *Šelomó Ibn Gabirol como poeta y filósofo* (Madrid-Barcelona, 1945).

6. Moses Ibn Ezra, *Kitāb al-muḥāḍara w'al-mudhākara*, ed. (Judeo-Arabic) and tr. (Hebrew) A. S. Halkin (Jerusalem, 1975). I am preparing an English translation. On Judah ha-Levy, see my article in Frank N. Magill, ed., *Critical Survey of Poetry: Foreign Language Series* (Englewood Cliffs, N.J., 1984) II, 776–82 (the dates given there for editions of the *Selected Poems* are incorrect and were gratuitously supplied by the editorial staff, as was the erroneous statement that his famous "Ode to Zion" is called "Shirei Ziyyon"!).

7. See my "Jewish Reactions to the *ʿArabiyya* and the Renaissance of Hebrew in Spain," *Journal of Semitic Studies* 28 (1983): 63–84.

most of the secular poetry, soon surpassed the Arabic model in originality and literary quality. This genre of literature, incidentally, influenced also the development of medieval Spanish fiction (though not, as has been suggested, the Hebrew branch; rather, the Arabic was the chief source of that influence). These works are today almost totally unknown except to a limited number of experts in Hebrew literature, almost exclusively in Israel, but they are fairly commonly known among Spanish scholars and have been the subject of research for over a century. The great literary historian Menéndez Pelayo already called attention to this literature in the last century, and since then Millás Vallicrosa, Gonzàlez Llubera, Riera i Sans, Gonzalo Maeso, and many other accomplished Hebraists in Spain have contributed greatly to our knowledge.[8]

This kind of world and life which unfolds before us in this poetry and literature is confirmed for us by other sources, both Jewish and Muslim, from al-Andalus. We are, in fact, in a position to know a great deal more about Jewish life in all respects in medieval Spain, and even in the Muslim period, than in almost any other country.[9] The very houses, synagogues, and cemeteries of the Jews in Spain have often survived to the present day.

The Jews who had been severely oppressed by the Visigoths were liberated by the invasion of the Berber Muslims from North Africa who crossed the narrow straits in 711 and took possession of most of Spain.[10] What must, nevertheless, have been a small remnant of the

8. See especially M. Menéndez Pelayo, *Origenes de la novela* (in his collected *Obras* edition), throughout on Hebrew literature; Millás's already-cited book on Ibn Gabirol and his companion volume on *Yehudá ha-Leví como poeta y apologista* (Madrid-Barcelona, 1947); Ignacio Gonzàlez Llubera, "Literatura hebrea en Cataluna," Anglo-Spanish Society of the British Empire and Spanish-speaking countries, *Report and Transactions* (London, 1920), pp. 109–25, and his translation of Josep ben Meir Ibn Sabara (Joseph Ibn Zabarra) *Llibre d'ensenyaments delectables* (Barcelona, 1931) replaced only to a degree by the new Castilian translation *Libro de los entretenimientos* by Marta Forteza-Rey (both of which are better than the English translation of Moses Hadas, *The Book of Delight* [New York, 1932]); Jaume Riera i Sans, "Literatura en Hebreu dels jueus catalans," *Miscellanea Barcinonensia* 13 (1974): 33–47; David Gonzalo Maeso, *Historia de la literatura hebrea* (Madrid, 1959). Also Alejandro Díez Macho, *Mosé Ibn ʿEzra como poeta y preceptista* (Madrid-Barcelona, 1953) and *La novelística hebraica medieval* (Barcelona, 1951). This represents only some of the most important work done in Spanish on Hebrew literature and poetry.

9. For a general survey of Jewish life in Muslim Spain, but limited only to the very early centuries and somewhat unsatisfactory, see Eliyahu Ashtor, *The Jews of Moslem Spain* (Philadelphia, 1973; two vols.). While this English translation, unlike that of Baer, is not severely abridged, it is an incomplete translation of the Hebrew original. See also my "Some Aspects of Muslim-Jewish Relations in Spain," *Estudios en homenaje a Don Claudio Sánchez Albornoz en sus 90 anos* (Buenos Aires, 1983 [1984]) II, 179–214.

10. See my "Jews and the Muslim Conquest of Spain," *Jewish Social Studies* 37 (1976): 145–58.

former Jewish population—many if not most of whom had been forcibly converted by the Visigoths—was soon expanded through a constant influx of immigration from the area the Jews still called Babylon (Iraq), Syria, and North Africa. This coincided with a similar influx of Muslim immigration from those countries.

The result, for both the Muslim and the Jewish communities of Spain, was a cosmopolitan and highly sophisticated culture. Until the restoration of the ill-fated caliphate of Córdoba under ʿAbd al-Raḥmān III in 929, the Muslims of Spain had really been dependent politically and culturally on the official center of Muslim life at Baghdad. Now they at last attained independence. The Jews, too, depended on the academies (*yeshivot*) and their heads, called *geonim*, in the same region near Baghdad to determine their life according to Jewish law in all areas: religious, social, and economic. Jewish communities and individual scholars of Spain sent their requests for answers to legal problems and for copies of books to the Babylonian scholars, but increasingly in the tenth and early eleventh centuries there was a tendency toward independence from these Babylonian centers of learning. It is not unlikely that this growing movement toward Jewish self-sufficiency in religious and social control in Spain, which coincides with that of the independence of the Muslims of al-Andalus from Baghdad, was to an extent influenced by the latter. Certainly it was no longer politically wise for the Jews to be seen as having such close ties with hostile Baghdad. Another factor, of course, was the constant growth of learning and the development of scholarship and academies of learning also among the Jews of Spain.

Significantly, it was during the reign of ʿAbd al-Raḥmān III that we find the first important Jewish official, a vizier at the court, who also played a leading role in developing indigenous Jewish culture in Spain. This man, Ḥasdai Ibn Shapurt, is one of the most fascinating figures in medieval Jewish culture. He supported Talmudic learning and the establishment of the first academies in Spain, served as a patron for the earliest Hebrew poets and grammarians, sponsored and perhaps personally had a hand in the Arabic translation of the famous Greek pharmaceutical work of Dioscorides, and established the first contact with the kingdom of the Khazar converts to Judaism in the Crimea. He was also the first Jew living in Muslim Spain of whom we know that he had frequent contact also with Christian rulers. His position at the court of the caliph of Córdoba was something like that of a secretary of state for foreign diplomatic missions, from Constantinople, Italy, the Holy Roman Emperor, and the Christian rulers of northern Spain. Arabic, of course, was totally unknown to these Christian rulers and their diplomats, but they sent Jewish envoys who communicated with Ḥasdai, presumably in Hebrew, and he translated their messages into Arabic and negotiated on behalf of his king.[11]

Córdoba was certainly, as it still is, one of the loveliest cities of the world. Glowing golden in the sunset, its inner administrative capital area was called the "golden city." The hills surrounding the city were covered with all kinds of flowers, which belonged to the public and which they picked to decorate their homes in the charming manner still seen today in Spain.

It is extremely difficult to estimate population figures for the medieval period with any hope of accuracy. Certainly that of Muslim Córdoba has been wildly exaggerated—as high as 500,000 according to some medieval sources, and over a million in the tenth century according to some modern writers. The city could never, of course, have contained a population anywhere near these figures. It is even more hazardous to attempt to guess the Jewish population in the cities of Spain. Ashtor, who made an effort to do so, has usually erred on the conservative side. He suggested that close to a thousand Jews lived in the southwest section of the city, but there was another Jewish quarter in the northern part, and we know also that there were Jews living mingled with Muslims in other neighborhoods. In short, if we were to at least double Ashtor's estimate we might not be far off.[12]

What is of importance is not the number of Jews, but the conditions under which they lived. They were not restricted to any particular section or quarter, or at least there is no evidence in either Muslim or Jewish sources to suggest that they were. If the majority of Jews seemed to prefer a certain area, often the southwestern section of a city, this is for reasons unknown to us. We have the evidence of many interesting sources, for example, the famous *Dove's Neck Ring*, or book on love, of Ibn Ḥazm, who grew up in Córdoba and was an acquaintance of Samuel Ibn Naghrillah when the latter lived there, that Jews lived and worked freely among the Muslims. Indeed, there are almost as many favorable references to Jews in Spanish Muslim sources as

11. Some information, not without error, on Ḥasdai will be found in vol. I, chapter 5, of Ashtor, *Jews of Moslem Spain*; see also Baer, *Jews in Christian Spain*, vol. I. On the Khazar kingdom, the definitive study is that of D. M. Dunlop, *The History of the Jewish Khazars* (Princeton, 1954). Needless to say, a recent book called *The Thirteenth Tribe* by a popular novelist is totally devoid of historical value.

12. The best work on Muslim population of al-Andalus is, of course, that of Leopoldo Torres Balbás—e.g., "Extensión y demografía de las ciudades hispanomusulmanes," *Studia Islamica* 3 (1955): 35–59, and numerous other studies, generally reprinted in his *Ciudades hispanomusulmanes* (s.l.s.a. [Madrid, 1971?]). Ashtor's guesses were put forth in a Hebrew article on "The Number of Jews in Muslim Spain," *Zion* 28 (1963): 34–52.

there are negative ones. Ibn Ḥazm was something of an exception in this regard, because when he reached adulthood, and after the bitter civil war of 1015–1016 which ended in the destruction of much of Córdoba and terminated the independent caliphate, he became a fanatical theologian and judge and wrote a bitter polemic against his former friend Ibn Naghrillah. Of course, this was brought on not only by the fact that Ibn Naghrillah was serving as prime minister of a Muslim kingdom, but that he had dared to write a book attacking the Qur'ān. Ibn Ḥazm's more famous encyclopedic work on the history and doctrines of religions is devoted also largely to attacking Judaism, ancient and modern. Bitter as its denunciation is, however, it is not often inaccurate and is based on a careful reading in Hebrew of the Bible and even the *midrash* and some rabbinical writings.

Knowledge of Hebrew was not entirely uncommon among Muslims of Spain, in fact. Only in part can this be explained by the conversion of some Jews to Islam, for instance, Samau'al al-Maghribī, probably born in Spain, where his father was hardly a "minor" poet, as his editor claimed, but rather one of the more important. Incidentally, Samau'al's polemic against the Jews, *Ifḥām al-yahūd,* is influenced on almost every page by Ibn Ḥazm, and I have elsewhere attempted to demonstrate that Maimonides not only knew the work, but refuted it in part in his famous "Letter to Yemen."[13]

In addition to converts, however—and this is especially true of those such as Ibn Ḥazm who lived in a period when conversion of Jews to Islam on any significant scale was still almost unknown—the usually cordial relations between Jews and Muslims and the very close similarities of the two religions must have encouraged the desire of Muslim scholars to read the Scriptures in Hebrew, just as most Jews knew the Qur'ān. Maimonides himself not only cited the Qur'ān but drew some of his concepts from it.

One of the most reliable sources we have for the history of Muslim Spain, that of the North African geographer al-Idrīsī, states that Córdoba extends from east to west for a distance of three miles, and that the distance from the *Bāb al-qanṭara* ("gate of the bridge") to the *Bāb al-yahūd* ("gate of the Jews") in the north is one mile.[14] The adminis-

13. Samau'al al-Maghribī, *Ifḥām al-yahūd,* ed. and tr. (English) Moshe Perlmann (New York, 1964). Moses b. Maimon (Maimonides), *Epistle to Yemen* ed. and tr. (English, sometimes inaccurately) A. S. Halkin and Boaz Cohen (New York, 1952). Neither Perlmann nor the editors of Maimonides guessed at the influence of Ibn Ḥazm or of Samau'al on Maimonides, or of that of Ibn Ḥazm on Samau'al.

14. Abū Muḥammad Ibn Idrīs al-Sharīf, called "al-Idrīsī," *Description de l'Afrique et de l'Espagne,* ed. and tr. R. Dozy and M. J. de Goeje (Leiden, 1866), text, p. 208 (Arabic text rpt. in *Geografía de España,* ed. Antonio Ubieto Arteta [Valencia, 1974], p. 57).

trative capital, *Madīnat al-Zāhira,* was established near Córdoba itself by al-Manṣūr, the prime minister of Hishām II, in 978–79. There he built his magnificent palace, which was soon surrounded by the homes of courtiers and dignitaries. It was this famous city, to the east of Córdoba and not the west as some writers have erroneously stated,[15] which was totally destroyed and burned in the civil war which broke out in 1009.

Following al-Manṣūr, his son al-Muẓaffar took control until his death in 1008, when his brother ʿAbd al-Raḥmān, called Sanchul, ruled for a brief period until Muḥammad ibn Hishām, great-grandson of ʿAbd al-Raḥmān III, proclaimed himself caliph in 1009. The father of Ibn Ḥazm served as vizier to all of these rulers until the accession of Muḥammad II, when he apparently fell out of favor and left his home in *Madīnat al-Zāhira* and moved back to his family home on the west side of Córdoba. It is apparently here that the young Ibn Ḥazm became acquainted with Jews, and we may surmise that there were few if any Jews living in the administrative capital itself.

So important was the Jews' population of Córdoba, even after the civil war brought about by Muḥammad's claim to the title, that a fifteenth-century Jewish chronicler (Joseph ibn Ṣaddiq of Arévalo) could even claim that Córdoba was "entirely Jewish" in the Muslim period. He may have been confused by the apparent existence of a suburb of Córdoba, called *al-Isālah,* where the Almohad ruler Abū Yūsuf Yaʿqūb exiled Averroes when he became angry with him, and which a thirteenth-century Muslim historian tells us was "formerly inhabited by Jews." On the other hand, I have found no name even resembling this in the Muslim geographical sources, and I suspect it may be a misprint for Alyūsana (Lucena), which could conceivably be called "close to" Córdoba, especially by a writer with no first-hand acquaintance with Spain.[16]

This claim must, in any event, take its place among the numerous legendary references to supposedly totally Jewish cities in Muslim Spain. The list of these simply includes all the major communities

15. E.g., Rafael Castéjon, "Medina Zahira, una Córdoba desparecida y misteriosa," *Boletín de la Real Academia de Ciencias, Bellas Letras y Nobles Artes de Córdoba* 3 (1924): 151–74; cf. the more accurate account of Leopoldo Torres Balbás, "Al-Madīna al-Zāhira, la ciudad de Almanzor," *Al-Andalus* 21 (1956): 353–59. It is unfortunate that Torres did not utilize the important information provided by Ibn Ḥazm, nor that of Muḥammad ibn ʿAbd al-Munʿim al-Ḥimyarī, *Kitāb al-rawḍ al-miʿṭār,* ed. E. Lévi-Provençal (Leiden, 1938), p. 80, where he also states that it was to the east of Córdoba.

16. "*Qiṣṣur zekher la-ṣaddiq,*" ed. Adolph Neubauer, *Medieval Jewish Chronicles* (Oxford, 1887) I, 93. The account concerning Averroes is by Ibn Abī ʿUṣaybiʿa, found in Aḥmad ibn Muḥammad al-Maqqarī, *The History of the Mohameddan Dynasties in Spain,* tr. Pascual de Gayangos (London, 1840–43), I, Appendix A, p. xix (not in the Arabic text).

where Jews lived, such as Lucena, Seville, Granada, and even Tarragona and Barcelona! That Muslim writers, followed later by some Jewish ones, could be so gullible only shows again the significant impact which Jewish culture had upon the Muslims, as well as the converse.

While Córdoba was thus first made famous because it was the seat of the Andalusian caliphate, a remarkable city where Muslims and Christians shared the great mosque for their respective services (Fernando III showed no such toleration when, upon reconquering the city in 1236, he immediately placed a cross on the same mosque and converted it into a church, just as Alfonso VII had done in 1146 when the city was first conquered by the Christians), it became and remained famous largely because of the two philosophers who were undoubtedly its most famous sons: Ibn Rushd (Averroes as he was known to the Latin West) and Mūsā b. Maymūn (Maimonides). Thus, a fifteenth-century writer and chronicler, Fernán Pérez de Guzmán, of an aristocratic family, wrote in his praise of famous men of Spain:

> The pagan Averroes, his commentary [on Aristotle] pleases us; so also the learned Egyptian Rabbi Moses [Maimonides], who remembers the Spanish kingdom; truly not in vain did he call Córdoba another Athens.[17]

In fact, Maimonides never made such a statement, but as I have shown elsewhere, he always regarded himself not an "Egyptian," but a Spaniard and spoke in glowing terms of his native country and its inhabitants.[18]

But if Maimonides did not characterize Córdoba as another Athens, it is a description not wide of the mark. The Muslims, particularly in the former Persian empire, inherited a cultural tradition which can only be described as remarkable, and which today we unfortunately can only appreciate in part, since much of it is lost. More than a little has been written about the transmission of Greek science, medicine and philosophy to the Muslim world, but almost nothing has been done on the very important influences of ancient India, Persia, Babylon and Egypt on Muslim civilization. When we read the beautifully prepared edition of Abraham Ibn Ezra's Latin astronomical tables, prepared by the great Spanish scholar Millás Vallicrosa, we find constant references to these ancient sources, many of which remain only names to us, and concerning the others we have only vague infor-

17. *Loores a claros varones de España* (N.B.A.E. 19, p. 238).

18. *Maimonides: Essays and Texts*, p. 139 ff., "Maimonides as Spaniard" (paper presented to I Congreso Internacional sobre la vida y obra de Maimónides, Córdoba, Sept. 8–11, 1985).

mation.[19] In the writings of Maimonides himself, there are references like these, which scholars have for the most part ignored. In the margins of my copies of his works, I have been able to trace the nature of some of these sources, but by no means all. What Maimonides said of the culture of the Jews prior to his own period, that many books had been written which were lost and whose nature were unknown, can be multiplied for us today a thousandfold with regard to the wisdom of ancient civilizations.[20] The greatest single loss for the history of culture, the destruction of the library of Alexandria, was almost repeated in the fifteenth century when the fanatical Cardinal Cisneros of Spain burned most of the remaining Arabic manuscripts which survived in his land.

The ideal of education in the medieval Muslim and Jewish world, particularly in Spain, is something which we can only envy. It was an ideal, nevertheless, which was attained in practice and not just advocated in theory. Following Aristotle, all knowledge was divided into two categories: practical and theoretical. (It is, incidentally, one of the more unfortunate results of medieval Latin translation that the Arabic term *ʿulūm* was rendered in Latin as "sciences," which despite its broader meaning came to have a more narrow focus in its English equivalent.) It was considered absolutely necessary to acquire a mastery of all the knowledge of both types.

Of course, we must hasten to add that there was often a discrepancy between the ideals of education and the reality, at least for the lower classes who could seldom afford the prolonged and intensive kind of study available to the aristocracy. It is surprisingly difficult to obtain a significant amount of contemporary or near contemporary information on education in Muslim Spain. Nevertheless, the scarce source material that is available provides a contradictory picture. For example, al-Marrākushī says that the Almohad ruler Abū Yaʿqūb Yūsuf (1163–84) had studied languages since the days when he governed Seville for his father, and that he found there "philologians, grammarians, exegetes of the Qur'ān." He further praises the ruler for pronouncing the Arabic of the Qur'ān correctly, obviously not a common characteristic among the Muslims of al-Andalus (as it is not among Muslims today), as we know from other sources. On the other hand, the same historian reports a statement he found in the "annals

19. Abraham Ibn Ezra, *El libro de los fundamentos de las tablas astronomicas*, ed. José Ma. Millás Vallicrosa (Madrid-Barcelona, 1947).

20. See, e.g., Moses b. Maimon, *Guide of the Perplexed*, tr. Shlomo Pines, p. 175 (I, 71) and p. 276 (II, 11). On this notion of lost ancient Jewish wisdom, see my "The 'Theft of Philosophy' by the Greeks from the Jews," *Classical Folia* 22 (1978): 53–67.

of the history of Córdoba" (what wouldn't we give if these had survived?) that seventy women were kept busy there writing copies of the Qur'ān in the elaborate and difficult *kūfī* script.[21] We may be inclined to be somewhat skeptical about this statement; however, learning among Muslim women in Spain is attested by the relatively large number of women poets. There is also the famous passage in Ibn Ḥazm where he relates that he was raised as a youth only among women, who taught him the Qur'ān, poetry, and calligraphy.[22]

Christian education, it should be noted, also flourished in Muslim Córdoba. According to an apparently authentic text, there was even a kind of university there in the tenth century (unnoticed by all the historians of medieval learning, this may have been the first such medieval institution), in which the martyrs St. Amador de Tucci, St. Fandila de Acci, and St. Sisenado Pacense studied. The more famous St. Eulogio introduced the study of Latin, previously neglected by Mozarabic Christians, there.[23]

Muslim boys, and undoubtedly Jews as well, began their religious schooling at five to seven years of age and even earlier. Schools for such young children were not in the mosque, for fear of their defiling their clothes in a religious place, but rather in the bazaar or public street. Among the specific things which Muslim teachers were instructed they must avoid were writing charms in *Hebrew* and taking presents of money or special food on Jewish holidays. This is important further evidence, if any were needed, that Jewish boys were sent to study also with these Muslim teachers. There was, however, a theoretical prohibition against sending Muslim children to Christian schools to learn arithmetic, or accepting Jewish children to learn Arabic.[24] In spite of this, we know that Jews did learn Arabic from Muslim teachers.

Normally, instruction in Spain began with Arabic language and po-

21. ʿAbd al-Wāḥid al-Marrākushī, *Kitāb al-muʿjib fī talkhīṣ akhbār al-maghrib*, ed. R. P. Dozy (Leiden, 1881), p. 270. For the *kūfī* script, see the examples in the *Cambridge History of Iran*, vol. 4, following p. 352, Plates 15, 24; and see M. Ocana Jiménez, *El cúfico hispano y su evolución* (Madrid, 1970).

22. Abū Muḥammad ʿAlī b. Aḥmad Ibn Ḥazm *Ṭauq al-ḥamāma*, ed. and tr. Léon Bercher (Alger, 1949), p. 126 (text), p. 127 (tr.); *El collar de la paloma*, tr. E. García Gómez (Madrid, 1952), p. 144; *The Ring of the Dove*, tr. A. J. Arberry (London, 1953), p. 101. (Bercher's text and translation are the best of many; Garcia's Spanish translation is good; Arberry's English translation is very poor.)

23. Enrique Flórez, ed., *España sagrada* (Madrid, 1747), 10, 261.

24. Most of this can be found in Arthur S. Tritton, *Materials on Muslim Education in the Middle Ages* (London, 1957), which should be supplemented by the important studies of George Makdisi, such as "Muslim Institutions of Higher Learning in Eleventh-Century Baghdad," (London University) *Bulletin of the School of Oriental and African Studies* 24 (1961): 1–56.

etry (indeed Ibn al-ʿArabī, 1076–1148, complained that these disciplines were often studied to the exclusion of other subjects[25]), then arithmetic, the Qur'ān, principles of religion, law, logic and religious tradition. There was no *madrasa,* or so-called university, in Spain until the late fourteenth century, when one was built in Granada. Thus, the majority of the advanced students who went on to become scholars studied privately with learned individuals both in Spain and in other Muslim countries. Many of the important Muslim scholars had an impressive list of "masters" under whom they had studied various subjects and from whom they received the *ijāza,* or written license to teach what they had learned. An interesting example is one fourteenth-century Muslim scholar in Spain who studied with no fewer than 104 masters, and yet he had only seven students of his own. One of these, however, the great Ibn al-Khaṭīb, was more famous than all of the 104 masters together.[26]

Advanced education, beyond the elementary religious education which for the Jew included the learning of both Arabic and Hebrew, the Bible and the Qur'ān, meant that one was required to master arithmetic, algebra, geometry (Euclidean and non-Euclidean), trigonometry (which was known not only in Arabic treatises, but in the Hebrew work of Abraham b. Ḥiyya of Barcelona), astronomy, physics, optics, logic, and then Greek and Muslim philosophy. This included the study of all the work of Aristotle; most of Plato, Alexander of Aphrodisias, Themistius, Ibn Sīnā (Avicenna), al-Fārābi, al-Ghazālī; and the Spanish Muslim philosophers such as Ibn Bājja and Ibn Ṭufayl. One's study then culminated, almost invariably, in pharmacology and medicine.

Certainly, we must not go to the extreme of assuming that every Jew or even most of them in Spain received such a rigorous education. Nevertheless, we have incontrovertible proof that quite a significant number did so. This can be easily confirmed simply by reading the numerous works produced by the Jews of Muslim Spain dealing with all these areas of study, very often several volumes on different sub-

25. Juan Vernet, *La cultura hispanóarabe en Oriente y Occidente* (Barcelona, 1978), p. 34: a seminal study by the major scholar of medieval Muslim culture and science in Spain.

26. Muḥammad b. Aḥmad Ibn Marzūq (1310–79), *El Musnad,* tr. from MSS María J. Viguera (Madrid, 1977), pp. 26–34, gives the list of teachers. For the *madrasa,* see Tritton, *Materials on Muslim Education,* pp. 106–7. Al-Maqqarī also confirms that no official schools existed in al-Andalus (*History of Mohammedan Dynasties* I, 140–41). However, for the *madrasa* which did exist in Granada, see L. Seco de Lucena, "El ḥayib Riḍwān, la madraza [sic] de Granada," *Al-Andalus* 21 (1956): 289–96. A slightly earlier one also existed in Málaga; cf. María Jesús Rubiera Mata, "Datos sobre una 'madrasa' en Málaga anterior a la Naṣrī de Granada," *Al-Andalus* 35 (1970): 223–26.

jects from the hand of one man. Several of the Hebrew poets, for example, earned their livings by practicing medicine, and all were well educated in the sciences and astronomy. Education was of primary importance in the Jewish community always, and we possess a number of treatises on the subject, as well as the personal testimony of those who studied these subjects.

Maimonides himself wrote in the *Guide* (I, 34) that a proper understanding of the difficult philosophical notions he proposed to discuss could only be attained after sufficient preparation of the preceding disciplines, and that in particular, knowledge of God can only be acquired through study of natural sciences; and these and similar observations recur frequently throughout his writings, such as the *Mishneh Torah,* his *responsa,* and his *Eight Chapters on Ethics.*[27] He also wrote in the dedicatory letter to his student for whom he wrote the *Guide*—who, of course, was Joseph Ibn Shimʿon of Ceuta, and not, as is still frequently said, Joseph Ibn ʿAqnin of Barcelona—that he, Maimonides, had personally instructed him in mathematics and astronomy.

Maimonides gives us only fleeting references to some of those with whom he himself studied. In *Guide* II, 9, he says that he knew the son of Jābir Ibn Aflaḥ of Seville, the celebrated astronomer whose abridgment of Ptolemy's *Almagest* was also translated into Hebrew.[28] Yet Maimonides incorrectly states there that Ibn Aflaḥ concurred with Ptolemy on the subject under discussion, whereas in fact he disagreed with him. Maimonides also says that he studied under one of the students of Ibn Bājja, and of course the influence of Ibn Bājja on Maimonides has been in part examined, particularly with regard to political philosophy and the concept of perfection.[29]

Indeed, the names cited by Maimonides in his work read like a *Who's Who* of classical and Muslim philosophy and science: Plato and Aristotle, of course; but also Alexander of Aphrodisias, Themistius, John Philoponus, Euclid, Ptolemy, Pythagoras, and almost all of the Muslim

27. Further details on these subjects, including translations of some of the important passages, may be found in my *Maimonides: Essays and Texts.*

28. See Sarton, *Introduction to the History of Science* II, 1, pp. 206 and 296 (that Sarton confused the name of Maimonides' student was then understandable; it is less forgivable for more contemporary scholars).

29. Lawrence Berman, *Ibn Bajjah and Maimonides: A Chapter in the History of Political Philosophy* (Hebrew, with English summary; Jerusalem, Hebrew University dissertation, mimeographed, 1959); Alexander Altmann, "Ibn Bajja on Man's Ultimate Felicity," *Harry A. Wolfson Jubilee Volume* (Jerusalem, 1965) I, 47–87, and his "Maimonides' Four Perfections," *Israel Oriental Studies,* vol. 2, p. 15 ff. (cf. on this my "Attaining 'Happiness' [Eudaimonia] in Medieval Muslim and Jewish Philosophy," *Centerpoint* 4 [1981]: 21–32).

philosophers (besides the places where names are specifically cited, there are numerous instances of influence without specific citation).[30]

To turn our attention again to the political and historical climates of al-Andalus at the time of Maimonides, the generally idyllic situation of the Jews changed significantly with the Almoravid invasion from North Africa. The exact date is a matter of debate in the Muslim sources, but probably 1090, confirmed also by the usually reliable Christian chronicler and archbishop of Toledo, Rodrigo Jiménez de Rada.[31]

However brutal the Almoravids may have been in their campaigns against the Christians in Spain, they certainly were not "barbarians" as the renowned Islamicist Dozy called them.[32] True, they could be fanatically intolerant of philosophical notions with which they disagreed, and Muslim sources repeatedly relate that the second ruler, ʿAli b. Yūsuf, burned the work of al-Ghazālī.[33] They also attempted, unsuccessfully, to banish boy prostitutes from Seville, and to institute puritanical sexual reforms in general. Nevertheless, poetry and literature continued to flourish. If the rigid and discriminatory regulations against both Christians and Jews in Seville, which have been preserved in an Almoravid manual, were actually enforced, then life for the *dhimmis* (the so-called protected minorities) must have been rather grim.[34] Yet, as is the case with most legal codes, we should not take these too literally.

We know, for instance, of a Jewish tax collector in Seville who was removed from his post when the Almoravids took control, then became involved with a dispute with a Jewish merchant who defrauded him. He took his case to the Muslim judge of Seville, who demanded an oath from the merchant in accord with Jewish law. When this was refused, the judge ordered the matter turned over to the Jewish officials for action. The fact that a Muslim judge was perfectly willing to decide a case involving two Jews in accord with Jewish law, and that he cooperated with the officials of the Jewish community of Seville, is

30. See, for example, the chapter "Maimonides and Some Muslim Sources" in Roth, *Maimonides: Essays and Texts.*

31. Muslim chronicles give various dates; the *Annales Toledanos* (ed. Flórez, *Espana sagrada* XXIII) I (erroneously there, II), 385, has 1086; Jiménez de Rada, *Historia Arabum* in his *Opera* (Valencia, 1968), p. 282.

32. On Dozy's judgment, and Codera's refutation, see Ambrosio Huici Miranda in his edition of Ibn ʿIdhārī, *al-Bayan al-mugrib* [sic] *nuevos fragmentos* (Valencia, 1963), p. 137, n. 14.

33. Al-Marrākushī, *Kitāb al-muʿjib*, tr. E. Fagnan (Alger, 1893), p. 149.

34. Muḥammad b. Aḥmad Ibn ʿAbdūn, *Seville musulmane au début du XII siècle,* tr. E. Lévi-Provençal (Paris, 1947), p. 149 ff.; a partial English translation, with some inaccuracies, by Bernard Lewis, *Islam* (New York, 1974) II, 162–65.

significant.[35] Nor was this by any means the only case, as we learn from the (admittedly scarce) rabbinical *responsa* from the period, when Muslim courts were voluntarily sought by Jews. In fact, routinely the rabbis ruled that documents written in Arabic and made in Muslim courts were valid.

There was scarcely any sort of general collapse of Jewish life and culture in this period. On the contrary, poetry and literature, science and philosophy, flourished during this time perhaps to an unparalleled degree.

Far more serious was the threat posed by the more fanatical Almohads, who invaded Spain in 1145 but did not gain effective control until 1163. Abū Yaʿqūb Yūsuf, the first Almohad ruler in Spain (1163–84), is reported to have ordered the seizure of the library of a scholar in Seville; yet we must consider, on the other hand, the apparently reliable testimony concerning the love of learning shown by this ruler later in his career and the fact that two great philosophers, Ibn Bājja and Ibn Ṭufayl, were attached to his court.[36]

Jewish historians have all too often held to the erroneous view that the Almohad period was a disaster and tragedy in Jewish history, when Jews throughout North Africa and al-Andalus were forced to convert to Islam or be annihilated. It has even been suggested, by scholars who ought to know better, that Maimonides himself converted to Islam, although this false report was exposed as such many years ago.[37] What Salo Baron has aptly called the "lachrymose conception" of Jewish history is no more evident than in the picture usually presented of the Almohad persecutions, and, of course, even more in the interpretation of the events of the fifteenth century in Spain and the expulsion of the Jews. Medieval Jewish sources dealing with tragic events

35. Isaac al-Fasi, *She'elot u-teshuvot*, ed. David Rotstein (New York, 1975), No. 33, pp. 103–08 (since this book is very rare, apparently only available at Yale, I give also the page numbers).

36. Al-Marrākushī, *Kitāb al-muʿjib*, ed. Dozy, p. 171; tr. Fagnan, p. 206.

37. This absurd legend was properly dismissed by D. S. Margoliouth, "The Legend of the Apostasy of Maimonides," *Jewish Quarterly Review* (o.s.) 13 (1901): 539–41; cf. also David Yellin and Israel Abrahams, *Maimonides* (Philadelphia, 1944), pp. 34–35 and 220–21, n. 9. Richard Gottheil and Salo Baron also rejected the authenticity of the story; see Baron, ed., *Essays On Maimonides* (New York, 1941), pp. 10, 13. It was not, incidentally, Ibn Abī Uṣaybʿiah who was the source of this accusation, but rather Ibn al-Qifṭī (d. 1248), whose entire account of Maimonides is obviously biased and is flatly contradicted by other Arabic sources (including Ibn Abī Uṣaybʿiah). Nevertheless, the positive report has been ignored and the already refuted charge of Maimonides' apostasy naively accepted as fact by no less a scholar than Bernard Lewis (*The Jews of Islam* [Princeton, 1984], p. 100; his representation of Maimonides' position on the Christian and Muslim creeds, p. 84, is also completely incorrect). Ibn al-Qifṭī's account, but again not Ibn Abī Uṣaybʿiah's, is translated in Lewis, *Islam* II, 190.

naturally took such models as the book of Lamentations in the Bible. Medieval Hebrew poets and chroniclers tended to portray every calamity which befell the Jews in apocalyptic terms. Whole communities were destroyed, no less, and Jews were either slaughtered or forced to embrace Islam or Christianity. The facts are always considerably different—as, for example, with the First Crusade in Germany—and careful analysis of actual sources concerning the Almohad period reveals that most of the communities which were supposedly "destroyed" in Spain were hardly affected at all. The careful researches of one scholar concerning the situation in North Africa, particularly with regard to Fez, correctly give the same picture. Indeed, the Jews were neither persecuted nor forced to convert in Fez, and this explains what had long bothered some Jewish writers: namely, why Maimonides and his family chose to go from Córdoba to Fez.[38]

Moses' father was Maymūn, a religious judge (*dayyan*) of Córdoba.[39] We possess a treatise written by him, in Arabic, concerning the situation under the Almohads. This "Letter of Consolation," as it is called, was written in 1160. The letter has been published, with an English translation which contains several errors.[40] It is of interest not only in showing us his opinion concerning the situation, but in its containing some elements which are very similar to views later expressed by his son. He says,

> a man must strive his best secretly and publicly in whatever he has to perform of the law [the Torah] and obey of the commandments in the heart, to lay hold of the cord of the law and not loosen his hand from it; for one in captivity is like one who is drowning. We are almost totally immersed, but we remain grasping something. Overwhelmed with humiliation, contumely and contempt, the seas of exile surround us, and we are submerged in its depths.

He warns that there are two trials given to man against which he must stand. One is the love of women, and the other the love of this world and its goods.

Maimonides himself responded to a letter which was in circulation, written by a rabbi living in a non-Muslim land (perhaps Christian Spain), which argued that even accepting the appearance of conversion to Islam is a complete denial of God. Maimonides strongly dis-

38. David Corcos (Abulafia), "Le-ofey yaḥasam shel shelitey ha-Almuḥadun le-yehudim," (Hebrew), *Zion* 32 (1967): 137–60, with English summary. There are, admittedly, some slight objections that could be raised, but the conclusions are sound.

39. The name *Maymūn* (not *Maimun* or *Maimon*) is Arabic (Berber), and fairly common for Jews and non-Jews of Muslim Spain and North Africa.

40. "Letter of Consolation," ed. (Judeo-Arabic) and tr. L. M. Simmons, *Jewish Quarterly Review* (o.s.) 2 (1889): 62–101 (tr.); text following p. 334.

agreed with this view, pointing out that according to this there would be no distinction between a forced convert and a willful one. Nor is Islam idolatry, a view which Maimonides repeatedly reaffirmed elsewhere in his later writings, and certainly a Jew should not choose death rather than to recite the formula of belief. No act of violation of Jewish law is required, even of those who actually convert, but only the confession of faith. He adds, "they [the Muslims] well know that we do not believe in this speech [the confession], and the only intent is to save oneself from the king, to appease him with simple words." As to the practical issue of how to behave if there is persecution, Maimonides says that he advises people certainly to utter the confession rather than die, "but not to remain in the dominion of that ruler, but dwell in their houses until they go out"—that is, until they can leave the country. Sarcastically, he assures the rabbi that "never has there been heard the like of this wondrous persecution, in which there is no force except on speech alone." He concludes his letter:

> The advice which I take for myself and the opinion which I find desirable for me and my companions and all who seek my advice is to leave these places and go to a place where one is able to establish his religious law and fulfill his Torah without duress and fear, and leave [if necessary] his home and children and all his possessions.

This was a statement which he also repeated later in his letter to the Jews of Yemen: "It behooves the victim for the sake of his religion to escape and flee to the desert and wilderness, and not to consider separation from family or loss of wealth."[41]

It is instructive to contrast the view held by Maimonides' contemporary—not, as we have said, his student—Joseph Ibn ʿAqnin of Barcelona (who may himself have fled from al-Andalus during the Almohad reign). In a still unedited work, he wrote that the Almohad persecution was indeed a real religious persecution as viewed by Jewish law; contrary to the opinion of Maimonides (whom he does not mention). Thus, the sanctification of God's name through martyrdom is required by law, and the "saints" of certain communities he names in North Africa who acted thus (chose death) did correctly; by implication, those who did not do so, sinned. Indeed, he says that they and "we" (by which he includes himself) are to be considered desecrators of God's name in public, although by compulsion and not willfully, because they did not choose death. Nevertheless, those who even now

41. *Iggeret ha-shemad,* published often. I have used the edition in Moses b. Maimon, *Iggrot,* ed. Joseph Kafiḥ (Jerusalem, 1972). The authenticity of the letter has been disputed, with no good reason. It almost certainly could not have been written in Fez. Maimonides' *Epistle to Yemen* (see n. 13), p. 34 (text); p. vii (tr.).

remain in the lands of persecution and do not flee must be considered willful and intentional violators. He gives very clear testimony that the Jews who have converted to Islam have only done so for appearance's sake and remain secretly Jews. "As much as we seem to listen to their [the Muslims'] voice in all that they command us, and incline after their law, so they make heavier their yoke upon us and treat us harshly."[42]

Also in his commentary on Song of Songs, he says that Jews hide their true service of God and only appear to receive the religion of the nations because of their fear of them. In yet another work, his commentary on *Pirqey Avot* ("Ethics of the Fathers"), he explains the teaching "Do not separate yourself from the community" as an injunction not to separate from the correct opinions held by the community, so that if the people of a community have lost the right opinion and are doing evil, "you must leave immediately from among them [and go] to another province." Concerning Malachi 3:14 ("you have said, It is futile to serve God. What did we gain by carrying out his requirements and going about like mourners before the Lord Almighty?"), he says that this applies to those who are now "sighing" (complaining) because of the persecution and the great troubles; they make all these complaints, and yet God deals justly and mercifully.[43]

Thus, in spite of the fact that Ibn ʿAqnin disagreed completely with Maimonides' assessment of the nature of Islam and of the Almohad situation, both were agreed that there was only one desirable solution—to leave the land of persecution.

It is sad to reflect that, in spite of all the attention that has been paid to Maimonides throughout the world by Jewish and non-Jewish scholars, we do not have a definitive biographical study, nor even one that is at least factually accurate. Writers too often rely on the early inaccurate and romanticized books that have established myth in place of history. It is not true, for example, that the Almohads "obtained no real hold in Spain" because they were "governed from Morocco." Nor is it correct that Maimonides and his family "endured more than ten years of peril" and wanderings in Spain because of the Almohad presence there.[44] As we have stated, the Almohads invaded al-Andalus in 1145, but were not firmly in control until 1163. They were certainly not "governed from Morocco," but ruled by Abū Yaʿqūb Yūsuf, the

42. *Ṭibb al-nafs,* ch. 6 (cited here from Abraham S. Halkin, "*Le-toldot ha-shemad bimei ha-Almuḥadin,*" *Joshua Staff Memorial Volume* (New York, 1953), pp. 101–10).

43. Ibn ʿAqnin, *Hitgallut ha-sodot ve-hofaʿat ha-me'orot (Inkishāf al-asrār wa-ẓuhūr al-anwār),* ed. and tr. (Hebrew) Abraham S. Halkin (Jerusalem, 1964), p. 361. Ibn ʿAqnin, *Sefer ha-musar,* ed. Wilhelm Z. Bacher (Berlin, 1911; photo rpt., Jerusalem, 1967), pp. 31, 35, 65.

44. Yellin and Abrahams, *Maimonides,* pp. 17, 33.

second ruler, who had been governor of Seville and even as king spent more time in al-Andalus than in North Africa. The dynasty firmly governed Muslim Spain for many years. We know that Maymūn wrote his "Letter of Consolation" in 1160, and Maimonides' letter in reply to the rabbi who urged martyrdom was probably composed at that time or shortly after. We know that Judah ha-Kohen Ibn Sūsan, religious judge of the community of Fez and Maimonides' teacher there, was killed in 1165. Thus, Maimonides and his family left Spain no earlier than 1160, and perhaps sometime after that, but not later than 1164. It would seem unlikely, though we have no definite evidence, that the Almohads could have begun any serious practice of anti-Jewish measures in Spain much before 1163.

This, of course, is not the end of the story, but rather the beginning. Maimonides began writing while still in Spain, including his *Treatise on Logic* and at least the beginning of the great commentary on the *Mishnah*. Medieval Christian writers invariably referred to him as "Moses the Egyptian." Yet he was not Egyptian and always signed himself simply *Mosheh ha-Sefardiy*, "Moses the Spaniard."[45] In this, as well as in several statements he made, he thus continued to show his love for his Spanish homeland and heritage.[46]

University of Wisconsin, Madison

45. In his *responsa*, even where we have the Arabic text he always signed with the Hebrew form of his name. Specific sources relating to Maimonides' perception of himself as Spanish are in my *Maimonides: Essays and Texts*.

46. It is fitting that Spain, which led the world in commemorating Maimonides in the celebrations in 1936 and again in 1956, should have again taken the lead in the anniversary year, 1986. We note with gratitude and amazement the beautiful commemorative volume containing a cassette and script and numerous beautiful slides which the Spanish embassy has provided as a gift to Jewish studies programs at universities in this country. In his native Córdoba, an entire year of commemorative events culminated in an international symposium, and there is the promise of the opening of a library and a center for Jewish studies there. Recently there has appeared the splendid Spanish translation of the *Guide* by Prof. David Gonzalo Maeso, a scholar who has devoted his life to Jewish culture.

Indeed, we must take this opportunity to do something which is all too rarely done: to acknowledge with gratitude the eminent place which Spanish scholars have given to Jewish studies for well over a century. As we commemorate Maimonides, let us recall with veneration those scholars such as Menéndez Pelayo, Amador de los Ríos, Fernández y González, Gonzàlez-Llubera, Millás Vallicrosa, Cantera Burgos, Díez Macho, and many others who have pioneered in Hebrew and Jewish studies; and let us similarly honor the great scholars and historians now living in Spain, including but by no means limited to Gonzalo Maeso, Fernández Esteban, Carlos del Valle Rodríguez, José Luis Lacave, Luis Suárez Fernández, Emilio Mitre, Juan Torres Fontes, and the many others who have worked and continue to work to bring to life the civilization and history of the Jews of Spain. We stand on the shoulders of giants. Maimonides has honored his country, and his country continues to honor Maimonides in the way he would most have appreciated, through scholarship.

2 Maimonides' Egypt*

MARK R. COHEN

Around the year 1165, Moses ben Maimon arrived in Egypt after fleeing Spain and then Morocco and staying briefly in the Holy Land. For the remainder of his life and the bulk of his literary career, Maimonides lived in the land of the Nile, though he continued to call himself "the Spaniard"—*al-andalusī* in Arabic, *ha-sefaradi* in Hebrew. This was, to be sure, natural: immigrants generally went by the toponymic of their native lands. However, for Maimonides the designation "Spaniard" reflected something more: pride in his origins and a nostalgic identification with a cultural center not duplicated in his new home. Compared to Spain, Egypt, indeed the Eastern Islamic world in general, possessed little Jewish intellectual distinction. Near the end of his life Maimonides wrote from Egypt to the flourishing new center of Jewish scholarship in southern France where many Andalusian refugees had settled:

> You, members of the congregation of Lunel, and of the neighboring towns, stand alone in raising the banner of Moses. You apply yourselves to the study of the Talmud and also cherish wisdom. The study of the Torah in our communities has ceased; most of the bigger congregations are dead to spiritual aims; the remaining communities are facing the end.[1]

If not letters and religious piety, what then distinguished Maimonides' Egypt? What was the setting in which the "Great Eagle," as later generations would style him, flourished and penned the works which earned him so towering a reputation in his own day? And how did he respond to living in a Jewish environment that he felt was intellectually

*This paper does not attempt to break new ground but rather to summarize the current state of knowledge about Jewish Egypt during Maimonides' time with an eye toward sketching a picture of the milieu in which he produced the great works discussed in other chapters in this volume of conference papers. See the Bibliographical Note at the end of this essay.

1. Letter cited from Isadore Twersky, *A Maimonides Reader* (New York, 1972), p. 481.

so inferior to the cultured aristocratic Jewish milieu of his native Andalusia?

In the sixties of the twelfth century, Egypt appeared to be and indeed was the most flourishing and pacific country in the Islamic world. Iraq, and its capital, Baghdad, had long lost the centrality it had boasted between the eighth and early tenth centuries during the heyday of the Abbasid Caliphate. Palestine and parts of Syria had been in the hands of the Crusaders since the beginning of the 1100s. Tunisia, with its capital of Qayrawan, had entered a precipitous decline in the middle of the eleventh century. Muslim Spain, a worthy rival of the Abbasid Caliphate from the tenth to midtwelfth century, was threatened by the steady advance of the Christian kingdoms of the north and overrun by the fanatic Almohades of Morocco in the 1140s—it was from Almohade terror in Spain that the Maimonides clan had fled.

The preeminence of Egypt at the time of Maimonides' arrival stemmed from successful efforts of the Fatimids, who had conquered the land in the middle of the tenth century. A Shiite dynasty, the Fatimids had made it their mission to supplant the Sunnite Abbasids as leaders of the Islamic world. To that end they had declared themselves independent caliphs and built in 969 a new imperial city to rival Baghdad, which they called Cairo ("the victorious" [*al-qāhira*]). Of equal importance, they fostered commerce with a laissez-faire policy toward the economic activities of Egyptian merchants and with an anti-Abbasid strategy of diverting the India trade from its time-honored route through Iraq and the Persian Gulf to Upper Egypt and the Red Sea. Thanks to the Fatimids, Egypt became a magnet attracting settlers from both the eastern and western parts of the Islamic world. Jews, too, were drawn to the country by its economic opportunities. The Fatimids, in addition, were exceptionally tolerant of non-Muslims, Jews and Christians alike. With one notable exception in the eleventh century that proves the rule, episodes of persecution were rare. Jewish merchants, and even Jewish administrators of Egyptian public affairs, played prominent roles in building the Fatimid state, while Jewish physicians faithfully served the medical needs of individual Fatimid rulers. A notoriously powerful Jewish courtier in mid-eleventh-century Cairo was apparently the person who provoked the following lines of satirical poetry expressing indignation at the Fatimids' indulgent attitude toward unbelievers:

> The Jews of this time have attained
> Their utmost hopes and have come to rule.

Honor is theirs, wealth is theirs too,
And from them come the counsellor and ruler.
People of Egypt, I have good advice for you—
Turn Jew, for Heaven itself has become Jewish.[2]

Maimonides, of course, arrived in Egypt at the moment when Fatimid rule was crumbling. In 1171, the famous Saladin overthrew the Fatimid dynasty in a bloodless coup and restored Egypt to Sunnite orthodoxy. For a brief time, the campaign to purge the land of Shiite perversions spelled difficulty for the non-Muslim inhabitants of Egypt. Saladin activated some of the discriminatory laws that the Fatimids had let lie as a dead letter for nearly two centuries. However, these and other repressive measures soon gave way, along with the general waning of religious reforming fervor, to a more friendly attitude toward Jews and Christians in Egypt, and the decades that Maimonides lived in Egypt were ones of continued prosperity and substantial security for non-Muslims, and of continued Jewish and Christian service to the Muslim court.

Most of what we know about Maimonides' Egypt, and, indeed, many important details of his own biography, we owe to the discovery in the nineteenth century of the Cairo Geniza. This famous cache of discarded sacred and nonsacred writings, stored for centuries in a room in a medieval synagogue in Old Cairo (also known as Fustat), contains a wealth of information about the life and society of Jews and non-Jews alike during the centuries of Fatimid rule and that of their successors, the Ayyubids and the Mamluks.

Thanks to the Geniza, we are able to identify about ninety Jewish settlements in Egypt during the time of Maimonides. These include not only the large cities of Cairo-Fustat and Alexandria, where the Spanish Jewish traveler Benjamin of Tudela, passing through Egypt in 1168, shortly after Maimonides' arrival there, counted seven thousand and three thousand Jews, respectively, but also smaller settlements such as al-Mahalla, in the central Delta; Damietta, on the Mediterranean coast; Fayyum, up the Nile from Cairo; and distant Qus, a bustling entrepôt on the fringes of the Sudanese desert commercially linking densely populated Lower Egypt and the Mediterranean littoral with Arabia, India, and points farther east. Incidentally, Benjamin of Tudela does not mention Maimonides among the Jewish notables of Egypt; the new immigrant from Spain had not yet made his mark.

2. Quoted, among other places, in Norman A. Stillman, *The Jews of Arab Lands: A History and Source Book* (Philadelphia, 1979), p. 51.

Any guess at the size of the Jewish population of Maimonides' Egypt is hazardous. Benjamin of Tudela's figures must be used with caution, as it is not certain whether he was counting souls, or only poll tax-paying mature adult males. In addition, there are discrepancies in the numbers given in the different manuscripts of his Itinerary. On the basis of data culled from Geniza relief rolls, the late S. D. Goitein calculated that the total Rabbanite population of Fustat around the time of Benjamin of Tudela's visit was about thirty-three hundred persons. To this must be added a fair number of Karaites. The late Eliyahu Ashtor estimated the total Jewish population of Egypt at the end of the twelfth century at no more than twelve thousand.

Two statements that can be made with certainty about the Jewish population of Egypt help establish the social context of Maimonides' permanent resettlement in that country. One is that the community comprised a very high percentage of immigrants. These included several groups: (1) Jews from Palestine, older settlers, perhaps tracing their ancestry as far back as the pre-Islamic Byzantine era, as well as refugees from Crusader rule; (2) Babylonian Jews, whose separate synagogues in major cities, whose custom of completing the reading of the Torah in one year as opposed to the three-year Palestinian cycle, whose spiritual attachments to the Babylonian *yeshivot*, and whose self-characterization as *Irāqiyyūn* ("people from Iraq") set them apart from their Palestinian neighbors; (3) North African Jewish merchants, those who had settled in Egypt after long experience traversing its territory en route to commercial destinations eastward, as well as more recent arrivals fleeing Almohade persecution; (4) Jews fleeing Almohade terror in Muslim Spain; (5) Jews from Byzantium and from Sicily; and (6) other immigrants from Europe, swept into Egypt on the heels of the revival during the Fatimid period of European shipping in the Mediterranean. In short, as immigrants to Egypt, Maimonides and his family participated in one of the major demographic trends of the time.

The second safe assertion that can be made about the Jewish population of Maimonides' Egypt is that it was at its all-time peak. A devastating famine and plague in 1201–1202, two years before Maimonides' death, dealt a heavy blow to the Jewish community's demographic strength. And despite a continuous flow of Jews into the country during the Mamluk period, the medieval Jewish population never recovered to its twelfth-century level. During Maimonides' time, however, the Jewish community of Egypt still possessed the vitality of a growing and self-assured entity and held out the promise of economic security to the wandering Andalusian émigré family.

Indeed, as is so abundantly clear from the documents of the Cairo Geniza, the Jewish community of Maimonides' Egypt shared in the prosperity begun by the Fatimids and was well integrated into the general economic life of the society around it. This contrasts sharply with the picture of economic life known for the Jewish settlements of northern Europe, the so-called Ashkenazic lands. The Jews of those parts were concentrated largely in marginal professions, increasingly in money lending by the twelfth century. Those of Maimonides' Egypt, by contrast, participated in all walks of life. And while it is true that in the twelfth century a high proportion of Egyptian Jews engaged in mercantile occupations, they were not, like their brethren in France, Germany, and England, economic outsiders. Rather, they were social counterparts of the Muslim (and Christian) members of the merchant class. Moreover, many Jews were represented in industry, farming, fishing, and civil service. In commerce and industry Jews regularly formed partnerships with Muslims. Not surprisingly, Maimonides' *responsa* are filled with queries relating to the wide variety of economic pursuits of the Egyptian Jews. And as is clear from passages in these and other writings of his, the great rabbinic sage and philosopher, whose younger brother David plied the trade routes in order to support the entire Maimon clan, was quite familiar with the ins and outs of the trading life.

Extreme mobility characterized the Jewish merchants of Maimonides' Egypt. In his time Jews regularly traveled the enormous distance between Egypt and India in search of precious spices, perfumes, pharmaceuticals, and textiles much in demand in the Mediterranean lands. It was during a commercial voyage to India that David Maimonides drowned in a shipwreck. His death, coming shortly after the family's arrival in Egypt, caused enormous personal grief to Maimonides, who had advised David against the perilous sea journey, and dealt a severe blow to the material resources of the family. From that moment on Maimonides had to seek employment as a physician at the court in Cairo in order to support his kin.

The Jewish community of Maimonides' Egypt had a well-established self-governing organization. At its head stood an official called the *ra'īs al-yahūd,* "Head of the Jews," who was chosen, normally, by the notables of the community and whose authority was recognized by the Muslim government. The Head of the Jews functioned as liaison between the Jews and the non-Jewish authorities. He possessed supreme judicial and administrative authority over the community; he appointed chief judges in the capital and local magistrates, as well as local administrators, in the provincial communities. He provided succor for those in need, strove to keep peace among his Jewish flock, and regulated religious life.

The Egyptian office of Head of the Jews came into existence during the last third of the eleventh century. Prior to that time, the chief religious and administrative authority over the Jews of Egypt had been the Head, or *Gaon*, of the Jewish yeshiva of Palestine. His position of sovereignty over Jewry in neighboring Egypt, rooted in the dominance of Palestinian Jewry, in general, during the period of Roman and Byzantine rule in Syria-Palestine and Egypt, gained a new lease on life following the Fatimid unification of Egypt and Palestine into an empire centered in Cairo. However, with the general disruption of security in Palestine in the eleventh century and the decline of the Palestinian yeshiva due to conflict within its walls, and following the detachment of Palestine from even nominal Fatimid control at the time of the Seljuk conquest of the 1070s, the yeshiva lost its grip on Egyptian Jewry. Encouraged by a certain policy trend of the Fatimid government to centralize minority self-governing institutions near the caliph's court in Cairo, the leaders of the Jewish community in the capital fell back on their own political resources and evolved a locally based central ruling institution that eventually replaced the weakened Palestinian gaonate.

By the middle of the twelfth century, these developments had reached an advanced stage. The Headship of the Jews was the fully recognized institution of central Jewish administrative and religious authority in Egypt. An immigrant to the country, like Maimonides, could truly feel that Cairo with adjacent Fustat was the most important Jewish capital in the Muslim world. Even the Palestinian *geonim* had come to accept this fact of life, and several representatives of ruling families of the Palestinian yeshiva actually occupied the office of Head of the Jews during the second, third, and fourth quarters of the twelfth century. The most important of these was Masliah ha-Kohen b. Solomon, who held the post from 1127 to 1139. Grandson of the head of the Jerusalem yeshiva from 1062 to 1083, Masliah's own father occupied the leadership of that formerly august institution in its exile in the city of Damascus. Masliah transferred the trappings of authority of the Palestinian yeshiva from Syria to Egypt, and while it has been customary in Jewish historiography to refer to his arrival there as the beginning of the "Gaonate of Fustat," how much actual learning occurred in Masliah's Fustat yeshiva we do not know. The very fact that he did not succeed in reestablishing continuity for his family in the leadership of Fatimid Jewry suggests that his yeshiva lacked rabbinic prestige. In fact, he was succeeded in the Headship of the Jews by another local Egyptian Jewish notable, the court physician Abū Manṣūr Samuel b. Hananya, who was a scholar in his own right.

At the time of Maimonides' arrival, during the very last, turbulent years of Fatimid rule, the office of Head of the Jews was itself experiencing instability. The incumbent Head of the Jews around 1165 was a member of another one of the leading families of the Palestinian yeshiva, and also a court physician to the Fatimids, by the name of Nethanel (Hibat Allah) ha-Levi b. Moses. A Geniza document dated April–May 1169, when Nethanel ha-Levi was still alive (he died after 1184), names a certain Saadya as the incumbent Head of the Jews. A year later, Nethanel's brother, Sar Shalom ha-Levi, appears as Head. At this time of confusion accompanying the demise of the Fatimid Caliphate, however, a troublemaker, nicknamed pejoratively Zuta ("Mr. Small"), who several years earlier had successfully attained office by securing the temporary deposal of Samuel b. Hananya as Head of the Jews, again made a bid to gain power.

Exactly at this juncture, in 1171, Moses Maimonides entered the public arena in Egypt—hence, he appears there for the first time in our sources—as defender of the community against the usurpations of the impostor Zuta as Head of the Jews. Perhaps connected in some way with Saladin's rise to power in that very year, Maimonides' accession to the leadership of Egyptian Jewry so soon after his arrival in the country certainly had some relation to the recognition he earned in the struggle against that Jewish evildoer. It may also have resulted from his tireless efforts helping raise money to rescue Jewish captives from Crusader captivity following the Frankish invasion of Egypt in 1168.

Maimonides served in office for just a few years. Sar Shalom ha-Levi returned to power around the year 1177 and ruled the community until approximately 1195. At that time, Maimonides entered office as Head of the Jews once again and reigned until his death in 1204. Between 1177 and 1195—during what must surely be classed as the longest "sabbatical" ever—the great sage had completed the two most important of his three magna opera: the *Mishneh Torah* and the *Guide of the Perplexed*. With this second administration as communal leader of Egyptian Jewry, Moses b. Maimon inaugurated a long-lived dynasty of Maimonidean Nagids—for such became the regular Hebrew title of the office beginning with the reign of his son Abraham—that lasted until the close of the fourteenth century.

Maimonides' fame among the Jewish intelligentsia of his day may have rested on his brilliant literary output. But his renown among the masses of Egyptian Jewry arose more immediately from his official role as Head of the Jews. In this capacity he communicated regularly with local communities, answered pleas for assistance from individuals, and organized general relief efforts for groups of Jews in distress. A man of thought to most of us today who read his halakhic and philosophical masterpieces, to most of his contemporaries in Egypt, Maimonides was, in the words of the late Professor Goitein, a consummate "man of action."

As we know, Maimonides was less than enthusiastic about his manifold public duties; he preferred the spiritual and intellectual ambience of the house of learning. Egypt, however, had not witnessed the emergence of academies of stature such as those that had grown up in Spain and North Africa during the tenth and eleventh centuries. Only once, at the close of the tenth and beginning of the eleventh centuries, had Egyptian Jewry seemed to be moving in this direction. In those years, two illustrious Babylonian-trained rabbinic scholars, Shemarya b. Elhanan and his son, Elhanan b. Shemarya, presided in Fustat over a Talmudic school. The institution was called a "midrash" to distinguish it from the ancient and venerable ecumenical *yeshivot* of Baghdad and Jerusalem. Nonetheless, the efforts of these two scholars to establish a permanent center of rabbinic learning in Egypt were ultimately interpreted by the Palestinian *geonim,* with some justification, as an attempt to create an independent center of self-government. For this and other reasons apparently, the midrash founded by Shemarya b. Elhanan did not last longer than the lifetime of his son, who died around 1025.

During the first quarter of the twelfth century, two generations prior to Maimonides' arrival, a distinguished Spanish Jew living in Egypt brought illustrious rabbinic learning into the bosom of the community. His name was Isaac b. Samuel ha-Sefaradi, "the Spaniard." He wrote *responsa,* an Arabic commentary on books of the prophets, a commentary on at least one Talmudic tractate, and liturgical poetry. Many of his writings are lost, and our only record of their existence is contained in the book lists preserved in the Cairo Geniza. This shows that his works were read and studied by contemporaries in Egypt, and, by extension, that there were many in the country hungering for advanced knowledge of the sacred Jewish texts.

The last dated reference to Isaac b. Samuel the Spaniard in our sources is in the year 1127. It seems that no scholar of similar stature graced the Egyptian Jewish community during the following generation; certainly we have no evidence that the Palestinian Gaon Masliah ha-Kohen shone for his rabbinic brilliance. It is against this immediate background that Maimonides' overnight rise to the spiritual leadership of all of Egyptian Jewry, shortly after his settlement in the country, can best be appreciated. Almost at once, the scholarly newcomer from Andalusia began to receive religious questions. His numerous *responsa*—the extant corpus numbers around five hundred—testify to his active role as jurisconsult for the Jews of the country, as well as points beyond its borders. Maimonides also opened an academy of higher learning for a small circle of advanced students. This institution came to be called *yeshivatah shel torah,* "the yeshiva of Torah study": not a midrash, as in the days of Shemarya b. Elhanan, who chose a more modest and subordinate title for his academy of rabbinic instruction, but a full-fledged yeshiva, drawing upon the title traditionally reserved for the exclusive use of the ancient academies of Palestine and Babylonia.

With his students Maimonides introduced a new item into the curriculum of advanced halakhic study: they were to learn his massive Hebrew code of Jewish law, the *Mishneh Torah,* to the exclusion of the Talmud itself. This innovation in the methods cherished by the ancient *yeshivot* and their medieval continuators, where tractates of the Talmud formed the centerpiece of daily instruction, raised eyebrows in certain circles. Not the least of the opposition came from the contemporary head, or *gaon,* of the yeshiva of Baghdad, who rightly saw in the *Mishneh Torah* and its incorporation into the course of study in an academy of higher Jewish learning, a usurpation of the time-honored prerogatives and preeminence of the yeshiva of Babylonia. The fiery controversy over the rationalistic writings of Maimonides that set camp against camp in Spain and southern France and whose embers kept smoldering until the beginning of the fourteenth century had its near equivalent in the Near East already during the lifetime of the sage of Fustat in the political opposition to the teaching of the *Mishneh Torah.*

Maimonides composed and taught the *Mishneh Torah* because, as he stated explicitly in his introduction to that work, "in our days, severe vicissitudes prevail, and all feel the pressure of hard times. The wisdom of our wise men has disappeared; the understanding of our prudent men is hidden."[3]

This claim reflects the despair of a representative of the generation that had witnessed the abrupt end of what we today call the Golden Age in Spain, as well as Maimonides' realization in Egypt that measures to ensure the continuity of a learned and pious Jewish existence in this now most important center of Jewry in the Islamic world were

3. Cited from Twersky, *A Maimonides Reader,* p. 39.

necessary. To this end, the great sage of Fustat embarked on several projects to reinforce and even reform religious life.

The threat to the proper pious practice of Judaism in Maimonides' Egypt came in part from within. The Karaites, members of a branch of Judaism that rejected the authority of post-Biblical Jewish law, constituted a powerful force in the Jewish community. Representing a wealthy segment of the Jewish population that often had close connections with the Muslim government, they were vigorously cultivated by the Rabbanite Jewish majority, who did not hesitate to marry off their children to Karaite spouses.

Maimonides, who hailed from a region where Karaites do not seem to have played much of a role in Jewish daily affairs, was rather surprised by the free intercourse, on all levels of existence, between Rabbanites and members of the heterodox denomination. In principle he did not object to such socialization, and in *responsa* he ruled that orthodox Jews should respect the Karaites; circumcise their newborn sons, even on the Sabbath, as commanded by Rabbinic law; bury their dead; and comfort them when they were in mourning.[4] However, he vigorously objected to Karaite influence over the religious practice of Rabbanite Jews. Thus, in a campaign reminiscent of Ayyubid measures to eliminate Shiite influence in Egypt, Maimonides, aided by other immigrant Jewish scholars in Egypt, instituted procedures to neutralize Karaite tendencies among the Rabbanite majority. He ruled, for example, that a Karaite-Rabbanite intermarriage could only be terminated by a bill of divorce drawn up in accordance with Talmudic stipulations. A more serious perversion in Maimonides' eyes concerned the laws of family purity. Karaite wives, limited in their monthly ablutions only by the laws of the Torah, did not follow the rigorous procedures dictated by Talmudic law. Rabbanite husbands of Karaite women tended to acquiesce, agreeing to have sexual relations with their wives under circumstances thoroughly frowned upon in Rabbinic legislation. Worse, many Rabbanite wives adopted the less meticulous procedures of Karaite purity laws in their own marriages, a latitudinarianism that led some to the complete neglect of ritual ablutions following menstruation and even to cohabitation with their husbands during their unclean days of the month.

In order to put a stop to these grave violations of Talmudic precept, Maimonides and his judicial colleagues in the Egyptian capital issued in the year 1176 a strongly worded legislative ordinance (*taqqana*)

4. *Responsum* 449 in Yehoshua Blau's edition, *Teshuvot Ha-Rambam (Rabbi Moses b. Maimon Responsa)*, vol. 2 (Jerusalem, 1960), pp. 729–732.

proscribing the adoption of Karaite practices of marital purity. It stipulated that any wife who failed to comply with the Talmudic standards in this matter would be automatically divorced, forfeiting all monies and other compensations owed her, and that complicit husbands would be placed under the ban.[5]

Maimonides' efforts to stem Karaite influence over orthodox Jewish life in Egypt met with a measure of success. The ordinance of 1176, along with other measures, marked the beginning of the religious exclusion of the Karaites from Rabbanite life in Egypt and of their consequent loss of status. This, in turn, apparently weakened Karaite resistance to the influence of Rabbanism and led to the conversion of many to Rabbanite Judaism during the time of Maimonides' son Abraham.

Another area of Jewish religious life in Egypt that caused Maimonides concern was the decorum of the synagogue. In Egyptian synagogues the prayer service was marked by a degree of disorder that offended the aesthetic and rationalistic impulses of the great philosopher. Maimonides writes that during the reader's repetition of the central prayer, the Eighteen Benedictions, congregants got up from their places, walked around, talked to their neighbors, turned away from facing east, the prescribed direction of prayer—he used the Islamic term, *qibla*—and even spit on the floor. Among other things, Maimonides realized that this kind of behavior constituted an embarrassment before the Muslims, for whom the service of the mosque was formalized and dignified, with every movement of the worshipper having religious meaning. Therefore, in a move fitting the leaders of modern Reform Judaism in Central Europe, Maimonides inaugurated a change in the synagogue service that entailed an alteration in Talmudic law. He decreed that henceforth there would be no reader's solo repetition of the Eighteen Benedictions. Rather, everyone must stand, facing the *qibla,* and recite the prayer attentively and in unison with the reader. In this way Maimonides hoped to bring Jewish worship in Egypt a little closer to the orderly and aesthetic model of the prayer service of the mosque and thus remove a blot on the reputation Jews had among their Muslim neighbors. The reform found acceptance in the main towns of Egypt. Maimonides' stature could not easily be challenged. In the following generation, however, his son Abraham, trying to expand his father's campaign to increase the piety of Egyptian Jewry, experienced tremendous opposition from some of the lay notables in the community.

5. Ibid., *Responsa* 242 and 320, pp. 434–444 and 588–589.

It seems, nonetheless, that in the twelfth century, and increasingly in the thirteenth, some Jews in Egypt were powerfully attracted to pietism of a Muslim variety, namely, Islamic Sufism. This was the period of time indeed when the mystical Sufi brotherhoods were gaining in popularity in the Near East, and for some intellectuals, theosophic Sufism was assuming the place once held by Islamic rationalism. The tendency among Jews became especially pronounced during the time of Abraham Maimonides, who himself was a kind of Jewish Sufi and wrote an Arabic code of Jewish law that climaxed with a guide for the mystical believer. However, already in Maimonides' day the trend could be discerned. In his commentary to the Mishna tractate *Avot,* Maimonides wrote:

> Should those of our co-religionists—and it is of them alone that I speak—who imitate the followers of other religions, maintain that when they torment their bodies, and renounce every joy, that they do so merely to discipline the faculties of their souls by inclining somewhat to one extreme, as is proper, and in accordance with our recommendations in this chapter, our answer is that they are in error.[6]

Elsewhere in the commentary, Maimonides tells us that these Jews wore woolen clothing and practiced isolation in the mountains[7]—in short, typical Sufi behavior. It is quite likely that in instituting his pietistic reforms of the synagogue service in Egypt, Maimonides was attempting to prevent defections from the community of Jews who preferred the ascetic mentality and praxis of the Muslim Sufis to the uncouth religiosity of their bourgeois co-religionists.

Maimonides' Egypt was a far cry from Maimonides' Spain. The relatively unlearned middle-class mentality of most of Egyptian Jewry stood in bold contrast to that of the refined aristocratic Jewish courtier society that the Maimon family had left behind on the Iberian peninsula. Yet Maimonides ultimately became a true son of Egypt. He did not withdraw from society. He was adopted by it and, in turn, adapted himself to its realities. In executing his manifold public duties as Head of the Jews, in founding a dynasty of Nagids who ruled Egyptian Jewry for the next two centuries, in opening an academy to teach the sons of Egyptian Jewish families, and even in writing his monumental Hebrew code of Jewish law, Maimonides was addressing himself to the needs of the Jews of his new homeland. Egypt did not become, like

6. Moses ben Maimon, *Eight Chapters,* ed. and trans. by J. I. Gorkinkle (New York, 1912), p. 64 (English).
7. Ibid., pp. 62–63.

southern France, a center of a transplanted Andalusian Jewish culture. But it was not to be in Provence, but rather in Egypt and in such places as Yemen, where Jews were spiritually oriented toward Cairo in Maimonides' time, that the future of the Jews of Islam would be charted. In some respects, therefore, the Maimonidean legacy lived on more authentically in Egypt and its environs than it did elsewhere in the centuries of the later middle ages.

Princeton University

BIBLIOGRAPHICAL NOTE

An essay similar to this one, written on the occasion of the 800th anniversary of Maimonides' birth and based on the state of knowledge about Maimonides' Egypt fifty years ago, was published in Hebrew by Simha Assaf under the title "Yehudei Mitzrayim Bi-zmano shel Ha-Rambam" ("The Jews of Egypt during the Time of Maimonides") *Moznayim* 3 (1934–35): 414–432; reprinted in a collection of Assaf 's essays entitled *Be-Oholei Ya'akov: Essays on the Cultural Life of the Jews in the Middle Ages* (Jerusalem, 1943). Today we know somewhat more about Maimonides' life and a great deal more about the character of the Egyptian Jewish community in which he settled. For more extensive discussion of the subject and for documentation of many of the generalizations made in the present short survey, the reader should consult the following publications.

S. D. Goitein, *A Mediterranean Society,* 5 vols. to date (Berkeley and Los Angeles, 1967–1988), vol. 6 forthcoming, contains a wealth of information about the economic, political and social history of the Jews of the Islamic Mediterranean in the eleventh through thirteenth centuries, based on the rich documents of the Cairo Geniza. Because the Geniza was located in Egypt, a good deal of Goitein's portrait applies directly to the Jews there. An older book that served as Assaf 's main source in 1935 and that is still worth consulting is Jacob Mann, *The Jews in Egypt and in Palestine under the Fatimid Caliphs* (1920–1922; new edition, 2 vols. in 1 with preface and reader's guide by S. D. Goitein, New York, 1970). On the topography and demography of Jewish Egypt, see Norman Golb, "The Topography of the Jews of Medieval Egypt: Inductive Studies Based Primarily upon Documents from the Cairo Genizah," *Journal of Near Eastern Studies* 24 (1965): 251–270 and 33 (1974): 116–149; and Eliyahu Ashtor, "The Number of the Jews in Medieval Egypt," *Journal of Jewish Studies* 18 (1967): 9–42 and 19 (1968): 1–22. The second part of Walter J. Fischel's *Jews in the Economic and Political Life of Mediaeval Islam* (1937; rpt., New York, 1969) tells the story of Jewish notables who achieved prestigious positions and considerable influence in the Fatimid court. A newer and more complete treatment of one pair of courtiers featured in Fischel's book is to be found in Moshe Gil's *Ha-Tustarim (The Tustaris, Family and Sect)* (Tel Aviv, 1981). On the continued favorable status of Egyptian Jewry during Maimonides' time and on some of the developments in the community during the last decades of the twelfth century, see E. Strauss (Ashtor), "Saladin and the Jews," *Hebrew Union College Annual* 27 (1956): 305–326. On the economic life of Egyptian Jewry see, in addition to the first volume of Goitein's *Mediterranean Society*, his *Letters of Medieval Jewish Traders, Translated from the Arabic* (Princeton, 1973), and Norman A. Stillman's "The Eleventh Century Merchant House of Ibn 'Awkal (A Geniza Study)," *Journal of the Economic and Social History of the Orient* 16 (1973): 15–88. On the revenue system of the Jewish community and its social services see, in addition to the relevant sections in the second volume of *Mediterranean Society*, Moshe Gil's *Documents of the Jewish Pious Foundations from the Cairo Geniza* (Leiden, 1976). On communal organization see, apart from the comprehensive survey in the second volume of *Mediterranean Society*, two books: Moshe Gil's *Eretz Yisrael Ba-Tequfa Ha-Muslimit Ha-Rishona (Palestine during the First Muslim Period [634–1099])*, 3 vols. (Tel Aviv, 1983), which deals with the period of the ascendancy of the Palestinian yeshiva over Jewish public affairs in Egypt and has much to say about political doings among Egyptian Jewry in the eleventh century; and my own *Jewish Self-Government in Medieval Egypt* (Princeton, 1980), which documents the evolution of the Egyptian office of Head of the Jews from the last third of the eleventh century through the first quarter of the twelfth. I have discussed the period prior to the rise of the office of Head of the Jews in "Administrative Relations Between Palestinian and Egyptian Jewry During the Fatimid Period," in *Egypt and Palestine: A Millennium of Association (868–1948)*, ed. by Amnon Cohen and Gabriel Baer (Jerusalem and New York, 1984), pp. 113–135. New biographical data from Geniza documents concerning Maimonides' rise to power in the Egyptian Jewish community are presented in Goitein's article "Moses Maimonides, Man of Action: A Revision of the Master's Biography in Light of the Geniza Documents," in *Hommage à Georges Vajda*, ed. by G. Nahon and C. Touati (Louvain, 1980), pp. 155–167. On Maimonides' and later his son's pietistic reforms see Naphtali Wieder, *Hashpa'ot Islamiyot al Ha-Pulhan Ha-Yehudi (Islamic Influences on the Jewish Worship)*, (Oxford, 1947); S. D. Goitein, "Abraham Maimonides and His Pietist Circle," in *Jewish Medieval and Renaissance Studies*, ed. by Alexander Altmann (Cambridge, 1967), pp. 145–164; G. D. Cohen, "The Soteriology of R. Abraham Maimuni," *Proceedings of the American Academy for Jewish Research* 35 (1967): 75–98 and 36 (1968): 33–56.

3 Demonstrative, Dialectical and Sophistic Arguments in the Philosophy of Moses Maimonides

ARTHUR HYMAN

That Maimonides had an ongoing interest in logic, that he was a competent logician and that his views on logic had an important influence on his *Guide of the Perplexed*[1] require little proof. He began his literary career with a *Treatise on the Art of Logic*,[2] which, while a rather conventional work, showed that he had mastered this discipline already at an early age. Logic, he reports in the letter with which he begins the *Guide* (I, Epistle Dedicatory, 3) formed part of the program of studies which he undertook with Joseph son of Judah—the addressee of the work—before revealing to him the secrets of the Law (Torah); and logic, he advises, must be studied before one can go on to mathematics, the natural sciences and metaphysics—those sciences required for the attainment of human perfection (*Guide* I, 34, 75). A question of logic also formed part of Joseph's purposes in studying with Maimonides, for he wanted to know whether the opinions of the Mutakallimūn were based on demonstrations or whether they belonged to some other part of logic (*Guide* I, Epistle Dedicatory, 3–4). And finally, there is the rather large number of incidental remarks, scattered throughout the *Guide*, devoted to points of logic, particularly to the nature of arguments used by Maimonides and his opponents.

1. The following versions of the *Guide of the Perplexed* were used: Arabic: ed. I. Joel (Jerusalem, 1931–32); Hebrew: trans. Samuel ibn Tibbon, ed. Y. Even Shemu'el (Jerusalem, 1981–82); English: trans. S. Pines (Chicago, 1963). References are to part and chapter of the *Guide* and the pages of the Pines translation. For example, *Guide* I, 34, 75, refers to part I, chapter 34, and page 75 of the English translation.

2. Arabic: ed. M. Türker, "Mūsā ibn-i Meymūn'un *Al-Maḳālā fī Sināʿat al-Manṭiḳ*," in Publications of the Faculty of Letters, Istanbul University, Review of the Institute of Islamic Studies, 3, 1–2 (1959–60); Arabic in Hebrew Letters: ed. I. Efros, in *Proceedings of the American Academy for Jewish Research* 34 (1966); Medieval Hebrew translations of Samuel ibn Tibbon, Aḥitub, Joseph ibn Vivas as well as English translation, ed. and trans. I. Efros, *Maimonides' Treatise on the Art of Logic* (New York, 1938). The Hebrew terms cited are taken from the ibn Tibbon translation.

This paper is meant as a preliminary investigation of the various kinds of arguments, those of both Maimonides and his opponents, which appear in the *Guide*. Since Maimonides' discussion is derived from Aristotle, I shall review some salient points of what the Philosopher had to say about demonstrative, dialectical and sophistic arguments. Next, I shall consider the *Treatise on the Art of Logic*. And finally, I shall investigate what light these logical distinctions throw on the discussions in the *Guide*.

I

Aristotle devoted three books of his *Organon* to kinds of arguments: the *Posterior Analytics* to demonstration, the *Topics* to dialectic and the *On Sophistical Refutations* to sophistic arguments. Of these arguments, demonstration is the most important, since it is only demonstration that leads to scientific knowledge. Aristotle writes: "By demonstration (*apodeixis*) I mean a syllogism productive of scientific knowledge (*syllogismos epistēmonikos*), a syllogism, that is, the grasp of which is *eo ipso* such knowledge" (*Posterior Analytics* I, 2, 71b, 17–19). While demonstration shares its syllogistic structure with other kinds of arguments, it is distinguished from them by the nature of its premises. These must meet the following conditions: they must be (1) true, (2) primary and indemonstrable, (3) immediate, (4) better known than the conclusions following from them and prior to these conclusions and (5) their causes (ibid., 19 ff.). These premises are available to everyone, not just to some special group, and they cannot be simply definitions of terms, but must state some "basic truth"—a truth appropriate to the science with which they deal. In summary fashion Aristotle states:

> An argument is 'demonstration' when the premises from which the reasoning starts are true and primary, or are such that our knowledge of them has originally come through premises which are primary and true (*Topics* I, 1, 100a, 27–29).

The role of dialectic in Aristotle's thought has been debated by modern scholars. Some see his account of dialectic as an early stage of his philosophy which, as W. D. Ross holds,[3] was superseded by his *Analytics*. Others consider dialectic as an integral part of Aristotle's mature thought. To these belongs J. D. C. Evans to whose *Aristotle's Concept of Dialectic*[4] I am indebted for some of the points that follow. Maimonides, I believe, would have been sympathetic to this approach.

3. W. D. Ross, *Aristotle*, (5th ed.; London, 1949; rpt., 1977), p. 59.
4. (Cambridge, 1977). For a summary account of the state of research and Evans's own thesis, see pp. 1–6.

For Aristotle, dialectic has a variety of uses. It is important for establishing principles of human conduct, that is, ethical judgments, as can be seen from examples occurring in the *Topics* and other works, especially the *Nicomachean Ethics*. "A dialectical problem," he writes, "is a subject of inquiry that contributes to choice and avoidance (*pros airesin kai phygēn*) . . ." (*Topics* I, 11, 104b, 1–2). Many of Aristotle's examples of dialectical problems and propositions are ethical. (Maimonides follows Aristotle on the dialectical nature of ethical problems.[5]) Dialectic is also important for establishing the basic premises of demonstration. In this paper I shall, however, not be concerned with these two uses of dialectic. What remains then is the use of dialectic for refuting false claims to knowledge and for establishing correct opinions for problems (*problemata*) and questions (*aporiai*) for which no demonstrative knowledge exists. These two uses of dialectic become fundamental for Maimonides' thought.

That dialectical arguments can have cognitive significance is clear from Aristotle's statement that "a dialectical problem is a subject of inquiry that contributes . . . to truth and knowledge (*pros alētheian kai gnōsin*)" (ibid.) and from his listing as an example of a dialectical problem the question "whether the universe is eternal or not?" (*Topics* I, 11, 104b, 8).[6] Whatever arguments one may offer, one of the alternatives must be true, the other false, though dialectic can offer only plausible opinions for the view accepted as true.[7]

While demonstrative propositions are available to everyone, dialectical propositions rest on agreement or general acceptance. "Reasoning . . . is dialectical," writes Aristotle, "if it reasons from opinions that are generally accepted (*endoxa*)"[8] (*Topics* I, 1, 100a, 29–30). Dialectical propositions also deal with opinions of particular groups of people. Aristotle states:

Now a dialectical proposition consists in asking something that is held by all men or by most men or by the philosophers, i.e. either by all, or by most, or

5. See my article "A Note on Maimonides' Classification of Law," *Fiftieth Anniversary Volume of the American Academy for Jewish Research* (Jerusalem, 1979), pp. 323–43, esp. 335–38.

6. A parallel passage reads: "Of propositions and problems there are . . . three divisions: for some are ethical propositions, some are on natural philosophy, while some are logical. Propositions . . . such as this are on natural philosophy, e.g. 'Is the universe eternal or not'" (*Topics* I, 14, 105b, 19–25). For a discussion of the variety of examples that Aristotle uses, see I. Düring, "Aristotle's Use of Examples in the *Topics*," in *Aristotle on Dialectic*, ed. G. E. L. Owen (Oxford, 1968), pp. 202–29.

7. Aristotle writes: "For purposes of philosophy we must treat these things according to their truth (*kat'alētheian*), but for dialectic only with an eye to general opinion (*pros doxan*)."

8. On *endoxa*, see Evans, *Aristotle's Concept of Dialectic*, pp. 77–85.

by the most notable of these, provided it be not contrary to the general opinion. . . (*Topics* I, 10, 104a, 8–11).

While this imposes a certain subjective character on dialectical propositions, they are by no means arbitrary. Aristotle writes: "Dialectic does not construct its syllogisms out of any haphazard materials, . . . , but out of materials that call for discussion" (*Rhetoric* I, 2, 1356b, 34–36). He similarly states that dialectic must address a proposition held by someone, for "no one in his senses would make a proposition of what no one holds, nor yet make a problem of what is obvious to everybody or to most people. . ." (*Topics* I, 10, 104a, 5–7). Cognitive dialectical arguments, then, seek plausible answers to genuine and significant questions for which no demonstrative answers exist.

Another argument against the totally subjective character of dialectic is that dialecticians offer reasons for the opinions that they accept and against those that they reject. The role of reason in dialectical arguments is discussed by Aristotle in an account of *aporiai* about friendship:

we accept the reasoning which will both best explain to us the views held about these matters and will resolve the difficulties and contradictions; and we will achieve this if we show that the conflicting views are held with good reason. For such reasoning will most closely accord with the agreed facts; and it will allow the conflicting views to be retained if analysis can show that each is partly true and partly false (*Eudemian Ethics* VII, 2, 1235b, 13–18).[9]

This interesting passage makes a number of points relevant to our investigation. It states, first of all, that the parties to a genuine dialectical argument must have reasons for the opinion they propose. Second, reasoning will help to resolve difficulties and contradictions in the opinions held. And third, dialectic can reconcile conflicting views by retaining what is true in each and rejecting what is false. From what has been said earlier and from the preceding passage it follows that there are two kinds of resolutions for dialectical questions: (1) those in which one of the opposing opinions is to be accepted because it is more plausible, while the other is to be rejected and (2) those in which the conclusion provides a plausible answer by combining what is true in the opposing opinions and rejecting what is false in them. A Maimonidean example of the first case is his account

9. See Evans, *Aristotle's Concept of Dialectic,* pp. 55 ff. The translation of the passage from the *Eudemian Ethics* is taken from this volume.

The *Eudemian Ethics* was not known to medieval Muslims and Jews. I use it here because it provides a convenient framework for a point I shall have to make about Maimonides' conception of dialectic.

of creation; examples of the second, his accounts of prophecy and providence.

Sophistic arguments agree with dialectical ones in that they aim to persuade, but they differ from them in the premises they employ and in intention.[10] Whereas dialectical arguments are based on premises that are generally accepted, sophistic arguments are based on premises that appear to be generally accepted but are not so (*On Sophistical Refutations* 2, 165b, 7–8). Concerning motivation, Aristotle writes in the same work:

> the art of the sophistic is the semblance of wisdom without the reality, and the sophist is one who makes money from an apparent but unreal wisdom (*On Sophistical Refutations* 1, 165a, 21–23).[11]

One gains the impression that sophistic arguments are primarily arguments that are meant to deceive, but they can also be arguments that are based on false premises regardless of intention.

II

In his *Treatise on the Art of Logic,* Maimonides tersely describes the three kinds of Aristotelian arguments, adding to them, as had become customary by his time, rhetorical and poetic arguments. In chapter 8 of the *Treatise*[12] he first of all enumerates and describes the premises upon which arguments are based. These premises are known immediately without any arguments in their support. As Maimonides writes: "they are known to be true and require no proof (*dalīl, re'ayah*) for their truthfulness." They are of four kinds: (1) sense percepts (*al-maḥsūsāt, ha-muḥashim*), (2) first intelligibles (*al-maʿqūlāt al-awwal, ha-muskalot*), (3) generally agreed upon opinions (*al-mashūrāt, ha-mefursamot*) and (4) opinions received through tradition (*al-maqbūlāt, ha-mequbalot*).[13] Of these, the second and third are important for our investigation.

Maimonides does not define these premises, but he offers examples.

10. On the distinction between dialectical and sophistic (eristic) arguments, see G. E. L. Owen, "Dialectic and Eristic in the Treatment of the Forms," in *Aristotle on Dialectic*, pp. 103–25.

11. See also, *On Sophistical Refutations* 11, esp. 171b, 25–34. In this passage Aristotle distinguishes between sophistic and contentious (eristic) arguments.

12. What follows is based on this chapter. For a discussion of the kinds of arguments among Muslims, see I. Madkour, *L'Organon d'Aristote dans le monde arabe* (2nd ed.; Paris, 1969), pp. 221–39.

13. Cf. Maimonides, "Letter on Astrology," ed. A. Marx, in *Hebrew Union College Annual* 3 (1926), 350 (English: trans. R. Lerner, in *Medieval Political Philosophy*, ed. R. Lerner and M. Mahdi [New York, 1963], p. 228).

He also notes that there is no disagreement concerning sense percepts among human beings having normal sensations, nor is there any disagreement about the first intelligibles among those having sound minds. As examples of sense percepts he lists the perception that a given substance is black, another white, another sweet, and still another hot. First intelligibles are self-evident propositions on which demonstration rests. Maimonides' examples are that the whole is greater than the part, that two is an even number and that things equal to the same thing are equal to each other.

Generally agreed upon opinions and opinions received through tradition differ from sense percepts and first intelligibles in that they are accepted only by special groups, not by all human beings. Maimonides writes:

> But as to generally agreed upon opinions, there is a difference and rivalry for superiority, since there are propositions that have become known among one people and not among another; and whenever a precept is known among many people its acceptability is stronger. Similarly, in the case of traditions, a tradition among one group may be lacking in another.

Generally agreed upon propositions are the premises of dialectical arguments. Maimonides' examples are the following: to uncover the privy parts is shameful; to compensate a benefactor generously is good. While Maimonides' two examples in the *Treatise* are ethical, a number of dialectical propositions appearing in the *Guide* are theoretical. Traditional premises are more restricted than those based on agreement, since they are received from a "chosen person" or from a "chosen assembly." Maimonides does not provide examples for such premises, but one gains the impression that he has in mind opinions received from a religious authority.[14] Traditional propositions provide the premises of rhetorical arguments.[15]

From the enumeration and description of these premises, Maimonides proceeds to a discussion of the arguments to which they lead. Demonstrative arguments or syllogisms (*al-qiyās al-burhānī, ha-heqqesh ha-mofti*), the only ones productive of scientific knowledge, must rest on premises that are true and available to everyone. Dialectical ar-

14. In the passage from the "Letter on Astrology" cited in the previous note Maimonides states, "The third [kind of trustworthy knowledge] is a thing that a man receives from the prophets or from the righteous."

15. As one would expect, rhetorical arguments based on traditional premises play a small role in the *Guide*. There are, of course, many references to Biblical and rabbinic sources, but these either are the starting point of a discussion or support some point that is made. For the role of "traditional authority" (*taqlīd, kabbalah*) prior to philosophic speculation and in the beliefs of ordinary people, see *Guide* I, 33, 71; 34, 75; 35, 80. For an incidental reference to "rhetorical statement," see *Guide* II, 15, 291.

guments (*al-qiyās al-jadalī, heqqesh ha-niṣuaḥ*) are those one or both of whose premises rest on generally agreed upon opinions, while rhetorical arguments (*al-qiyās al-khaṭabi, heqqesh ha-halasah*) are those one or both of whose premises rest on tradition. To these Maimonides adds sophistic arguments which are "for deception or falsehood." Rather carefully, Maimonides describes the premises of these arguments as "leading to error" (*ghawlaṭa bihā, taʿah ʿimah*), "erroneous" (*ghaliṭa fīhā, taʿah bah*) or "misleading" (*mawwaha fīhā, shiqqer bah*), suggesting thereby that sophistic arguments may be badly intentioned, but leaving open the possibility that they are based on premises that are simply false.

III

Maimonides offers little terminological help for locating the various kinds of arguments appearing in the *Guide*. While the term 'demonstration' (*burhān, mofet*) and verb forms such as "to be demonstrated" (*tabarhana, hitba'er be-mofet*) appear with some regularity in the *Guide*, the other kinds of arguments are barely mentioned by name. He mentions the three kinds of arguments incidentally when, criticizing the Mutakallimūn, he states that they mistakenly believed that they had demonstrative arguments for the creation of the universe because they "do not know the difference between demonstration, dialectics and sophistic arguments" (*Guide* I, 71, 180). Similarly, he praises a certain Mutakallim for accepting the unity of God on the authority of the Law rather than on the basis of Kalām arguments, for in rejecting these arguments he "was averse to the acceptance of sophistries" (*Guide* I, 75, 226). And attacking the Kalāmic proofs for creation, he writes:

> I approve of nothing in those proofs and I do not deceive myself by designating methods productive of error as demonstrations. If a man claims that he sets out to demonstrate a certain point by means of sophistical arguments, he does not, in my opinion, strengthen assent to the point he intends to prove, but rather weakens it and opens the way for attack against it (*Guide* II, 16, 293).

Since, then, terminological considerations provide little help in determining whether an argument is dialectical or sophistic, one must turn to the previously mentioned characteristic of these arguments to determine their nature and use.

Before we proceed to the use of demonstrative and dialectical arguments in the *Guide* (the arguments of the Mutakallimūn seem to be the only sophistic ones mentioned in the work), we must make a terminological observation. Maimonides uses two Arabic terms for the arguments he discusses and uses: *burhān* and *dalīl*. *Burhān*, in Maimonides' usage, refers to demonstrations, that is, arguments leading to certain knowledge, while *dalīl* refers to persuasive arguments, that is, arguments leading to opinion. Ibn Tibbon's Hebrew translation reflects this distinction when he translates *burhān* as *mofet*, *dalīl* as *re'ayah*.[16] S. Pines translates *burhān* as "demonstration," *dalīl* as "proof" (sometimes, however, as "argument").

The distinction between demonstrative and dialectical arguments is apparent not only in the substance of the *Guide*, but also in its literary style. Aristotle had stated that demonstrative arguments are not subject to disagreement, a sentiment which Maimonides echoes in the following:

> For in all things whose true reality is known through demonstration (*burhān*, *mofet*), there is no tug of war [disagreement] and no refusal to accept a thing proven . . . (*Guide* I, 31, 66).

In line with the principle that demonstrated propositions are not subject to disagreement, Maimonides presents such propositions anonymously. (It should be noted that, similarly, Maimonides in *Mishneh Torah* presents authoritative legal [halakhic] decisions anonymously.)[17]

16. Samuel ibn Tibbon distinguishes between the two terms as follows: *Mofet* . . . But inasmuch as the proofs (*re'ayot*) for something are of two kinds: strong proof (*re'ayah ḥazaqah*) concerning whose veracity there is no doubt and proof (*re'ayah*) below it in its veracity, I distinguished the strong proof concerning whose veracity there is no doubt by the term "*mofet*" (demonstration), the other by its generic name "*re'ayah*" (proof). But sometimes the second kind of proof [namely, "*re'ayah*"] is called "*mofet*" metaphorically and figuratively. At the beginning [of my translating the *Guide*] I wrote in place of "*re'ayah*" "*mofet*," but afterwards I corrected all [such translations]. (*Perush ha-Milim ha-zarot*, in Y. Even Shemu'el, ed., *Guide of the Perplexed*, appendix, p. 63).

Examples of propositions that have been demonstrated will be given further on. How careful Maimonides was in his terminology can be seen from the way he describes persuasive (dialectical or sophistic) arguments. He speaks of the "proofs" of the Mutakallimūn for creation and the unity of God (*Guide* I, 74, 215; 75, 223). Similarly, he describes Aristotle's arguments for the eternity of the universe as "proofs" (*Guide* II, 14, 285; 15, 289; 16, 293). And finally, he characterizes his own arguments in support of creation as "proofs" (*Guide* II, 16, 294; 21, 316).

Maimonides uses a number of phrases to indicate that a proposition or proof is dialectical. Among them are the following: "strong arguments" (*Guide* I, 33, 72); "our strongest proofs" (*Guide* II, 2, 253); "an opinion that has been shown to be the fittest to be believed" (*Guide* II, 2, 254); "opinions . . . that are exposed to the smallest number of doubts" (*Guide* II, 3, 254); "proofs . . . [that] involve a lesser number of doubts" (*Guide* II, 15, 289); "an opinion . . . [that] is not impossible" (*Guide* II, 16, 293–94); "arguments (proofs) that come close to being demonstrations" (*Guide* II, 19, 303); "speculative philosophic proofs devoid of falsification" (*Guide* II, 21, 316); "[an opinion that is] nearer . . . to intellectual reasoning" (*Guide* III, 17, 471).

17. On anonymity in Maimonides, see I. Twersky, *Introduction to the Code of Maimonides (Mishneh Torah)* (New Haven, 1980), pp. 97–102, and the references there to Maimonidean works discussing this issue.

Of the many instances in the *Guide*, the following citation is a typical example: "It is known (*maʿlūm, yaduʿa*) that existence is an accident attaching to what exists" (*Guide* I, 57, 132). While it is well known that this view is that of Avicenna, Maimonides sees no need to mention that philosopher's name, since, as he sees it, this proposition is true, requiring no authority for its support.

The stylistic presentation of dialectical arguments is different. These arguments, as we have seen, address significant questions about which people disagree. It is the dialectician's task to find reasonable support for the varying opinions and then find the most plausible solution. Invoking the authority of the Hellenistic commentator Alexander of Aphrodisias, Maimonides presents the following account of the dialectical method:

> Alexander has explained that in every case in which no demonstration (*burhān, mofet*) is possible, the two contrary opinions with regard to the matter in question should be posited as hypothesis and it should be seen what doubts attach to each of them: the one to which fewer doubts attach should be believed (*Guide* II, 22, 320).

In place of anonymously presented demonstrations, we now hear of conflicting opinions among which Maimonides sets out to discover that which has the most plausible reasons or, according to the passage cited, "to which the fewest doubts attach."

It has become fashionable in recent research to picture Maimonides as a philosopher of a skeptical or even agnostic bend of mind. To be sure, he speaks of the limitations of human intellect (*Guide* I, 32),[18] and his reduction of essential attributes predicated of God to "negations of privations" (*Guide* I, 58) raises the question of what can really be known about God. However, these discussions must be balanced by frequent references to propositions that have been demonstrated. Since, in the *Guide*, Maimonides forgoes the full discussion of topics that have been demonstrated in books and treatises on physics and metaphysics (*Guide* II, 2, 253–54), one can expect demonstrations only of issues that are germane to the work.

Since one of the purposes of the *Guide* is to show Joseph, the addressee, that the Kalām arguments for the existence, unity and incorporeality of God are false, but that correct demonstrations of these three attributes exist, it is not surprising that the main demonstrative arguments appearing in the work deal with these topics. (As we shall

18. See S. Pines, "The Limitations of Human Knowledge According to Al-Fārābī, Ibn Bājja and Maimonides," in *Studies in Medieval Jewish History and Literature*, ed. I. Twersky (Cambridge, Mass., 1979), pp. 82–109.

see, the case of creation, for which the Mutakallimūn also claimed to have demonstration, is different.)[19] Having set down twenty-five propositions which are required for these demonstrations (we shall hear more of them presently), Maimonides goes on to present four demonstrations for the existence of God: from motion, from composition, from necessity and contingency, and from potentiality (*Guide* II, 1).[20] Attached to these are demonstrations that God is one and incorporeal.

Besides presenting these demonstrations, Maimonides, in several passages of the *Guide,* states that he "will demonstrate" or "has demonstrated" the existence, unity and corporeality of God. He writes, for example: "Now with respect to that which ought to be said in order to refute the doctrine of the corporeality of God and to establish His real unity . . . you shall know the demonstration (*burhān, mofet*) of all of this from this Treatise [the *Guide*]" (Guide I, 1, 21). Similarly: "For God, may He be exalted, is not a body, as shall be demonstrated to you in this Treatise" (*Guide* I, 18, 44). And he comments on his own demonstrations of the existence, unity and incorporeality of God: "All these are demonstrative methods of proving the existence of one deity, who is neither a body nor a force in a body . . ." (*Guide* II, 1, 249).

While Maimonides presents full demonstrations for the existence, unity and incorporeality of God, there are many passages in the *Guide* in which he characterizes propositions as having been demonstrated without, however, presenting the demonstrations in their support. Since the presentation of these demonstrations lies outside the purpose of his work, Maimonides refers the reader to the extant philosophic literature. Foremost among these demonstrated propositions are the twenty-five physical and metaphysical propositions on which he bases his proofs of the existence, unity and incorporeality of God (*Guide* II, Introduction). Concerning these propositions he writes:

> The premises needed for establishing the existence of the deity, may He be exalted, and for the demonstration that He is neither a body nor a force in a body and that He, may His name be sublime, is one, are twenty-five—all of which are demonstrated without there being a doubt as to any point concerning them. For Aristotle and the Peripatetics after him have come forward with a demonstration for every one of them. . . .

19. Maimonides holds that the existence, unity and incorporeality of God can be demonstrated, but that the Kalām proofs are false. However, concerning creation he holds not only that the Kalām proofs are erroneous, but that creation is not subject to demonstration, only to dialectical arguments (*Guide* I, 71, 180).

20. See H. A. Wolfson, "Notes on Proofs of the Existence of God in Jewish Philosophy, *Hebrew Union College Annual* 1 (1924), 575–96 (rpt. in *Studies in the History of Philosophy and Religion,* eds. I. Twersky and G. H. Williams [Cambridge, Mass., 1973], pp. 561–82).

Among other demonstrated propositions to which Maimonides refers are the following: God has no magnitude and hence, no motion or rest (*Guide* I, 26, 57); transparency is not a color (*Guide* I, 28, 61); the moral virtues are required as preliminaries for the intellectual virtues (*Guide* I, 34, 76–77); affirmative attributes cannot be ascribed to God (*Guide* I, 59, 137); natural things do not come about by chance (*Guide* II, 20, 312; III, 17, 464); and a vacuum does not exist (*Guide* II, 24, 324).

Maimonides' discussion of providence provides a good example of his use of the dialectical method.[21] As in all sections of the *Guide* in which the arguments are dialectical, he begins with an account of the opinions that have been held. In the case of providence there are five such opinions. First of all, there is the opinion of Epicurus, who, holding that everything occurs through chance, denies providence of any kind. This opinion can be disregarded since it has been demonstrated that it is philosophically unsound. Next, there is the opinion of Aristotle. Relying on the nature of what exists, he held that the universe functions in regular fashion and in accordance with necessary laws. Identifying this natural order with providence, Aristotle maintained that providence extends to the celestial region and, in the sublunar world, to the species. But whatever happens to individuals in the sublunar world, including human beings, occurs by chance. According to Aristotle there is no distinction between the mouse that is eaten by a cat and the prophet who is devoured by a lion.

The opinion of the Ashʿarites is the opposite of that of Aristotle. Whereas Aristotle admitted providence in the sense that nature functions in orderly fashion, the Ashʿarites denied such independent order and ascribed everything to the direct will of God. Not only are natural events directly determined by the divine will, but also human actions. Since, according to their view, he who wills must know what he wills, it follows that God's knowledge (and with it His providence) must extend not only to human beings, but to animals, plants and minerals as well.

The next opinion is that of the Muʿtazilites, who maintained that

21. The analysis which follows is based on *Guide* III, 17–18. For Maimonides' discussion of providence, see the following: A. Nuriel, "Providence and Governance in *Moreh ha-Nevukhim*," *Tarbiz* 49 (1979–80), 346–55 (Hebrew); A. Reines, "Maimonides' Concepts of Providence and Theodicy," *Hebrew Union College Annual* 42 (1972), 169–206; C. Touati, "Les deux théories de Maimonide sur la providence," in *Studies in Jewish Religion and Intellectual History: presented to Alexander Altmann on the occasion of his seventieth birthday*, ed. S. Stein and R. Loewe (University, Alabama, 1979), pp. 331–43. See also "Translator's Introduction," in *Guide*, trans. S. Pines, pp. lxiv–lxvii.

man is free and that all of God's actions are consequent upon His wisdom and that all He does is just. This led them to affirm that divine justice requires that God rewards and punishes not only human beings according to their deserts, but also animals. The mouse eaten by a cat must be rewarded for its suffering in the World to Come. Since God rewards and punishes in accordance with His wisdom, His knowledge must extend to animals, no less than human beings.

Having presented these three opinions (that of Epicurus had been ruled out), Maimonides went on to show that cogent reasons had brought the proponents of these views to the opinion they held:

To my mind no one among the partisans of these three opinions concerning providence should be blamed, for every one of them was impelled by strong necessity to say what he did (*Guide* III, 17, 468).

Aristotle had denied that providence extends to individual human beings, because he had found that the order of the universe went no further than the sublunar species. The Ashʿarites, by contrast, held that since God is the direct cause of everything within the world, his providence and hence his knowledge extend not only to human beings, but to animals, plants and minerals as well. Emphasizing that God is just and that His justice is in conformity with His wisdom, the Muʿtazilites maintained that His providence and hence His knowledge, extend to animals, no less than human beings.

Having considered the opinions he rejects, Maimonides turns to the opinion of the Law and then to his own opinion. Affirming that man is free and that God is just, the Law teaches that divine providence extends only to human beings, not to animals:

I was impelled to adopt this belief by the fact that I never found in the book of any prophet a text mentioning that God has a providence watching over one of the animal individuals, but only over a human individual (*Guide* III, 17, 472).

But Maimonides accepts this opinion not only on the authority of prophets, but on the basis of rational arguments as well. These arguments, however, are not demonstrative, but dialectical. He writes:

In this belief that I shall set forth, namely, that divine providence extends to individual human beings, not animals, *I am not relying upon the conclusion to which demonstration has led me,* but upon what has clearly appeared as the intention of the book of God and of the books of our prophets. This opinion, which I believe is less disgraceful than the preceding opinions and *nearer than they to intellectual reasoning (al-qiyās al-ʿaqlī, ha-heqqesh ha-sikli)* (*Guide* III, 17, 471—italics mine).

Commentators on Maimonides have disagreed on whether his own opinion is an interpretation of the opinion of the Law or whether it differs from it. Be that as it may, we need only be concerned with his own account, which is "nearer to intellectual reasoning." This account is based on certain cosmological and psychological teachings that he accepted. The universe, according to this account, consists of a series of celestial spheres each of which is governed by a soul and an incorporeal intelligence. The lowest of these incorporeal intelligences is the Agent Intellect, which is the intellect that governs the sublunar sphere. This intellect is the "Giver of Forms" as well as an efficient cause in the production of human knowledge. Unlike sublunar bodies which act through contact with the bodies they affect, the Agent Intellect (as all incorporeal intellects) causally affects whatever it affects through "emanation" or "overflow" (*fayḍ, shefaʿ*).[22]

Maimonides uses the notion of "overflow" to develop his account of divine providence. While the opinion of the Law leaves open the possibility that providence may be the result of direct divine intervention, Maimonides develops his view against the background of the cosmological and psychological theories that we have sketched. Providence, for him, is not the result of direct divine intervention, but depends on the development of man's intellect. The greater the development of the intellect, the greater the providence. He writes, "According to me, divine providence is consequent upon the divine overflow" (*Guide* III, 17, 471) and again, "Accordingly divine providence does not watch in equal manner over all of the human species, but providence is graded as their human perfection [that is, the development of their intellect] is graded" (*Guide* III, 18, 475). In holding that providence depends on the development of human intellect, he rules out that it may extend to animals, plants or minerals.

In the light of his own understanding of providence, Maimonides completes his dialectical argument by criticizing the three opinions that he rejects. Some of these opinions, he holds, are excessive (that is, they extend providence too far); others fall short (that is, they extend providence not far enough). While he does not mention any names, it seems that the Ashʿarites and the Muʿtazilites are those that are excessive, Aristotle and his followers those that fall short. If, as Maimonides asserts, the correct opinion (that "closer to intellectual reasoning") is that providence is limited to human beings, the Ashʿarites go too far in extending it to animals, plants and minerals, and the Muʿtazilites in extending it to animals.[23] By contrast, Aristotle and

22. See *Guide* I, 72; II, 4 and 11–12.

23. See S. Munk, *Le Guide des Égarés* (rpt. Paris, 1981), III, p. 136, n. 2. Shem Tob

his followers fall short since they limit providence to the species, denying thereby that it extends to individual human beings (*Guide* III, 17, 474).

Having examined one example of Maimonides' use of the dialectical method, we turn now to one example of each of the different ways in which he resolves dialectical problems. Recalling that Aristotle had maintained that there are dialectical problems in which one of the two alternatives should be accepted, while there are others in which the resolution consists of a combination of what is true in the divergent opinions, we shall consider Maimonides' account of creation as an example of the first kind and his account of prophecy as an example of the second kind.

Maimonides begins his discussion of creation by enumerating three opinions that have been held.[24] The first of these is that of all who believe in the Law of Moses. According to it, God created the universe by His will (and by His wisdom), after absolute nonexistence, out of nothing and apart from time. The second opinion is that of Plato and others who maintained that God created the universe out of some preexistent matter; the third that of Aristotle and his followers, who affirmed that the universe is eternal. Since according to Maimonides, the Platonic position is equivalent to the belief in the eternity of the world, only two alternatives remain: the universe is either created or eternal. That the issue is dialectical is clearly indicated by Maimonides' justifying the doubts he had raised about Aristotle's opinion that the universe is eternal:

> We have acted in this way when it was to our mind established as true that, regarding the question whether the heavens are generated or eternal, neither of the two contrary opinions could be demonstrated. For we have explained the doubts attaching to each of the opinions and have shown to you that the opinion favoring the eternity of the world is the one that raises more doubts and is more harmful for the belief that ought to be held with regard to the deity (*Guide* II, 22, 320).

Whereas commentators, including al-Fārābī, had maintained that Aristotle believed that he had demonstrated the eternity of the universe, Maimonides undertakes to show that the Philosopher was well aware that his arguments for eternity were only plausible opinions.

---

ben Joseph ibn Shem Tob, the fifteenth-century commentator on the *Guide*, adds the opinion of the Law to the excessive opinions. It is excessive since, according to it, providence extends indiscriminately to all human beings, while according to Maimonides, it is contingent on the development of the human intellect (in *Guide* [Warsaw, 1872; rpt. Jerusalem, 1960–61], part III, p. 26b).

24. See my essay, "Maimonides on Creation and Emanation," in *Studies in Medieval Philosophy*, ed. John F. Wippel (Washington, D.C., 1987), pp. 45–61.

Maimonides argues this interpretation on textual grounds. The close examination of the Aristotelian texts discloses that Aristotle was well aware that his arguments were only dialectical. For example, he states in the *Physics* that all the physicists prior to him believed that motion (and, hence, the universe) is eternal. Maimonides comments that had Aristotle had demonstration for this proposition, he would not have needed to invoke the opinion of his predecessors (*Guide* II, 15). However, in spite of his awareness of the dialectical nature of the problem, Aristotle held that the arguments in support of eternity are more convincing.

To counter Aristotle, Maimonides argues, first of all, that the Philosopher was brought to his opinion by holding that creation was a kind of change and that the laws of change operative within the world also have to apply to creation. Maimonides grants Aristotle that were this line of argumentation correct, it would follow that the universe is eternal, but it is precisely this argument that is at stake. Taking issue with Aristotle, Maimonides sets out to present evidence that, in fact, the laws of motion applicable within the world are not applicable to creation. Hence, creation is at least possible (*Guide* II, 17).

But Maimonides goes beyond arguing merely for the possibility of creation; there is evidence that creation is more plausible than eternity. This evidence is provided by certain astronomical features of the world. Observation discloses that there exists a certain disorder in the celestial realm: planets having the same velocity differ in position, and planets having slower motions are above those having faster motions, and sometimes the reverse is seen to be the case. These and other celestial irregularities cannot be explained on the Aristotelian view that the universe is totally ordered, and they provide evidence for creation through the divine will (*Guide* II, 19 and 24). Against Aristotle, Maimonides concludes that this evidence makes creation the more likely solution of the dialectical question.

The case of prophecy is different.[25] Once again Maimonides begins by enumerating the positions that have been held. There was, first of all, the opinion of pagans who believed in prophecy, and this opinion was followed by some of the common people who adhere to the Law. These held that prophecy was caused directly by the divine will: God could make a prophet whomever He wishes. Then there was the opinion of the philosophers (the Aristotelians) who maintained that prophecy was a natural phenomenon. If a person possessed the moral

25. See H. A. Wolfson, "Halevi and Maimonides on Prophecy," *Jewish Quarterly Review*, n.s., 32 (1942), 345–70; 33 (1942), 49–82 (rpt. in H. A. Wolfson, *Studies in the History of Philosophy and Religion*, II, 60–119).

and intellectual virtues and had a well-developed imagination, he would automatically become a prophet. Finally, there was the opinion of "our Law." It agreed with the opinion of the philosophers in maintaining that only someone who had the requisite qualifications could become a prophet, but it made room for the first opinion in holding that the divine will may prevent prophecy in someone otherwise qualified for it (*Guide* II, 32). The case of prophecy provides, then, an example of the resolution of a dialectical problem by combining what is true in the divergent opinions and rejecting what is false.

Having described Maimonides' conception of dialectical arguments and having provided some examples of his use of the dialectical method, we may now ask, What is the function of dialectic in the *Guide*? Three possible answers suggest themselves to this question. The first of these is that dialectical arguments are a device used by Maimonides to hide his true opinion. Thus, for example, Maimonides presents lengthy philosophical and speculative arguments to show that creation or eternity is a dialectical problem and that creation is the more plausible alternative, while he really believes, with the Aristotelians, that the eternity of the world has been demonstrated. But if this interpretation is correct, it would seem to follow that such arguments are sophistic and that the *Guide*, to a large extent, is a sophistic rather than a dialectical work. On this supposition, how would Maimonides' overt arguments differ from the Kalāmic arguments he rejects?

According to a second interpretation, there are dialectical arguments in the *Guide*, but these lack cognitive value and have only a utilitarian function. They would then belong to the category of "beliefs, belief in which is necessary for the sake of political welfare" (*Guide* III, 28, 512), that is, beliefs required to establish the authority of the Law and to motivate obedience to it. This interpretation receives some textual support from a passage such as the following: "the belief in eternity the way Aristotle sees it . . . destroys the Law in its principles, necessarily gives the lie to every miracle, and reduces to inanity all the hopes and threats that the Law has held out" (*Guide* II, 25, 328).

While dialectical arguments may have a utilitarian function, I wish to argue for a third interpretation, namely, that they have cognitive significance as well. According to this view, the *Guide* contains physical and metaphysical propositions that can be supported by demonstrations, but there are also others—such as propositions about creation, prophecy and providence—for which only dialectical arguments can be offered. The distinction between these two kinds of propositions is not so much their truth or falsity—though demonstration leads to certain knowledge, dialectic only to true opinions—but the kinds of arguments offered in their support. On this interpretation it follows that both demonstrative and dialectical arguments are part of Maimonides' logical method for the solution of physical and metaphysical problems. There is textual evidence for this interpretation, perhaps the most striking example being the parable of the royal palace (*Guide* III, 51). Describing in the parable the positions of various kinds of human beings in relation to the palace and its ruler (God), Maimonides states of those who have reached the inner chamber and are in the presence of the king:

> He, however, who has achieved demonstration to the extent that that is possible, of everything that may be demonstrated; and who has ascertained in divine matters, to the extent that that is possible, everything that may be attained; and *who has come close to certainty* (*qārib al-yaqīn, we-yikrab 'el 'amitah*) in those matters in which one can only come close to it—has come to be with the ruler in the inner part of the habitation (italics mine).

From this it seems to follow, with the stricture noted, that dialectical no less than demonstrative arguments have cognitive significance.

Yeshiva University

4 Maimonides on Aristotle and Scientific Method*

JOEL L. KRAEMER

I

In his Translator's Introduction to the *Guide of the Perplexed*, Professor Shlomo Pines notes that many of the quotations from Aristotle's works on the natural sciences and from the *Topics* "serve to build up an image of Aristotle regarded as an earnest seeker of truth tentatively propounding more or less plausible theories."[1] This description is a far cry from the conventional image of the Greek thinker as he is generally portrayed in Maimonides' environment.[2]

In this paper I shall try to show that Maimonides' interpretation of Aristotle finds surprising confirmation in the exegesis of some modern exponents of his thought. It will also become clear that Maimonides' understanding of the mode and power of Aristotle's argumentation flowed from certain insights of Alexander of Aphrodisias. But my aim is not simply to grasp how Maimonides understood Aristotle. In view of the fact that Maimonides esteemed Aristotle and had high regard for his teachings in logic and scientific method, it is legitimate, I submit, to infer that Maimonides' conception of Aristotle's method illu-

*The research for this paper was supported by the Lucius N. Littauer Foundation and by the Rosenberg School of Jewish Studies, Tel Aviv University. A Hebrew version will appear in a volume of studies dedicated to Professor Shlomo Pines.

1. S. Pines, "Translator's Introduction: The Philosophic Sources of The Guide of the Perplexed," in *The Guide of the Perplexed* (Chicago, 1963), pp. lxii–lxiii.

2. In the European Middle Ages (thirteenth century), "the masters of arts" discovered in Aristotle a new model for science and for the destiny of a university person, for they found in Aristotle an investigator who poses questions—the hunter (*thēreuein*) (*Prior Analytics* 46a11), the discoverer (*heurēsis*) (*Nicomachean Ethics* 1112b19) and the investigator (*zētēsis*) (*Metaphysics* 983a23). See C. H. Lohr, "The Medieval Interpretation of Aristotle," in *The Cambridge History of Later Medieval Philosophy*, ed. N. Kretzmann et al. (Cambridge, 1982), p. 91.

mines significant aspects of his own conception of scientific theory. Furthermore, treating these themes will enable us to draw conclusions concerning Maimonides' objectives in the *Guide of the Perplexed* and to gain insight into the dialectical character of that work.

In his "Tithenai ta Phainomena," G. E. L. Owen drew attention to what appears to be a serious discrepancy between Aristotle's statements concerning scientific methods of reasoning in the *Analytics* and the methods that he actually employs in the *Physics*.[3] Whereas in the *Posterior Analytics* Aristotle attempts to depict scientific reasoning as a tight system of demonstrative truth based upon a rigid system of formal deductive reasoning, in the *Physics* (where he is expected to carry out this procedure) his mode of argumentation is rather tentative and relaxed.

A more dramatic incongruity, Owen observes, concerns the means by which scientific principles are discovered. Owen claims that in the *Prior Analytics* and elsewhere Aristotle presents a "Baconian picture" of scientific explanation. Accordingly, one must first grasp and collect the *phainomena* ("empirical observations") and thereafter elaborate the proofs in the various sciences. Aristotle explicitly relates this procedure to the enterprise of the *Physics*. Now, says Owen, while this Baconian method is eminently applicable and attested in Aristotle's biological works and in the *Meteorology*, it is not actually followed in the *Physics*, for in this work Aristotle's discussions are often not founded upon empirical observations. These data are used instead to guide and illustrate his analyses. Consequently, Aristotle cannot maintain that his physical principles are really based upon grasping and collecting the phenomena.

Owen points out that Aristotle uses the term *phainomena* in a different sense when he discusses the subject of scientific inquiry. For example, he begins his discussion of *akrasia* in the *Nicomachean Ethics* 1145b1–6, by commenting on his scientific procedure, as follows:[4]

> Here, as in all other cases, we must set down the appearances (*phainomena*) and, first, working through the puzzles, in this way go on to show, if possible, the truth of all the beliefs we hold (*ta endoxa*) about these experiences, and if this is not possible, the truth of the greatest number and the most authori-

3. G. E. L. Owen, "Tithenai ta Phainomena," in *Aristote et les problèmes de méthode*, ed. S. Mansion (Louvain, 1961), pp. 83–85; reprinted in *Aristotle, a Collection of Critical Essays*, ed. J. M. E. Moravcsik (Notre Dame, 1968); and in *Articles on Aristotle, I. Science*, ed. J. Barnes et al. (London, 1975).

4. The translation is that of Martha Craven Nussbaum, "Saving Aristotle's Appearances," in *Language and Logos*, ed. M. Schofield and M. C. Nussbaum (Cambridge, 1982), p. 267. Prof. Hilary Putnam kindly drew my attention to this important study.

tative. For if the difficulties are resolved and the beliefs (*endoxa*) are left in place, we will have done enough showing.

Owen argues that in this text the term *phainomena* does not mean "observed facts" (as Sir David Ross translates), for when Aristotle goes on to explain what he has in mind he does not discuss observed facts or the like but rather *ta endoxa,* which are "the common conceptions on the subject," and he ends his comments by stating that "these are the *legomena* ('things said')" (1145b8–20), where *legomena* means "linguistic usage" or "the conceptual structure revealed in language." In this sense of the term, dialectical argument may be said to have its starting point in the *phainomena.*

Aristotle's *Physics* may, in fact, be taken as having its starting point in the *phainomena* in this second sense of the term, that is, as equivalent to the *endoxa* or the *legomena.* Aristotle's discussion of place, for instance, is based upon what he says appears to be the case according to established ways of speaking, what the theorists say, what the majority think—what he further on terms as *endoxon.* The puzzles (*aporiai*) that accompany the discussion of place are not difficulties that concern observed data but rather logical paradoxes and conceptual conundrums. If this is true, then the *Physics* is a philosophic work based upon dialectical arguments, not upon observed data.

Owen's line of interpretation is adopted and carried a step further by Martha Craven Nussbaum in "Saving Aristotle's Appearances," with the crucial difference that she rejects Owen's suggestion that Aristotle used the term *phainomena* in a dual or ambiguous sense.[5] Her starting point is the very same passage in the *Ethics* introducing *akrasia,* in which Aristotle comments on his scientific/philosophic method. She understands Aristotle to be saying, "If we work through the difficulties with which the *phainomena* confront us and leave the greatest number and the most basic intact, we will have gone as far as philosophy can, or should, go." Along with Owen, then, she interprets *phainomena* in this passage to be equivalent to "what we believe" or "what we say," thereby accepting Owen's association of *phainomena* with "language and ordinary belief." As stated, she does not believe, however, that Aristotle used the term equivocally. In her view, this is all he ever means by *phainomena.*

Nussbaum dismisses the traditional, or conventional, interpretation of Aristotle's scientific/philosophic procedure. According to this interpretation, Aristotle posited that the scientist first collects empirical

5. Nussbaum, "Saving Aristotle's Appearances," pp. 267–80.

data, avoiding at this stage the contamination of interpretation. He then goes on to devise a theory that gives a satisfactory explanation of the data. According to this conventional interpretation of Aristotle's method, when he speaks of the *phainomena* he means observational data in the Baconian sense, and his endeavor "to save" the *phainomena* is an effort to devise an adequate theory.

Aristotle's *phainomena* are, however, not observational data but rather *endoxa*, "the common conceptions or beliefs on a subject," and *legomena*, "the things we say." Thus far, with reference to Aristotle's scientific procedure, Nussbaum walks hand in hand with Owen. She then departs from him by contending that Owen was not sufficiently consistent in his critique of the traditional Baconian interpretation of Aristotle's procedure. In her view, Aristotle never means by *phainomena* neutral, theory-free observations of "hard facts." In his marine biology, for example, he depicts "the world as it appears to, as it is experienced by, observers who are members of our kind." Aristotle accepts "the data of human experience" as the limits of his scientific method. This procedure requires the scientist to establish the pertinent appearances, including common beliefs and ways of speaking and prior discussions of the problem—the opinions of "the many and the wise."[6] The phenomena are grasped by a class of members who share a certain way of life: in other words, members of communities like "ours." Once the relevant appearances have been harvested, the scientist enumerates the puzzles that accompany the appearances. The tug-of-war of opposing opinions requires that the scientist resolve the puzzles and difficulties and then return to the appearances to show that the adopted explanation is the one that is most adequate.

I shall have occasion to observe further on that this fresh understanding of Aristotle's scientific procedure is, *grosso modo*, anticipated by Alexander of Aphrodisias, and that Alexander is, in turn, followed by Moses Maimonides in this regard.

II

The image of Aristotle presented by Maimonides as one who seeks the truth earnestly and propounds more or less plausible theories in a tentative way is projected close to the beginning of the *Guide*, in part I, chapter 5. Maimonides speaks of Aristotle, whom he calls "the chief of the philosophers," as someone who strove to achieve correct beliefs to the extent that objective lies within human capacity. In this

6. Ibid., p. 275, citing *Topics* 100b21 and 104a8–12.

chapter, Maimonides stresses the limitations of human knowledge, a theme that recurs with great strength in part I, chapters 31 to 36.[7] Part I of the *Guide*, from chapter 1 to chapter 45, is concerned mainly with lexicographical questions, specifically with equivocal terms that occur in Scripture. The lexicographical discussions are occasionally interpenetrated by digressions on related matters. For instance, chapter 2 is concerned with a question that had been posed by "a learned man," which brings Maimonides to distinguish between intellectual cognition of the truth and awareness of "the things generally accepted as known" (*al-mashhūrāt/ta endoxa*).[8] The chapter also treats an equivocal term, namely, *elohim*. Chapter 5 also treats equivocal terms at the end, that is "seeing," "vision," and "looking" (which may mean "intellectual apprehension").[9] But the chapter begins with a statement concerning Aristotle's scientific procedure by way of a paraphrase of *De caelo* 291b24–28:[10]

When the chief of the philosophers[11] began to investigate very obscure matters and to attempt a proof concerning them, he excused himself by making a statement the meaning of which is as follows. A student of his books should not, because of the subject of his researches, ascribe to him effrontery, temerity, and an excess of haste to speak of matters of which he had no knowl-

7. On this motif in the *Guide*, see Pines, "The Limitations of Human Knowledge according to Al-Fārābī, ibn Bājja and Maimonides," in *Studies in Medieval Jewish History and Literature*, ed. I. Twersky (Cambridge, Mass., 1979), pp. 82–109.

8. The Arabic text has *rajul ʿulūmī*. I have used the edition of S. Munk and I. Joel (Jerusalem, 1930–31). See p. 15, 1.22 (15.22). (The numbers after the period refer to lines.) The expression is rather awkward and its meaning not entirely clear. It is used to render *ho mathēmatikos* in the Arabic translation by Isḥāq b. Ḥunayn of *De anima* (403b15). See S. M. Afnan, *A Philosophical Lexicon in Persian and Arabic* (Beirut, 1969), p. 200; ʿA. Badawī, *Aristotelis De Anima* (Cairo, 1954), p. 7.15.

9. At the end of I, 5, Maimonides says that his entire purpose was to show that when the terms "seeing," "vision" and "looking" occur in this sense, intellectual apprehension (*idrāk ʿaqlī*), and not eyesight, is meant. In other words, this chapter also treats lexicographical issues. In the lexicographical chapters philosophic motifs are interwoven—in chapters I, 1–5, intellectual apprehension is a dominant theme—and the reader is expected to discern and connect them.

10. For translations and paraphrases from the *Guide* I have used the English translation by Pines. On this text, see Pines, "Translator's Introduction," pp. lxi, lxiii.

11. The reference is, of course, to Aristotle. Note that Aristotle is the first philosopher mentioned in the *Guide* and that he appears quite close to the beginning. Maimonides' attitude toward Aristotle is adumbrated in his famous letter to Samuel b. Tibbon: "The works of Aristotle are the roots and foundations of all works on the sciences. But they cannot be understood except with the help of commentaries, those of Alexander of Aphrodisias, those of Themistius, and those of Averroes" (Pines, "Translator's Introduction," p. lix). See also *Guide* II, 14, beginning, where Maimonides says, referring to the discourse of the philosophers, that he will only pay attention, among those engaged in speculative discourse, to Aristotle, "for it is his opinion that ought to be considered." In II, 19 (p. 306), Maimonides calls attention to the "depth of Aristotle's penetration and to his extraordinary apprehension. . . ."

edge; but rather he should ascribe to him the desire and the endeavor to acquire and achieve true beliefs[12] to the extent to which this is in the power of man.[13]

It may readily be assumed that Maimonides was in sympathy with Aristotle's modest and tentative approach to the investigation of very obscure matters. The burden of Aristotle's apologia is indeed the very message that Maimonides strove to convey to his pupil Joseph son of Judah in part I of the *Guide*, in which he warns against excessive haste in tackling obscure matters. The obscure matters in the text paraphrased in chapter 5 are concerned with celestial mechanics. Maimonides moves from his paraphrase of the text to the lesson one may derive from Aristotle's disavowal of boldness and excessive haste. Maimonides infers that one should not rashly hasten to attain what he calls "this great and sublime matter" (that is, the divine science, or metaphysics) without the necessary prerequisites.[14] These include training in the various sciences, moral preparation by refinement of character, and subduing of one's desires and cravings that come from the imagination.

Maimonides often stresses that purification of the imagination is a necessary condition for the attainment of knowledge. Investigation of this great and sublime matter also presupposes familiarity with logic. One needs to attain a knowledge of true and certain premises and of the methods of syllogism and inference, as well as means of preservation from the pitfalls of sophistical thinking. The one who strives for this knowledge should not jump to conclusions, and he should not excessively strain his mind to reach apprehension of the deity. He should rather advance gradually and with reticence and awe.[15] In this

12. Text: *iʿtiqādāt ṣaḥīḥa* (p. 19.17). *Ṣaḥīḥa* is best rendered by "correct." Ibn Tibbon uses *amiti* ("true") instead of *nakhon* ("correct").

13. The words "to the extent to which this is in the power of man" recall one of the definitions of philosophy that the Falāsifa received from the Alexandrian commentators on Aristotle, that were usually included in introductions to Porphyry's *Eisagoge*, namely, "assimilation to God according to human capacity." See, e.g., D. M. Dunlop, "The Existence and Definition of Philosophy," *Iraq* 13 (1951): 86, where the definition appears in what has been identified as being a work of Ibn al-Ṭayyib; see S. M. Stern, "Ibn al-Ṭayyib's Commentary on the *Isagoge*," *BSOAS* 19 (1957): 419–25.

Maimonides uses the phrase rather often; see especially *Guide* III, 54, *ultimo*, where speaking of human perfection Maimonides says that it is apprehension of God and knowledge of His providence manifested in bringing creatures into being and governing them "in a measure corresponding to his capacity."

14. See, e.g., the commentators Ephodi, Narboni and Shem Tov ad loc. On the relationship between intellectual apprehension of the deity and the notion of vision in the Bible in *Guide* I, 1–5, see chaps. 1 (p. 15.6), 2 (16.28), 3 (18.10–11), 4 (18.18), 5 (20.24–25).

15. One of the overall aims of the *Guide* is to lead the pupil through the sciences in

very sense it is stated in Scripture, "And Moses hid his face, for he was afraid to look upon God" (Exodus 3:6).[16] Moses was commended for this, Maimonides says, and God caused his bounty and goodness to overflow upon him, so that it was said of him, "And the figure of the Lord shall he look upon" (Numbers 12:8). The Sages say that this was Moses' reward for having "hidden his face so as not to look upon God." Moses' conduct contrasted with that of the nobles of the children of Israel, who were "overhasty, strained their thoughts, and achieved apprehension, but only an imperfect one" (trans. Pines, p. 30).[17]

The lesson of chapter 5 was, as stated, pertinent to the recipient of the *Guide*, Joseph son of Judah (and those like him). Maimonides notes in the Epistle Dedicatory (p. 3) his pupil's keen avidity for inquiry and his powerful desire for speculative matters.[18] It was because of his strong motivation that Maimonides acceded to his request to study with him. He studied under Maimonides' tutelage first mathematics, then astronomy, and thereafter logic, thus following the established syllabus of philosophic studies. At this point the pupil requested further knowledge, particularly concerning divine matters, that is, metaphysics, and also concerning the intentions of the Mutakallimūn. He wished to ascertain whether or not their procedures were based upon demonstrative proofs.[19] Realizing that his pupil was perplexed (*ḥāʾir*) and stupefied, Maimonides dissuaded him from this higher pursuit and urged him instead to go on with his studies in a systematic way. The *Guide*, then, is a work which, inter alia, points the way to the pursuit of philosophy in a careful, deliberate and systematic manner.

Maimonides returns to the *De caelo* passage in *Guide* II, 19 (p. 307). This time, however, he quotes the Arabic translation of the text verbatim. The passage is cited in a context pertaining to astronomy, which is in fact the topic treated by Aristotle in the *De caelo* text.[20] Maimonides once again suggests that the investigation in question goes beyond astronomy per se. He introduces the quotation by observing that Aristotle made his statement when he realized the feebleness of his com-

---

an orderly manner. We learn in the Epistle Dedicatory that Maimonides' pupil Joseph son of Judah was eager to plunge into metaphysical questions before he had received the necessary preliminary training.

16. Maimonides presents Moses here and elsewhere as the ideal knower.

17. See also II, 24.

18. *Guide*, Arabic text, pp. 1.7–8.

19. The expression "the intentions of the Mutakallimūn" (*maqāṣid al Mutakallimīn*, pp. 1.17–18) recalls the title of al-Ghazālī's work, *Maqāṣid al-falāsifa*.

20. Maimonides refers to the motion of the spheres in the passage immediately prior to this.

ments concerning the causation of these things.[21] Maimonides' quotation of the text is as follows:[22]

Now we desire to make a sufficient inquiry into two questions.[23] For it is obligatory for us to inquire into them and to speak concerning them according to the capacity of our intellects, our knowledge, and our opinion.[24] However, no one ought to attribute this undertaking[25] to overboldness[26] and temerity on our part, but rather should our desire and ardor for philosophy be admired.[27] When, therefore, we seek out noble and important questions[28] and are able to propound for them—though it be only to some small extent—a well-founded[29] solution, it behooves the hearer to feel great joy and jubilation. This is literally what he says.

Aristotle's text, on which this is based, reads (trans. J. L. Stocks):

There are two difficulties, which may very reasonably here be raised, of which we must now attempt to state the probable solution; for we regard the zeal of one whose thirst for philosophy leads him to accept even slight indications where it is difficult to see one's way, as a proof rather of modesty than of over-confidence.

In this instance, in II, 19 (p. 307), in contrast to the paraphrase in I, 5, Maimonides does not wish to stress Aristotle's tentativeness and modesty so much as he does his awareness of the weakness of his statements. Maimonides then tries to account for Aristotle's difficulties by observing that the feebleness of his arguments was compounded by the circumstance that the science of mathematics had not been brought to a state of perfection in his time, and also by the fact that the motions of the heavenly spheres were not as well known then as they were in Maimonides' own time, a view which he expresses elsewhere and which, incidentally, stands in bold contrast to the opinion

21. In referring to the causation of these things (the motion of the spheres, and so on), Maimonides alludes to adducing demonstrative (apodeictic) proof. Demonstrative proof, or scientific knowledge (*apodeixis*), is based, according to Aristotle, upon knowledge of (the four) causes; see, e.g., *Prior Analytics* 94a20.

22. *De caelo* 291b24–28. The English translation is that of J. L. Stocks. The Arabic translation used by Maimonides was that of Yaḥyā b. al-Biṭrīq, reworked by Ḥunayn b. Isḥāq; see the Arabic text edited by ʿA. Badawī (Cairo, 1961), pp. 269–70.

23. The two questions relate to the movements of the spheres and the stars. The word *question* (*masʾala*) may reflect Greek *aporia*.

24. Text (p. 214.16): *bi-mablagh ʿuqūlinā wa-ʿilminā wa-raʾyinā*. The word *ʿuqūlinā* is lacking in the Arabic text edited by Badawī. The Greek original reads simply *legein to phainomenon*.

25. Text: *an yunzila dhālika minnā*. Badawī: *an yarā dhālika minnā*.

26. Text: *qiḥa*. Badawī: *musāfaḥa*(!).

27. Badawī adds *ḥīnaʾidhin*.

28. The words *al-masāʾil* ("questions") and *al-sharīfa* ("noble") are lacking in Badawī. The Arabic text reflects Greek *tas magistas echomen aporias*.

29. Text: *mubraman;* Badawī: lacking.

of his contemporary Ibn Rushd, who believed that the sciences had reached perfection in the time of Aristotle.[30]

Note that whereas in the paraphrase of the *De caelo* passage in *Guide* I, 5, Maimonides had referred to acquiring correct beliefs according to human capacity, in II, 19, where we have a more literal rendering, he uses the expression "according to the capacity of our intellects, our knowledge, and our opinions." This limitation to human intellectual capacity is stated in connection with the claim that it is difficult to discover the ground and causes of celestial phenomena, in other words, to provide demonstrative arguments.[31] This assertion should be related to Maimonides' position, stated in II, 24, that the aim of the astronomer is not to give information concerning how the spheres are in reality but simply to determine what fits that which is visible, that is, the appearances, or the phenomena. Maimonides expounds the meaning of the expression "according to the capacity of our intellects . . ." in a new way that, he claims, he has not come across in the works of commentators. He explains that by the words "according to the capacity of our intellects" Aristotle intended "our incapacity to assign causes for things of such perfection and accomplishment. But he deemed that to a small extent these might be assigned, and he did this."

Let us recall that Maimonides had spoken of his pupil Joseph son of Judah as someone who had a "powerful desire for speculative matters." The passage before us likewise refers to "our desire and ardor for philosophy." This ardor may be well and good, but it is this natural inquisitiveness that, carried too far, drives a human being to seek knowledge of speculative matters that is beyond his intellectual capacity or stage of preparation.

Establishing the limitations of human knowledge is the main objective of part I, chapters 31 to 34. Maimonides begins chapter 31 by stating that while the human intellect has the natural power to apprehend certain things, there are also existent beings and matters that the intellect is totally incapable of apprehending. To be sure, there are variations among the intellectual capacities of different individuals, but the human intellect per se has an absolute limit.[32]

30. See also *Guide* II, 24. In Maimonides' view, as expressed there, Aristotle was unfamiliar with a certain astronomic fact because mathematics had not been perfected in his time. Maimonides' contemporary Ibn Rushd believed that the sciences had reached perfection in the time of Aristotle. He consequently attempted to justify Aristotle's notions concerning celestial mechanics. See also Pines, "Translator's Introduction," pp. lxiii and cx.

31. See below for further discussion.

32. See also Pines, "Limitations," p. 92. Pines also mentions *Guide* I, 37 (p. 86), and

Maimonides does not specify here why human beings are incapable of achieving knowledge of certain things. Elsewhere, in III, 9 (p. 436), for example, he explains that it is matter that precludes knowledge of what is separate from matter, that is, the separate intellects and God. On several occasions Maimonides alludes to the fact that Moses was capable of attaining knowledge of the separate intellects and the celestial bodies and their motions, namely, a knowledge that is actually beyond human capacity. This ability is related to his liberation from the bonds of matter, the "strong veil" that prevents apprehension of beings that are separate from matter. Moses is thus presented as the ideal knower, a position that Maimonides may have assumed for theological reasons.

Human beings are conscious of their cognitive limitations, Maimonides says (I, 31, p. 65), and consequently do not yearn for knowledge of things that are beyond their capacity, at least not when their ignorance pertains to phenomena such as the number of stars, whether this number is odd or even, or the species of living beings, minerals, plants, and so on. That is, people are perfectly aware that they cannot grasp the ostensibly innumerable; they cannot count the grains of sand on the seashore. But, says Maimonides, human beings do have a powerful desire to know certain matters that are, in fact, beyond their capacity, without their being aware that this is the case. Maimonides has in mind, he says, things that cannot be demonstrated, concerning which contradictory opinions and doubts abound. When demonstrative arguments can be marshaled, then disagreements do not occur. The various sciences may be arrayed in a hierarchy as regards their demonstrative power. Metaphysics contains many elements that engender perplexity, whereas these elements are few in physics and nonexistent in mathematics. Metaphysics, then, is the chief source of perplexity, and this is one of the main points Maimonides wishes to drive home in his discussion of the limitations of human knowledge.

Alexander of Aphrodisias, Maimonides recalls, had mentioned three causes for disagreement. The second is most relevant to Maimonides' discussion here. It is the "subtlety and obscurity of the object of apprehension in itself and the difficulty in apprehending it."[33]

38 (p. 87), relating to Moses' request to see the Lord's face (Exodus 33:23). In response to this request, the Lord gave him the capacity to apprehend even transcendental beings such as the separate intellects (see also I, 21, 54; II, 51, 456.9). Pines notes also (on p. 93) that Maimonides assigns to Moses a similar function in his discussion of astronomy and celestial physics (II, 24). Moses alone, it is suggested (p. 327), attained a knowledge of the celestial bodies and their motions. Pines is of the opinion that this view is also related to Exodus 33:23; Maimonides, in fact, quotes Numbers 12:8 (the idea is the same) and presumably assumed this position for theological purposes.

33. On the causes for differences of opinion enumerated by Alexander of Aphrodisias, see Pines, Translator's Introduction, pp. lxvii–lxviii, and "Limitations," 100–4.

Maimonides concludes the chapter (I, 31) by saying: "Do not think that what we have said with regard to the insufficiency of the human intellect and its having a limit at which it stops is a statement made in order to conform to Law. For it is something that has already been said and truly grasped by the philosophers without their having concern for a particular doctrine or opinion."[34] In short, this view has been embraced by the likes of Alexander of Aphrodisias, by philosophers who were not motivated at all to claim the insufficiency of the intellect for theological reasons. Nevertheless, it is possible, as Pines has argued, that Maimonides set limitations for human knowledge in order to make room for religion, as Kant did after him. The fact that his predecessors among the philosophers, particularly a pagan philosopher such as Alexander of Aphrodisias, had established such limits, made his case stronger.

Consequently, according to Maimonides, it is impossible to begin instruction with the divine science, or metaphysics. He lists five reasons for this (I, 34, p. 72). The first is the "difficulty, subtlety and obscurity" of the subject. Human beings, Maimonides says, have a natural desire to know ends. He apparently alludes to Aristotle's dictum in *Metaphysics* 980a11, "All men by nature desire to know."[35] But along with having this natural desire they are also impatient and unwilling to pursue preliminary studies. Whoever truly strives for perfection must undergo the necessary training, first in the art of logic, then in the mathematical sciences, thereafter in physics, and finally in metaphysics.[36]

As I have noted, this lesson is directed to Joseph son of Judah and to those like him, who in their overzealousness to know do not investigate the sciences in an orderly and systematic way but plunge into

34. Pines holds the view that by establishing limitations for human knowledge Maimonides intended to leave room for religion, as did Kant; see "Maimonides," *Dictionary of Scientific Biography* (New York, 1974), IX, 29; "Limitations," p. 100.

35. Cf. Aristotle, *Metaphysics* 980a11 (trans. Sir David Ross).

36. This lesson is directed to Joseph son of Judah and to those like him who as a result of overzealousness to know do not investigate the sciences in an orderly fashion but rather plunge into profound questions without adequate preparation. We know the order of study of the sciences, or the philosophic curriculum, from Arabic philosophy. See also *Guide* III, 51, where in the famous parable of the palace, Maimonides discusses the various levels of knowledge of the sciences. He mentions in order the mathematical sciences, the art of logic, physics and metaphysics. The classification of the sciences and their order of study (which should not be confused) are based upon an Aristotelian scheme. See, e.g., *Metaphysics* 1026a6–33; Maimonides, *Treatise on the Art of Logic*, ed. I. Efros (New York, 1938), c. 14. See H. A. Wolfson, "The Classification of Sciences in Medieval Jewish Philosophy," in *Studies in the History of Philosophy and Religion*, ed. I. Twersky and G. H. Williams (Cambridge, Mass., 1973), I, 511. On the classification of the sciences in Arabic philosophy, see the texts translated in F. Rosenthal, *The Classical Heritage in Islam* (London, 1965), pp. 54–63.

metaphysical questions without adequate grounding in the prerequisites. The order of study of the sciences set down here is similar to the syllabus familiar to us from al-Fārābī's *Enumeration of the Sciences* (*Iḥṣā' al-ʿulūm*) and kindred discussions. In *Guide* III, 51, in the famous parable of the palace, Maimonides treats the various levels of scientific knowledge. The order he sets forth there is the mathematical sciences, the art of logic, physics and metaphysics. This classification of the sciences and their order of study are ultimately derived from an Aristotelian model.

Maimonides presents (I, 34) Aristotle's views concerning the causes of the motions of the heavenly spheres, which entail the existence of intellects functioning as sphere movers, as hypotheses that cannot be demonstrated. Their advantage consists in the fact that they are less vulnerable to doubts than are other opinions that have been expressed on the subject, and they are also more susceptible of being elaborated in a systematic and coherent order. Thanks to these traits, namely, relative certainty and order, Aristotle's opinions conform with the criteria of scientific method established by Alexander of Aphrodisias in his work entitled *The Principles of the Universe* (*Fī mabādiʾ al-kull*). His views are also consistent with many (Maimonides does not say "all") statements in the Torah, and in particular with what has been elaborated in well-known *midrashim* that may be ascribed with certainty to the Sages.[37]

We shall see again, further on, that Maimonides takes the trouble to stress (for instance, in II, 24) that Aristotle's views on the separate intellects, which are the movers of the celestial spheres, conform with the opinions of the Sages of the Talmud. There is a hint in our text that the opinions of the Sages, contained in "well-known" *midrashim,* are dialectical. (The Arabic term translated by "well-known" is *al-mashhūra.*)

Maimonides' reference to Alexander of Aphrodisias is traceable to two passages in *The Principles of the Universe* in which the Great Commentator sets forth his views on scientific method.[38] In the first of these passages Alexander states:

37. We shall see further on that in *Guide* II, 24, Maimonides takes the trouble to stress that Aristotle's comments on the separate intellects, which are the movers of the celestial spheres, conform to the views of the Talmudic sages. There is a hint there, in my opinion, embedded in the word *al-mashhūra* ("well-known") that the *midrashim* are dialectical.

38. The full name of Alexander's treatise is *Mabādiʾ al-kull bi-ḥasab raʾy Arisṭāṭālīs—The Principles of the Universe (the All) according to the Views of Aristotle.* The text was published by ʿA. Badawī, *Arisṭū ʿinda al-ʿarab* (Cairo, 1947; reprinted 1978); see pp. 253–77. The first passage appears on p. 253; the second, on p. 276. See Pines,

Things of this kind[39] are best explained, in my opinion, when the principles upon which there is consensus[40] conform[41] with the manifest, clearly apparent, and well-known[42] phenomena. In connection with them the method of demonstrative arguments[43] is untenable. This is because the starting point of demonstration is prior things and causes, but the first principles have no prior things or causes.[44]

In the second passage Alexander first refers to the government of the universe according to "the divine Aristotle." He points out that everything in the world preserves its own nature and fulfills its nature's functions within the scheme of an ordered universe:

This opinion is not only more than any other in accord with divine government; it is also the one that more than any other is appropriate for speculation and that is verified because of its agreement with, and close relation to, the things existing in the world.[45] Everyone who philosophizes should, whatever the circumstances, use this opinion and prefer it to all others. For[46] it is the most correct[47] of all the opinions that have been propounded concerning God, the Great and the Sublime, and concerning the divine body. It alone among the various opinions preserves the coherence and order of the things that are produced because of this coherence and order. If it should occur to anyone that some [point] among those that we have set forth requires further and more subtle investigation, he should not, because of a slight difficulty that might become manifest, bring about a slackening of our vigilance and our effort [directed] toward defending[48] this opinion in its totality. [He ought not to do this], even if [this opinion] is obnoxious and repugnant to him. On the contrary, we ought not only to stick to this opinion, but also to defend it. For of all[49] the opinions that have been held concerning God, the Great and the

---

"Translator's Introduction," p. lxix. I have also consulted MSS Yahuda (Princeton) 605, Escorial 798, Jarullah 1279 (and thank the library authorities for making microfilms available to me). It is worthy of note that MS Jarullah 1279 contains the *Guide* in Arabic script, as was indicated by F. Rosenthal, "From Arabic Books and Manuscripts V," *JAOS* 75 (1955): 16–21. See also n. 77.

39. Apparently the principles of the physical world, which had been mentioned previously, are intended.

40. Text: *allatī tuwaṭṭaʾ lahā.*

41. Text: *tuwāfiq wa-talzam.* MS Yahuda 605: *muwāfaqa muṭābaqa.*

42. Text: *al-ashyāʾ al-mubayyana al-ẓāhira al-maʿrūfa.* MS Yahuda 605: *lil-umūr al-wāḍiḥa al-ẓāhira.* We may suppose that the word *phainomena* appeared in the Greek source.

43. Text: *al-aqāwīl al-burhāniyya.* On *qawl* in the sense of "sentence," "statement," "proposition" (=*logos*), see F. W. Zimmermann, *Al-Farabi's Commentary and Short Treatise on Aristotle's De Interpretatione* (London, 1981), p. xxi, n. 1.

44. Text: *ʿilla.* MS Yahuda: *sabab.*

45. Text: *al-umūr al-mushāhada lil-ʿālam.* In MS Escorial and MS Jarullah the reading is *al-umūr al-mawjūda fil-ʿālam.* Read perhaps: *al-umūr al-mawjūda al-mushāhada fil-ʿālam.* On the basis of Badawī's edition, Pines suggested that the last word should be taken to mean "the knower" (i.e., *ʿālim*) and not "the world" (*ʿālam*).

46. Text: *aw.* Jarullah: *idh.*

47. Text: *aṣwab.* Escorial: *alyaq.*

48. Text: *nuṣra.* Jarullah: *naẓra.*

49. Text: *jamīʿ.* Jarullah: *afḍal.*

Sublime, it is the most correct,[50] if we seek to solve[51] all the opinions opposed to it and to correct, as far as we are able, their errors. [We shall do this] after having first stated that it is difficult to find a speculative opinion exempt from doubts.[52]

Alexander is arguing, in other words, that since first principles have no prior causes, they can only be tested by their power to explain phenomena adequately. The hypothesis of an eternal ordered universe is subject to questions and objections as are all theories, but it is the most adequate explanation of the nature of what exists, the most coherent theory, and the most appropriate pertaining to God.

Elsewhere, in a brief treatise, Alexander explains that one cannot discuss principles by way of demonstrative proof, and that finding such proof for them is impossible. If this were not the case, he argues, then the principles would have to have principles. It is for this reason, he explains, that dialectical syllogisms are useful for establishing the principles of philosophy.[53]

Alexander's ruminations on scientific procedure undoubtedly flow from his close familiarity with Aristotle's treatment of the subject. Explaining the utility of the *Topics,* which concerns dialectical statements, Aristotle says (101a34–101b4), for example, that the work is useful for the philosophic sciences; for if we can arouse difficulties on two sides of a specific question, we can then reveal the truth and falsehood regarding all the points that arise. The *Topics* is also useful, Aristotle says, with respect to the principles of the sciences, for they cannot be discussed on the basis of the specific principles of a certain given science, as the principles are prior to everything else. It is consequently necessary to discuss them by means of the common opinions pertaining to each point. Now this task belongs to dialectic, or is more appropriate to dialectic, inasmuch as dialectic has a convenient approach to the principles of all the methods of research.

Aristotle's discussion of scientific procedure and the usefulness of dialectical propositions in the *Topics,* and Alexander's elaboration of the same themes, are pertinent to Maimonides' notion concerning the type of argumentation that Aristotle used in discussing the subject of

50. Text: *fī'l-ṣawāb.* Jarullah: *fī'l-ṣawāb.*

51. Text: *kull.* Jarullah: *li-ḥall.* Escorial: *ḥall* (?). Pines suggested that the text should be emended to *radd.*

52. The text has *shukūk,* a term that often renders Greek *aporiai.* See also II, 22, on the principle of minimal doubt. Pines notes that Maimonides' overemphasis on the uncertainty of Aristotle and Alexander regarding theories is a distortion of their ideas ("Limitations," p. 94). See also "Translator's Introduction," p. lxx.

53. ʿA. Badawī, *Commentaires sur Aristote perdus en grec et autres épîtres* (Beirut, 1971), p. 58.

the eternity of the universe. As Aristotle did not have a demonstrative proof for the eternity of the heavens, he was compelled, according to Maimonides, to fall back upon a weaker form of argument based upon the consensus of mankind. This manner of argumentation is manifestly dialectical.

Aristotle's argument for the eternity of the universe, Maimonides submits (II, 14, p. 289), is based inter alia upon an inference derived from the universal consensus among nations in the past. To illustrate this point, Maimonides quotes Aristotle's discourse in *De caelo* 270b5–11. In Maimonides' version, the text reads:[54]

> All men explicitly affirm the perpetuity and permanence of the heavens. And when they became aware that they were not subject to coming-about and passing-away, they asserted that they are the dwelling-place of God, may He be exalted, and of the spiritual beings—he means to say, of the angels. They attributed the heavens to Him in order to indicate their perpetuity.

Maimonides adds that Aristotle also exposits similar notions on this subject so as to support the view, which speculation has led him to believe is true, by means of beliefs that are universally held to be true.

Aristotle's text is as follows:

> For all men have some conception of the nature of the gods, and all who believe in the existence of the gods at all, whether barbarian or Greek, agree in allotting the highest place to the deity, surely because they suppose that immortal is linked with immortal and regard any other supposition as inconceivable. If then there is, as there certainly is, anything divine what we said about the primary bodily substance was well said.

A number of divergences between Maimonides' version of the text and the original may be noted. Maimonides, for instance, mentions "all men" of the Aristotelian text, but he does not use the phrase "whether barbarian or Greek," as do the Greek text and the Arabic translation, as this was obviously irrelevant. Aristotle used the expression "gods" and "divine" as synonyms. The Arabic translation of *De caelo* rendered "gods" by *ruḥāniyyīn* ("spiritual beings"), and it was on this basis that Maimonides introduced the term into his text. Maimonides' identification of the spiritual beings with the angels does not occur in the Arabic text.

Maimonides' understanding of the dialectical character of the *De caelo* passage may be easily supported. Aristotle introduces the text by saying the following: "It seems that our argument confirms appearances (*tois phenomenois*) and appearances confirm our argument." In

54. In the Arabic text, ed. Badawī, pp. 140–41.

the final analysis, the argument is based upon the *phainomena,* that is, prevalent beliefs of human beings, in other words, dialectical arguments.

In a similar way, Aristotle invokes the consensus of mankind ("the truth of the ancient and truly traditional theories") in *De caelo* 284a1–4, in order to support the view that there exists "some immortal and divine thing which possesses movement. . . ."[55]

And he appeals to ancient, venerable traditions in *Metaphysics* 1074a39–b14, to establish the belief in the divinity and eternity of the heavens. The passage is important for understanding the function of religious symbolism as grasped in the political writings of the Falāsifa and deserves to be quoted in extenso (trans. W. D. Ross):

> Our forefathers in the most remote ages have handed down to their posterity, in the form of a myth, that these bodies are gods and that the divine encloses the whole of nature. The rest of the tradition has been added later in mythical form with a view to the persuasion of the multitude and to its legal and utilitarian expediency; they say these gods are in the form of men or like some of the other animals. . . . But if one were to separate the first point from these additions and take it alone—that they thought the first substance to be gods—one must regard this as an inspired utterance, and reflect that, while probably each art and each science have developed as far as possible and have again perished, these opinions, with others, have been preserved until the present like relics of the ancient treasure. Only thus far, then, is the opinion of our ancestors and of our earliest predecessors clear to us.[56]

Maimonides alludes to the passage in *De caelo* 270b5–11, once again in *Guide* II, 18 (p. 302), where he states that Aristotle's assertion concerning the consensus (*ijmāʿ*)[57] of the nations in the past, that the angels and the deity dwell in heaven,[58] does not signify that the heavens are eternal, as he would have it. The consensus of mankind signifies rather the existence of the sphere movers—they being the spiritual beings and the angels—as well as the existence of the deity who is the mover and the governor of the heavens.[59]

55. Nussbaum, "Saving Aristotle's Appearances," p. 291, cites these two texts (her *De caelo* 285a1–4 should be 284a1–4) and connects them with the passage from the *Metaphysics* quoted here.

56. See also Ibn Rushd's *Great Commentary on the Metaphysics: Averroes, Tafsīr Mā baʿd aṭ-ṭabīʿah,* ed. M. Bouyges, 2nd ed. (Beirut, 1967), pp. 1687–90. In the Arabic translation of the text of Aristotle, the word *aḥādīth* translates Greek *en muthou.* In his comment ad loc. (p. 1688), Ibn Rushd refers the views of the ancients to the Chaldeans.

57. Note that whereas in II, 14, Maimonides uses the expression *mashhūr* ("well known"), here he speaks of consensus.

58. Maimonides adds here that this is the literal meaning of the Biblical text. In II, 14, he compares the spiritual beings of Aristotle (according to the Arabic translation) and the angels in rabbinic *midrashim.*

59. Maimonides adds that he will explain this; see II, 19.

Maimonides adds that no proof for the existence of the Agent equals the proof deriving from the heaven, and he observes that also according to the opinion of the philosophers the heaven indicates the existence of the Mover, and that He is not a body or a force within a body.[60] The cosmological argument for the existence of God receives strong support here. Elsewhere, as we shall see, Maimonides appears to contradict this position.

Maimonides explains (*Guide* II, 15, pp. 289ff.) that Aristotle was aware that he had no demonstration for the eternity of the universe, and that his arguments and proofs were simply the most appealing to the human mind. The superiority of these arguments, in the view of Alexander, is that they are beset by fewer doubts than alternative theories.[61] It is inconceivable, Maimonides says, that Aristotle, who instructed mankind in the methods of demonstration, would have believed that his views on the subject actually had demonstrative force.

Maimonides goes on to distinguish between Aristotle and the Aristotelians. "The latter-day followers" of Aristotle did him a disservice by claiming that he had really demonstrated the eternity of the universe. Maimonides remarks disdainfully that most of those who claim to philosophize adhere blindly to Aristotle on the question of the eternity of the universe,[62] and they regard his contentions as firm, indubitable demonstrations, deeming it unseemly to disagree with him. Maimonides contrasts the "true" Aristotle with his slavish followers. Aristotle himself never claimed that he had a demonstration on this question. His manner of arguing in the *Physics* indicates that he was well aware that his arguments were less cogent than demonstrative. Maimonides then paraphrases *Physics* 251b14–19 thus:

> All the physicists preceding us believe that motion is not subject to generation and passing-away, except Plato, who believes that motion is subject to generation and passing-away, and the heaven too according to him is subject to generation and passing-away.

Maimonides adds, "This is literally what he says."[63] But the citation

60. The cosmological argument for the existence of God is affirmed here. Elsewhere, Maimonides appears to contradict this; see n. 100.

61. See my discussion of this point in Section I above.

62. For the notion of blind adherence Maimonides uses the well-known term *taqlīd*, which generally means blind adherence in matters of religion and faith. On the meaning of the concept, particularly in the writings of al-Ghazālī, see H. Lazarus-Yafeh, *Studies in Al-Ghazzālī* (Jerusalem, 1975), pp. 488–502.

63. Cf. the Arabic translation in Isḥāq b. Ḥunayn, ed. ʿA. Badawī, *Arisṭūṭālīs: al-Ṭabīʿa* (Cairo, 1965), pp. 810–11.

There are several differences between Maimonides' formulation and the source. Maimonides mentions "motion," whereas Aristotle had spoken of "time." Maimonides

in the *Guide* is considerably attenuated, as we may judge if we compare it with the original text or even with the Arabic translation of Isḥāq b. Ḥunayn. Aristotle's text reads (trans. Hardie and Gaye):

But as far as time is concerned we see that all with one exception are in agreement in saying that it is uncreated: in fact, it is just this that enables Democritus to show that all things cannot have had a becoming: for time, he says, is uncreated. Plato alone asserts the creation of time, saying that it had a becoming together with the universe, the universe according to him having had a becoming.[64]

Maimonides comments in this connection that if Aristotle really had cogent demonstration on this issue, he would not have had to appeal to the consensus of previous physicists, nor would he have had to denounce the opinion of those who disagree. The consensus of "men of knowledge" does not add to or detract from something that has been demonstrated, nor can its certainty be undermined by universal denial of its validity.[65]

Maimonides goes on (II, 15, pp. 290–91) to adduce Aristotle's mode of argumentation in *De caelo* 271b4–13 as additional support for his contention that Aristotle himself did not claim to have had a demonstrative argument concerning the eternity of the universe. When Aristotle began to explain that the heavens are not subject to generation and passing-away, he posed the questions whether the heavens are to be regarded as generated from something or not, and whether they are likely to pass away or not.[66] Having posed these questions, Maimonides says, Aristotle then wanted to mention the contentions of the proponents of the view that the heavens are generated. And he justifies this procedure as follows:

If we wish to do this, our words will be more acceptable for, and more worthy of approval by, those who proceed correctly in speculation, and more particularly if they have first heard the arguments of those who disagree with us.[67]

---

adds passing-away, whereas Aristotle mentioned only coming-into-being. (The question whether the heavens come into being and pass away appears in the passage from *De caelo* that is quoted in the immediate sequel.) It is noteworthy that before our passage Aristotle had mentioned that time is the number of motion or itself a kind of motion, and so on. Another difference is that Aristotle had reference to Plato's view on the coming into being of time and the world, while Maimonides did not mention the world but only the heavens. Also, in the translation by Isḥāq b. Ḥunayn the word for heavens appears instead of the word for world.

64. Cf. Plato, *Timaeus* 38b.

65. Cf. *Topics* 100b21, 104a8–12. In contrast to dialectical arguments, demonstrative proof does not depend on the consensus of mankind.

66. Cf. the Arabic text, ed. Badawī, p. 196. And see the comment of Pines in his translation, p. 290, n. 5.

67. The words *awwalan fa-innā in qulnā naḥnu ra'yanā wa-ḥujajanā wa-lā nadhkur ḥujaj*

For if, without mentioning the arguments of those who disagree with us, we only mention our opinion and our arguments, these would appear too weak to be accepted by the listeners. It behooves him who wishes to judge according to the truth not to be hostile to those who disagree with him, but to be friendly to, and equitable toward them—meting out the same measure[68] in granting that their arguments were correct as he would with regard to his own arguments.

Maimonides adds that this is "literally the discourse of the man."[69] The text of *De caelo* reads:

Having established these distinctions, we may now proceed to the question whether the heaven is ungenerated or generated, indestructible or destructible. Let us start with a review of the theories of other thinkers; for the proofs of a theory are difficulties for the contrary theory.[70] Besides, those who have first heard the pleas of our adversaries will be more likely to credit the assertion which we are going to make. We shall be less open to the charge of procuring judgement by default. To give a satisfactory decision to the truth it is necessary to be rather an arbitrator than a party to the dispute.

Considering Aristotle's presentation of arguments for the eternity of the universe, Maimonides poses the question (II, 15, p. 291), addressing "the community of people who are engaged in speculation," whether one can really blame Aristotle ("that man") or suppose that he had actually found a demonstration concerning this question.[71] For no one, certainly not Aristotle, can possibly imagine that if opposing arguments are not first heard then the acceptability of something that has been demonstrated is weakened. Furthermore, says Maimonides, Aristotle was certainly aware of the difference between arguments and demonstrations, or between opinions that are more or less acceptable and demonstrative matters. And it is unnecessary and superfluous to appeal to a rhetorical argument, namely, that fairness to one's opponent fortifies one's own opinion.[72]

---

al-mukhālifīn (p. 203.1–2) are lacking in the Arabic translation of *De caelo* due to *homoioteleuton.*

68. The text of the *Guide* reads (p. 203.4), *yujīz lahu mā yujīz li-nafsihi,* literally, "permitting for him what he permits for himself." In the Arabic translation of *De caelo* the text reads, *yukhayyir lahu mā yukhayyir li-nafsihi,* "preferring for him what he prefers for himself." The latter appears preferable.

69. "The man" (*al-rajul*) is a common epithet for Aristotle in Arabic philosophy.

70. This sentence is lacking in Maimonides' quotation.

71. It is necessary to pay attention to Maimonides' apostrophes to various addressees. Although the *Guide* was ostensibly written for a single pupil, Maimonides occasionally addresses other specific audiences. I mean to discuss these apostrophes on another occasion.

72. The aim of rhetoric, according to Aristotle, is persuasion, and consequently the mode of presenting arguments and fairness to one's opponent are important. The aim of demonstrative science, however, is instruction, and the scientist does not need to persuade. See, for example, *Rhetorics* I, 1, 12–14.

Aristotle's whole purpose, Maimonides continues (II, 15, pp. 291–92), is to explain that his opinion is more correct than the opinions of his opponents. For example, there are those who profess that philosophic speculation implies that the heavens are subject to generation and passing-away but have never been nonexistent, or that the heavens are generated but do not pass away, and similar opinions.[73] Maimonides then acknowledges that Aristotle's opinion is in fact more correct than those of his opponents "in so far as inferences are made from the nature of what exists." He then adds the puzzling sentence "However, we do not think so, as I shall make clear." Maimonides' intention here is somewhat cloudy. Pines suggests in a note *ad locum* (p. 292, 11) that the sense is either that Maimonides disputes the Aristotelian doctrine of the eternity of the universe or else that he does not agree that inferences that are made from the nature of what exists may be invoked as demonstrative proofs. It is possible that both senses may be discerned in the passage. In any case, it is worth noting that Maimonides says elsewhere (II, 17, p. 295) that we cannot infer from the nature of something in its final state to the state it was in before it was generated. In other words, the possibility of the generation of the universe is not negated by an inference drawn from the nature of existence. As is well known, Maimonides rejected the proofs of the Mutakallimūn concerning creation (I, 71) for they are based, he says, upon premises that contradict the nature of existence as it appears to us. Maimonides argues in I, 71, that he succeeded in achieving the aim of the Mutakallimūn without denying the nature of existence or disagreeing with Aristotle concerning anything that he had really proved.[74]

Let us return to Maimonides' evaluation of the force of Aristotle's arguments (II, 15, p. 292). Speaking for himself, Maimonides states that he has no doubt that Aristotle did not succeed in providing demonstrations concerning the following points: (1) the eternity of the world, (2) the cause of the different motions of the spheres, and (3) the ordered hierarchy of intelligences of the spheres. Nor, claims Maimonides, did Aristotle imagine that he had done so. He stated instead that we have no access to inferential reasoning on these matters and

73. *Physics* 279b17–280a30.

74. See also Pines, "Maimonides," p. 30, and M. Fakhry, "The Antinomy of the Eternity of the World in Averroes, Maimonides and Aquinas," *Le Muséon* 66 (1953): 152–53; and cf. Warren Zev Harvey, "A Third Approach to Maimonides' Cosmogony-Prophetology Puzzle," *Harvard Theological Review* 74 (1981): 281–301. Harvey argues that Maimonides adopted the Aristotelian theory of the world's eternity on the basis of the assumption that this theory fits the nature of existence.

no principle from which to derive inferences.[75] He then cites Aristotle's statement in *Topics* 104b14–17:[76] "As for matters concerning which we have no argument or that are too great in our opinion, it is difficult for us to say: Why is this so? For instance, when we say: Is the world eternal or not?"[77]

Maimonides prefaces the citation from the *Topics* by saying, "You know the text of his words." And then following the quotation he adds the statement, "This is literally what he says." And in the immediate sequel he says, "However, you know Abū Naṣr [al Fārābī's] interpretation of this example." Clearly, Joseph son of Judah had already studied the *Topics* along with the *Commentary* of al-Fārābī, possibly with Maimonides.

Maimonides then reminds the recipient of the *Guide* that according to al-Fārābī's interpretation of this statement, the notion that Aristotle might have doubted the eternity of the universe was simply out of the question, and al-Fārābī held Galen in utmost contempt, says Maimonides, for professing that this question was obscure and undemonstrable.[78] This, Maimonides comments, is because Abū Naṣr believes that it is manifest and demonstrated that the heavens are in fact eternal.

Maimonides felt it necessary to elaborate these things, he says (II, 15, p. 293), only because most of those who consider themselves to have insight, despite the fact that they lack any understanding of the sciences, opt for the theory that the universe is eternal and follow the authority of prominent scientists who assert this, while rejecting prophetic discourses as unscientific.

Maimonides undoubtedly alludes here to Jewish intellectuals (not few in number) who adhered to Aristotelianism, bowing to the authority of contemporary science and disdaining the Biblical account of creation and other themes that were treated, in their view, more seriously by prominent scientists. Maimonides suggests that their enthusiasm for the scientific approach is not accompanied by a firm grounding in the sciences. It is his purpose, then, to direct these mis-

75. See Pines, "Limitations," p. 97.

76. The word is *ḥujja* which may also mean "proof."

77. See the Arabic translation of the *Topics* by Abū ʿUthmān al-Dimashqī, ed. ʿA. Badawī, *Manṭiq Arisṭū* (Cairo, 1948–59), pp. 485.15–16, and the edition of the *Guide* in Arabic script, ed. H. Atay (Ankara, 1972), where there are a number of variants from our text.

78. S. Munk, *Le Guide des égarés* (Paris, 1856–66) II, 127, n. 2, mentions Galen, *De Hippocratis et Platonis Placitis* IX, 7 (Kuhn, V, 780). In this passage Galen argues that the question whether the world came into being or not is useless (*achrēston*).

Al-Fārābī's comments on this passage of the *Topics* and on the eternity of the universe are preserved in MS Hamid 1, 812, fol. 105a. I plan to discuss them on another occasion.

guided intellectuals to a deeper understanding of Aristotle, scientific method and the true message of the prophetic discourses.

The main point, then, is that, contrary to the belief of many scientists and their followers (including, for instance, al-Fārābī), Aristotle himself never claimed that his arguments for the eternity of the universe were demonstrative and certainly never produced demonstrative arguments to prove this theory. The hypothesis of the world's eternity has at best the force of a dialectical argument.

Now Maimonides highlights the dialectical character of the hypothesis of the world's eternity in the introduction to part II of the *Guide*. Before enumerating the twenty-five premises Maimonides states (p. 235) that Aristotle and the Peripatetics after him produced a demonstration of each of the twenty-five premises required for asserting the deity's existence, incorporeality and unity. One premise, namely the twenty-sixth, affirming the eternity of the universe, Maimonides says he is prepared simply to grant them.[79] Again, having enumerated the twenty-five premises, Maimonides asserts (p. 239) that some of these premises become clear after scant reflection and are demonstrative premises and first intelligibles or the like. All of the premises have been demonstrated in a manner which leaves no room for doubt, either in the *Physics* and in the commentaries on the *Physics* or in the *Metaphysics* and in the commentary on the *Metaphysics*. There is one more premise, affirming the necessity of the eternity of the universe, which Aristotle regarded as correct[80] and the most appropriate for our assent. "We shall grant him this premise by way of a hypothesis," Maimonides says, "in order that the clarification of that which we intended to make clear should be achieved."[81] This premise, the twenty-sixth, asserts that "time and movement are eternal, perpetual, existing *in actu*." From this it follows, in Aristotle's view, that there exists a body, moving eternally, existing *in actu*,[82] namely the fifth body. Accordingly, heaven is not subject to generation and corruption. While Aristotle does in fact always strive to establish the truth of this premise, Maimonides asserts that in his view Aristotle does not really "affirm categorically that the arguments he puts forward in its favor constitute

79. Maimonides writes (p. 165.9): *wa-muqaddima wāḥida nusallimuhā lahum taslīman.* The word *taslīm* is related to dialectical argumentation. See, for instance, A.-M. Goichon, *Vocabulaires comparés d'Aristote et d'Ibn Sīnā* (Paris, 1939), p. 13 (297–98); *Posterior Analytics* 76b27–28; *Metaphysics* 995b24.

80. Text: *ṣaḥīḥa.* See n. 12.

81. Text: *fa-nusallimuhā lahu ʿalā jihat al-taqrīr.* In his translation (p. 239, n. 7), Pines suggests that we read *al-taqdīr* instead of *al-taqrīr,* in accordance with Ibn Tibbon. In his edition of the *Guide,* Y. Kafih brings this reading as a variant. Atay has *al-taqrīr.*

82. *Physics* 251b20 et seq.; *Metaphysics* 1071b5 et seq. (Pines, p. 240, n. 8).

a demonstration." Instead, this premise is, in the opinion of Aristotle (as Maimonides reads him), that which is most fitting and probable.

There are three points of view concerning this premise, Maimonides says (*Guide*, pp. 240–41). Aristotle's followers and commentators avow that the premise is necessary and demonstrated. The Mutakallimūn, on the other hand, wish to establish that it is impossible. Maimonides then expresses his own opinion, which is that the premise under discussion is possible, that it is not necessary, as claimed by Aristotelian commentators, nor impossible, as alleged by the Mutakallimūn.[83] The two premises, the one that affirms the eternity of the universe and the one that asserts the belief in temporal creation, enjoy the modal status of possibility.

We have seen that, in Maimonides' view (*Guide* II, 15, 292), there is no doubt that Aristotle did not produce cogent demonstrations concerning the eternity of the universe, the reason for the spheres' motion and the hierarchy of the spheres. And we have also seen that, in his view (I, 31, p. 61), the things causing perplexity are many in metaphysics, few in physics, and nonexistent in mathematics.

In the same spirit, Maimonides asserts (*Guide* II, 22, 319–20):

> Everything that Aristotle has said about all that exists from beneath the sphere of the moon to the center of the earth is indubitably correct, and no one will deviate from it unless he does not understand it or unless he has preconceived opinions that he wishes to defend or that lead him to a denial of a thing that is manifest. On the other hand, everything that Aristotle expounds with regard to the sphere of the moon and that which is above it is, except for certain things, something analogous to guessing and conjecturing. All the more does this apply to what he says about the order of the intellects and to some of the opinions concerning the divine that he believes; for the latter contain grave incongruities and perversities that manifestly and clearly appear as such to all nations, that propagate evil, and that he cannot demonstrate.[84]

Similarly, Maimonides says (in II, 19, p. 307) that what Aristotle has explained concerning the sublunar world follows an order that conforms with existence, has clear causes, and can be said to derive necessarily from the motion and powers of the sphere. But he has not given a clear cause accounting for matters relating to the sphere, nor has he indicated a necessary order for this. These problems, Maimonides says, are dealt with elsewhere (see II, 24).

83. It should be noted that if one of the premises adduced to prove the existence of God is possible, it follows that the proof which rests upon this premise has only the force of a dialectical proof. On the classification of modalities, see, for instance, A.-M. Goichon, *Lexique de la langue philosophique d'Ibn Sīnā* (Paris, 1938), p. 382 (672), p. 386 (678), p. 417 (744).

84. See Pines, "Translator's Introduction," p. lxx; and "Limitations," p. 94.

Maimonides, observes Pines, regards Aristotle's sublunar physics as adequate because the explanations put forth are mechanical. And adequate physical theory, in Maimonides' view, requires that scientific explanation provide only efficient causes. Even teleological aspects, says Pines, which should not be overlooked (for instance, the continuation of the universe in its present state), can be accounted for by means of efficient causes.

Maimonides requests (p. 320) that the reader refrain from criticizing him for raising doubts concerning Aristotle's opinion. Maimonides insists that he treats "this philosopher" as his followers have requested. Alexander of Aphrodisias, for example, has clarified that whenever no demonstration is possible, two rival opinions should be posited as hypotheses, and the hypothesis subject to the fewer doubts should be accepted. Alexander applies this technique to all the opinions concerning the divine that Aristotle propounds and for which no demonstration is possible. All those who came after Aristotle claim that his statements arouse fewer doubts than all else that might be said.[85]

Maimonides concludes II, 22, by stating:

> We have acted in this way when it was to our mind established as true that, regarding the question whether the heavens are generated or eternal, neither of the two contrary opinions could be demonstrated. For we have explained the doubts attached to each of the opinions and have shown to you that the opinion favoring the eternity of the world is the one that raises more doubts and is more harmful for the belief that ought to be held with regard to the deity. And this, in addition to the fact that the world's being produced in time is the opinion of Abraham our father and our prophet Moses, may peace be on both of them.[86]

The arguments put forth here are manifestly dialectical. The belief in creation, according to the opinion of Abraham and Moses, belongs to the class of propositions that have become well known within a specific nation. Such propositions are considered dialectical by Maimonides in his *Treatise on Logic*.

III

In Maimonides' time there was a severe crisis with regard to the Aristotelian paradigm of celestial physics. This crisis compounded his doubts concerning cosmological issues, including the question of the eternity of the universe.

The addressee of the *Guide* already knows, Maimonides says (II, 24,

85. *Topics* 101a34–36.
86. See *Guide* II, 15.

p. 322), that the ordering of the celestial motions and conformity of the stars with appearances depend upon either epicycles, eccentric spheres, or both.[87]

Maimonides had stated at the beginning of II, 24, that the addressee already knows astronomical matters which he has studied under his direction and what he has learned from Ptolemy's *Almagest*. He thus knows about epicycles and eccentrics. What he does not yet know is that these principles fall outside the limits of reasoning and natural science. The allusions throughout the chapter to what the pupil already knows indicate that he has already entered the mysteries of celestial physics.

Maimonides points out to his pupil that both the epicycles and the eccentrics fall outside the bounds of reasoning and that they conflict with all that has been expounded in physics.[88] For instance (p. 323), Aristotle made certain basic assumptions in the *Physics* according to which there must be some immobile thing about which circular motion takes place. It is consequently necessary that the earth be immobile. But the circular motion of the posited epicycles is not about something immobile.[89]

Maimonides mentions that he had heard that Abū Bakr b. Bājja claimed to have devised an astronomical system in which only eccentric circles came into play and to have dispensed with epicycles. Maimonides expresses some doubt concerning the accuracy of the report he had heard regarding this novel and original system of Ibn Bājja, as he did not hear about it from the students of Ibn Bājja whom he knew. In addition, he doubts the utility of this invention, if Ibn Bājja truly made such a claim, for even this theory exceeds the principles posited by Aristotle, which are exhaustive. Maimonides takes credit for having drawn attention to this point.[90]

Maimonides strives to clarify in this chapter (II, 24) why the as-

87. Note well Maimonides' reference to what his addressee already knows and does not yet know, which peg his stage of development and that of the writer's potential audience.

88. Pines states (*Guide*, p. 322, n. 1) that the word *qiyās* used here means "syllogism" and more broadly "reasoning" or "analogy." Maimonides intends, as we shall see immediately, Aristotelian physics and its attendant modes of thought. It is possible that *qiyās* here means demonstrative proof. See also n. 98.

89. Cf. J. L. E. Dreyer, *A History of Astronomy from Thales to Kepler*, 2nd ed. (New York, 1953), p. 263. Dreyer is of the opinion that Aristotle actually did not oppose epicyclic movement with a mathematical point at the center, for this was not proposed in his time. His principle of motion is accordingly not connected at all with the notion of a center of motion.

90. It is clear from here that Ibn Bājja's aim was reportedly to defend Aristotelian physics, although at the price of some concessions.

sumption of eccentrics is incapable of saving Aristotle's celestial physics, and he devotes considerable attention to other difficulties. In contrast to other philosophers of the Spanish Aristotelian school—for example, Ibn Bājja, Ibn Ṭufayl and Ibn Rushd—Maimonides does not attempt to defend Aristotle. On the contrary, he brings into sharp relief throughout the chapter the difficulties inherent in Aristotle's system.[91] "Consider now how great these difficulties are," he writes. If Aristotle's natural science is true, there can be no epicycles or eccentric circles and everything revolves about the center of the earth. But if this is so, then how can the various motions of the stars be explained? Aristotle's principle that motion is circular, uniform and perfect conflicts with appearances, at least without the aid of epicycles and eccentrics. These principles of Ptolemaic astronomy are justified by the exactitude of calculations relating to the course of the sphere of the moon, eclipses, their timing and duration, a star's retrogradation and other motions.[92] But even the Ptolemaic system does not bring contentment. For how, Maimonides asks, is it possible to conceive of a rolling motion (*daḥraja*) in the heavens or a motion about a center that is not immobile. This, he adds, is "the true perplexity" (*al-ḥayra al-ḥaqīqa*).[93]

Maimonides surmounts the perplexity to an extent by means of the claim (which he communicated to his pupil directly in oral instruction) that the function of the astronomer is not to inform us how the spheres are in reality but to devise an astronomical system, allowing for circular and uniform motions, that corresponds to appearances, whether things are this way or not.[94] "You know already," Maimonides says to his pupil (p. 326), that Abū Bakr b. al-Ṣā'igh, in his discussion of natural science, doubted whether Aristotle was aware of the sun's eccentricity and simply did not mention it or whether he was simply unaware of it.[95] Maimonides' own opinion is that Aristotle was unaware of it, because mathematics had not been perfected in his time.[96]

91. See my discussion below.

92. Cf. O Neugebauer, "The Astronomy of Maimonides and Its Sources," *HUCA* 22 (1949), p. 336. Neugebauer explains that the homocentric spheres (of Eudoxus and Aristotle) were invented to explain the phenomenon of retrogradation, among other things.

93. That is, the true perplexity stems from the fact that the solutions of Ptolemy are also unsatisfactory.

94. See also Thomas Aquinas, *In libros Aristotelis De Caelo et mundo exposito, Opera omnia* III (The Vatican, 1889), II, 17, pp. 186ff.; *Summa theologiae* I, q. 32, a. 1; Lohr, "The Medieval Interpretation of Aristotle," p. 94.

95. Ibn Bājja's Commentary on Aristotle's *Physics* is preserved in MS Bodleian, Pococke 206 and has been edited by M. Fakhry (Beirut, 1973).

96. See also *Guide* II, 4, 9; I, 72.

And even had he been aware of it, he would have rejected it, and had it been fixed as true in his mind, this would have led him to a state of utmost perplexity concerning his presuppositions on the subject.[97]

Maimonides reiterates in this connection (pp. 326–27) the statement that he had made in II, 22, namely, that all of Aristotle's assertions concerning what is below the sphere of the moon accord with syllogistic reasoning, that is, demonstration.[98] The reasons that Maimonides gives for the validity of Aristotle's physics are (1) these things have a known cause; (2) that they follow one upon the other; (3) and that it is clear precisely where wisdom and natural providence are effective. In contrast to terrestrial physics, man's knowledge of the heavens is restricted to but a limited amount of what is mathematical, which the addressee of the *Guide* knows. Maimonides then adds by way of what he calls "poetic *gnomai*,"[99] "The heavens are the heavens of the Lord, but the earth hath He given to the sons of man" (Psalms 115:16), interpreting the verse to mean that only God knows completely "the true reality, the nature, the substance, the form, the motions, and the causes of the heavens." But He has let human beings obtain knowledge of what is beneath the heavens. Maimonides then makes the puzzling statement "And even the general conclusion that may be drawn from them, namely, that they prove the existence of their Mover, is a matter the knowledge of which cannot be reached by human intellects" (p. 327).

The last statement contradicts Maimonides' affirmation of the knowability of this proof in other texts (I, 9, pp. 34–35; II, 18, p. 302). Ibn Tibbon's translation gives Maimonides' statement a different meaning. It reads (trans. Pines, p. 327, n. 12): "The general proof from them is that they indicate the existence of their Mover, but the knowledge of other matters concerning them cannot be reached by human intellects." This statement is, of course, consistent with what Maimonides says in I, 9, and II, 18, and we may suspect that Ibn Tibbon's translation was an effort to achieve this harmony. On the other hand, it is also possible that Ibn Tibbon had a different text before him. I propose that it may have read, *wal-istidlāl al-ʿāmm minhu annahu dallanā ʿalā muḥarrikihi* ⟨*ammā sāʾir amrihi*⟩ *la-amr lā taṣil ʿuqūl al-insān ilā maʿrifatihi.* (I have placed the hypothesized missing words in angle

97. The text (pp. 228.12–13) reads, *wa-law ṣaḥḥa lahu la-taḥayyara fī kull mā waḍaʿahu fī hādhā al-nawʿ ḥayra shadīda.*

98. Text (p. 228.16): *jarā ʿalā qiyās. Qiyās* here has the sense of demonstrative proof. See n. 88.

99. Text (p. 228.19): *ʿalā jihat al-nawādir al-shiʿriyya.* The word *nawādir* means "aphorisms, *gnomai*," and the like. It is possible that the adjective *al-shiʿriyya* alludes to the class of poetic statements.

brackets.) Translation: "And the general conclusion that may be drawn from them is that they prove the existence of their Mover. ⟨But as for other matters concerning them,⟩ human intellects cannot attain knowledge of them." This reading has the virtue of being consistent with what Maimonides says elsewhere, and it also fits the present context.[100]

Having stated that the deity has permitted human beings to attain knowledge of things in the sublunar world but not of heavenly things, save the inference from them concerning the existence of their Mover, Maimonides again warns the addressee against fatiguing the mind with ideas that cannot be grasped. What cannot be apprehended by syllogistic reasoning should be given over to the one whom the divine overflow reached, about whom it could be said, "With him do I speak mouth with mouth" (Numbers 12:8).[101]

Maimonides ends the chapter, which concerns the perplexity engendered by the incompatibility of Aristotelian physics and Ptolemaic astronomy, with an impressive show of intellectual honesty: "This is the end of what I have to say about this question. It is possible that someone else will find a demonstration by means of which the true reality of what is obscure for me will become clear to him. The extreme predilection I have for investigating the truth is evidenced by the fact that I have explicitly stated and reported my perplexity regarding these matters as well as by the fact that I have never heard nor do I know a demonstration as to anything concerning them."[102]

According to Maimonides, then, just as there has been progress in mathematics and astronomy from the time of Aristotle until his own time, so progress may be anticipated after his time. The limitations of human knowledge on these subjects, that concern celestial mechanics, are therefore not absolute. Perplexity is not a permanent condition.

This notion of scientific progress may be related to Maimonides' ideas on progress in other areas of human endeavor—in the sphere of law, for example, and in the ethical refinement of a people in the course of history.

The crisis in astronomical theory, which resulted from the clash between Aristotelian celestial physics and Ptolemaic astronomy, came

100. See also Munk, *Guide* II, 194–95, n. 4.

101. See Pines, "Limitations," pp. 92–93. Moses is the ideal knower.

102. Maimonides mentions perplexity (*ḥayra*) three times in this chapter, with reference to Ptolemy, Aristotle and then here. The word clearly arouses associations with the title of the book.

The words *ḥayra* and *taḥayyur* often render the Greek term *aporia*, which is a feature of the dialectic process.

to a peak in Spain in Maimonides' lifetime.[103] Ibn Bājja, as we have seen, apparently attempted to rescue Aristotle's system. Ibn Ṭufayl invented a theory critical of Ptolemaic hypotheses and advanced alternate explanations. And his disciple, al-Biṭrūjī, who reports this about his teacher, also aspired to improve astronomical principles so as to make them conform with Aristotelian physics.[104] Ibn Rushd, who was Maimonides' contemporary (and fellow Cordovan), and perhaps the greatest philosopher of the Spanish Aristotelian school, rejected epicycles and eccentrics as presuppositions that are opposed to nature—that is, Aristotelian physics. He argued inter alia that these assumptions conflict with the principle that circular motion must be around the true center of the universe, which (in his view) is the earth. In his opinion, nothing in mathematics justifies the existence of epicycles and eccentrics posited by the astronomers. Ibn Rushd believed that the correct system was known at the time of Aristotle, that the sciences then reached their perfection, and that it was imperative to return to the Aristotelian model.[105] Contrary to Maimonides then, Ibn Rushd diagnosed a retreat in the sciences from the time of Aristotle to his own time.

Although Maimonides is affiliated with the Spanish Aristotelian school, his criticism of contemporary astronomy sets him apart from his Spanish predecessors. They tended to criticize Ptolemaic hypotheses from an Aristotelian vantage point, whereas the main thrust of Maimonides' critique was directed against the difficulties of the Aristotelian system.[106] Maimonides exploited the crisis in the regnant paradigm in order to cast doubt on Aristotelian celestial physics. Contrary to Ibn Rushd, he had no intention whatever of trying to restore Aristotelian physics. And in contrast to Ibn Rushd, as stated, he thought that the Aristotelian astronomical model was underdeveloped; for in his opinion mathematics and astronomy had not achieved in

103. See Pines, "Translator's Introduction," pp. cix–cxi; and L. Gauthier, "Une réforme du système astronomique de Ptolémée," *Journal Asiatique*, 1909, Part II, 483–510; Dreyer, *A History of Astronomy*, pp. 262–67.

In a Conference on Maimonides in Egypt held at Tel Aviv University in June 1982, Dr. T. Langerman lectured on "The 'True Perplexity': *The Guide for the Perplexed*, Part II, Chapter 24." The article will appear in the volume of papers of the colloquium.

See also Z. Bechler, "The Methodological Basis of Maimonides' Attack on Aristotelian Physics" (Hebrew), *Iyyun* 17 (1966): 34–41, and English summary, 58–59.

104. S. Munk, *Mélanges de philosophie juive et arabe*, nouvelle édition (Paris, 1955), p. 412; B. Goldstein, *Al-Biṭrūjī: On the Principles of Astronomy* (New Haven, 1971), I, 3–4.

105. F. Carmody, "The planetary theory of Ibn Rushd," *Osiris* 10 (1952): 556–86.

106. Gauthier, "Une reforme," pp. 489–90; Neugebauer, "The Astronomy of Maimonides," p. 335.

Aristotle's time the station that they attained in his lifetime. Nevertheless, he was aware of the difficulties inherent in the Ptolemaic theory. He had had contact with pupils of Ibn Bājja and with a son of Jābir b. Aflaḥ, critics of the Ptolemaic theory, and was familiar with the objections of other scientists.[107]

Two main questions concerning Maimonides' position regarding the contemporary crisis in astronomy may be raised: First, was his skepticism motivated by religious considerations? Second, was his skepticism regarding the possibility of devising a unified physical theory incurable? Addressing himself to these questions, Shlomo Pines suggests that Maimonides stressed the weakness of the Aristotelian theory because its vulnerability gave him a weapon to wield in the theological-religious debate and *also* because of the requirements of scientific theory.[108] Pines suggests that, as far as his skepticism is concerned, perhaps his own purpose, at least in part II of the *Guide,* may have been to undermine the confidence reposed in the doctrine of the universe's eternity, which was intimately related to general confidence in Greek science. To this end he may have exaggerated in the course of setting forth his doubts. Despite this, Pines says, when Maimonides summarizes the main points of physical science and astronomy in *Guide* I, 72, he apparently accepts the Ptolemaic theory and does not intimate to the reader that there is any doubt concerning it.[109] The position of thoroughgoing skepticism, Pines states, may be, for the reasons Maimonides presented, the only one that is truly logical and consistent. He adds, however, that in his view this kind of agnosticism would undermine everything that Maimonides intended to achieve in the *Guide* and it would also be inconsistent with his overall position, exposited elsewhere, concerning a human being's ultimate aim and his capacity for knowledge.[110]

There are no clear-cut answers to these questions. But perhaps part of the solution may be found at the end of II, 24, where Maimonides confesses his own perplexity and expresses the hope that someone in

107. In *Guide* II, 24, Maimonides mentions also Thābit ibn Qurra and al-Qabīṣī. Langerman (see n. 103) raised the question whether Maimonides knew Ibn al-Haytham's *al-Shukūk ʿalā Baṭlamyūs;* see ed. A. Sabra and N. Shehaby (Cairo, 1971). He notes that Maimonides does not mention the work and that there is no firm evidence that he was familiar with it.

108. See n. 103.

109. See also *Mishneh Torah,* Foundations of the Law, III, 1–5; and see Neugebauer, "Astronomy of Maimonides," p. 336, who mentions that Maimonides does not express doubts concerning the Ptolemaic theory in the *Mishneh Torah,* either in the Foundations of the Law or in the Laws concerning the New Moon, where he makes intensive use of eccentrics and epicycles.

110. See Pines, Translator's Introduction, p. cx.

the future may produce a demonstration of what is obscure for him. Science does not stand still; it is not a system of petrified hypotheses. It develops gradually by overcoming doubts and difficulties and attaining more adequate theories. In the well-known vocabulary of Thomas Kuhn, it progresses from the paradigm, tradition and consensus of normal science through a stage of crisis to a scientific revolution and the devising of a new paradigm.

The criteria that Maimonides uses to test the validity of theories are their power to explain phenomena mathematically, without physical models, and their power to accomplish this in the simplest possible way. In Maimonides' view, the conflict between Aristotelian celestial physics and Ptolemaic astronomy is not a clash between two physical models of the universe. He asserts (II, 11, pp. 273–74) that the science of astronomy does not seek cogent demonstrations concerning the form and number of the spheres. Only some astronomical matters are founded on the demonstration that they are in a given way, as, for instance, the indubitable demonstration that the sun's path is inclined against the equator. But no demonstration can be adduced to determine whether the sun has an eccentric sphere or an epicycle. The astronomer, however, is not ruffled by this uncertainty, for the object of the science of astronomy is to posit by way of hypothesis an arrangement that allows for the star's motion to be uniform and circular, having no acceleration, deceleration or change, and "to have the inferences necessarily following from the assumption of that motion agree with what is observed." The astronomer concurrently tries, as far as possible, "to diminish motions and the number of spheres."[111] It is preferable to explain certain motions of a star on the basis of the assumption that there are three spheres rather than four.[112] Maimon-

111. Cf. also Ptolemy, *Almagest* XIII, 2: "We should try to find the simplest hypothesis we can by which we can harmonize the heavenly motions, and failing this be content with what is possible." This passage is cited by B. R. Goldstein, "The Status of Models in Ancient and Medieval Astronomy," *Centaurus* 24 (1980): 136. On Maimonides' views treated here see p. 139.

Goldstein compares Maimonides' position to that of Cardinal Robert Bellarmine as expressed in a letter to Paolo Antonio Foscarini, in which he reacts to Copernicus' hypothesis: "It seems to me that your reverence and Signor Galileo act prudently when you content yourselves with speaking hypothetically and not absolutely, as I have always understood that Copernicus spoke. To say that on the supposition of the Earth's movement and the Sun's quiescence all the celestial appearances are explained better than by the theory of eccentrics and epicycles is to speak with excellent good sense and to run no risk whatever. Such a manner of speaking is enough for a mathematician." See also G. de Santillana, *The Crime of Galileo* (Chicago, 1955), p. 99.

112. Cf. Aristotle's maxim that "Nature does nothing superfluous" in *The Generation of Animals* 739b20 and many other places. See Ibn Rushd in his *Great Commentary on the Metaphysics*, pp. 1662–63, citing Ptolemy's *al-Iqtiṣāṣ*, viz. *The Planetary Hypotheses*, on the

ides cites as an additional example of what came to be known as Occam's razor, or the law of parsimony, his preference for the hypothesis of the sun's eccentricity, as Ptolemy supposes, rather than the hypothesis of an epicycle.[113]

Maimonides, then, maintained that the natural sciences are capable of attaining the truth within certain limitations and that they should not exceed these limitations. Unlike the Mutakallimūn he refused to reject Aristotelian physics.[114] He found a different solution for the question of creation versus eternity. Maimonides' emphasis on the limitations of human knowledge, says Pines, may be his most significant contribution to general philosophy. And Pines adds that, like Kant, Maimonides marked these limitations in order to leave room for faith.

Maimonides' skepticism is qualified. He does not deny the possibility of attaining knowledge concerning sublime subjects such as celestial mechanics and metaphysics; he denies the possibility of attaining demonstrative truth in these subjects. In the absence of such knowledge human beings are compelled to settle for something less.

IV

Let us return to the beginning. According to G. E. L. Owen and Martha Craven Nussbaum, not only in ethics and metaphysics, but also in physics, Aristotle relied upon dialectical arguments, upon the phenomena in the sense of the *endoxa* and *legomena*, and he relied upon the opinions of his predecessors, particularly the wise among them. Once the consensus is established it is necessary to raise doubts and difficulties and to apply them in a specific direction.

My contention is that Maimonides, in the wake of Aristotle and the Great Commentator Alexander of Aphrodisias, approached the enterprise of science in the same way. He noticed that on crucial questions and obscure matters, such as celestial mechanics and the issue of creation versus eternity, Aristotle came forth with no better than dialectical arguments and at times even stooped to rhetorical claims. Ultimately, consensus is all we have. Now on the issue of creation versus eternity both alternatives are vulnerable, but the assumption

---

simplest way of explaining phenomena; and see Carmody, "The Planetary Theory of Ibn Rushd," p. 571.

113. At the end of the chapter, Maimonides explains that all the things that he explained do not contradict what is said by "our prophets and the sustainers of our Law." He adds that the innate and primordial wisdom of the community was lost under the conditions of Exile. See also *Guide* II, 8.

114. Pines, "Maimonides," p. 29.

of eternity, he claims, is more so. Consequently, one should prefer the well-known premises, or the consensus, of the Sages of the nation of Abraham and Moses to the consensus of Aristotle and his successors. Or, to put it in another way, one should accept the consensus of the practitioners of the religious laws (the *ahl al-sharīʿa,* or the *mutasharriʿūn*), meaning the Jews, Christians and Muslims, to that of Aristotle and the Ṣābians. Maimonides suggests that the demonstrative truth was accessible to Moses, the ideal knower, by the medium of the Active Intellect, but the degree to which this supposition was more than theological is open to question.

In his understanding of the meaning of dialectic Maimonides followed Aristotle. According to Aristotle, dialectic, or well-known, propositions conform with the knowledge held by everyone, or by most human beings, or by the wise among them.[115] Maimonides includes conventional, or well-known, propositions (*mashhūrāt/endoxa*) among the four kinds of propositions that are self-evident and do not require proof.[116] The other three are perceptions (*maḥsūsāt*), first ideas (*maʿqūlāt*) and traditions (*maqbūlāt*). There can be no disagreement among human beings of sound mind concerning perceptions and first ideas. There may, however, be differences of opinion concerning conventional propositions, or dialectical statements, for these are propositions that have become well known within a specific nation. Maimonides adds that to the extent that the matter is well known among more nations, so is assent (*taṣdīq*) to it greater. The traditions rest either upon one man or upon many. We need proof with respect to the traditions that the one from whom we transmit is trustworthy. It is possible, Maimonides adds, that what is accepted within one group is not accepted among others.

In the sequel Maimonides classifies syllogisms according to categories familiar to us from the Falāsifa: demonstrative, dialectical, rhetorical, sophistical and poetic.[117] According to this classification a demonstrative syllogism is one whose premises are true. A dialectical syllogism is one whose premises (or one of them) are well known. The premises of a rhetorical syllogism (or one of them) belong to traditions. There is also a syllogism that is sophistical, wherein the premises (or

115. *Topics* 100b21, 104a8–12. On Aristotle's notion of dialectic, see J. D. G. Evans, *Aristotle's Concept of Dialectic* (Cambridge, 1977).

116. *Treatise on Logic,* pp. 39–42 (trans. Ibn Tibbon); 47–49 (trans. Efros). And see the Arabic text in I. Efros, "Maimonides' Arabic Treatise on Logic," *Proceedings of the American Academy of Jewish Research* 34 (1966): 21–24.

117. Cf. D. M. Dunlop, "Al-Fārābī's Introductory *Risālah* on Logic," *Islamic Quarterly* 3 (1956–57): 267 (text); 275–76 (trans.); Al-Fārābī, *Iḥṣā' al-ʿulūm,* ed. ʿUthmān Amīn, 3rd ed. (Cairo, 1968), pp. 79–85.

one of them) are such that one errs or falsifies. A syllogism whose premise is used by way of imitation is a poetic syllogism. The art of the demonstrative syllogism is the art of demonstration; the art of the dialectical syllogism is the art of dialectic; the art of the rhetorical syllogism is the art of rhetoric; the use of the sophistical syllogism is sophism; and the art of syllogisms that explains the ways of imitation is the art of poetry.

It is, then, the art of dialectic that concerns us. It is a commonly held misconception that Maimonides (and his model, al-Fārābī) had a low opinion of dialectic and the practitioners of dialectic, namely, the Mutakallimūn. This misconception flows from a failure to recognize the critical difference between pernicious and constructive dialectic. The Falāsifa claimed that the Mutakallimūn did not understand the true function of dialectic and consequently abused an important tool. In their view, following the lead of Aristotle, dialectic had a useful, indeed vital, function.[118] Consider, for example, Ibn Rushd. In his Middle Commentary on the *Topics*, he elaborated upon Aristotle's remarks concerning the utility of dialectic. In the first place, it is important to observe that Ibn Rushd attempted, in the wake of Aristotle, to stress the proximity between dialectic and demonstrative proof, or philosophy.[119] Dialectic is useful for theoretical sciences insofar as it paves the way for philosophy proper. Furthermore, it is useful for the education of the masses to the extent that it teaches them what they require for the sake of political association, for the citizens must concur on certain issues so as to associate on the basis of justice and harmony. Dialectic, says Ibn Rushd, attains this aim more readily than does rhetoric or poetics.[120] This use of dialectic is appropriate for those who have already attained fundamental ideas concerning the sciences but have not succeeded in transcending opinion and arriving at demonstrative knowledge.

Ibn Rushd's principal aim is to accent the utility of dialectic as a tool for achieving demonstrative knowledge. He notes that Aristotle

118. With regard to the function and value of dialectic, the passage in *Topics* 101a25–b4 was a guiding light for the Arabic philosophers. Aristotle lists three functions: (1) It is useful for mental training for the purpose of arguing about whatever subject may be proposed. (2) It is useful for conversations with the many, for by enumerating opinions it is possible to deal with them. (3) It is useful for the philosophic sciences by way of clarifying difficulties on both sides of a question and establishing the principles of the sciences.

119. The following is based upon C. E. Butterworth's introduction to Ibn Rushd, *Talkhīṣ Kitāb al-jadal* (Averroes, *Middle Commentary on Aristotle's Topics*), ed. C. E. Butterworth and A. A. Haridi (Cairo, 1979), pp. 30–37.

120. Ibn Rushd, *Talkhīṣ Kitāb al-jadal,* par. 1; *Topics* 101a31–33. See also Ibn Sīnā, *Kitāb al-Shifā', al-Manṭiq, al-Jadal,* ed. I. Madkour (Cairo, 1965), pp. 11–14.

generally begins his investigations in the realm of physics, metaphysics and politics by means of a dialectical discourse, and that only thereafter does he raise the discussion to the level of demonstrative proof.[121] Moreover, dialectic, by means of a close link with demonstration, is useful in the enterprise of discovering the principles of the sciences.[122] Beyond this, dialectic, more than the demonstrative art, is useful for transmitting theoretical opinions to the masses. In this connection Ibn Rushd stresses that there is a hierarchy within opinions that are absorbed in this manner, and that the opinions of wise men are the most reliable. In sum, the main goals of dialectic are to serve philosophy as a stepping stone to demonstrative knowledge and as a means for discovering scientific principles, as well as to convey the truths of theoretical philosophy to the masses.

Ibn Rushd clarifies the difference between the philosopher and the dialectician.[123] Accordingly, the philosopher uses demonstrative syllogisms. He carries on an internal discussion with himself and persuades himself. His loftiest aspirations center upon the question of the validity of his premises. In contrast to the philosopher, the dialectician formulates questions and answers, and he always must turn to another person, to an addressee.[124]

In his Short Commentary on the *Topics*, Ibn Rushd says, in a similar vein, that dialectic conveys belief that is close to certainty and is consequently closer to demonstrative philosophy than rhetoric or poetics.[125] In this work he levels a sharp critique against the Mutakallimūn. He blames them inter alia for being ignorant of the art of dialectic, and he illustrates their distortion of this art by citing their proof for the creation of the universe.[126] He also exposes the flaws of the Mutakallimūn in his Short Commentary on the *Rhetoric*, where he claims that they are in fact not dialectical theologians but rather rhetorical theologians. And adding insult to injury, he claims that even qua rhe-

121. Ibn Rushd, *Talkhīṣ*, par. 5; *Topics* 101a34–37. In the light of Ibn Rushd's comment, it is possible to understand Narboni's criticism of Maimonides in his commentary on *Guide* II, 15 (ed. J. Goldenthal, Vienna, 1852, p. 31). Narboni claims that not only with respect to the creation of the universe (as Maimonides claims) but also in other matters of the *Physics*, Aristotle tends to begin with generally known propositions, the opinions of the ancients and doubts, and only then to go on with demonstrative proofs.

122. Ibn Rushd, *Talkhīṣ*, p. 52 and n. 19.

123. Ibid., pp. 44–45.

124. Ibid., par. 302; *Topics* 155b3–18. See also Ibn Sīnā, *Kitāb al-Shifā'*, (n. 120), pp. 11, 13.

125. C. E. Butterworth, "Averroes: Politics and Opinion," *American Political Science Review* 66 (1972): 894–901, esp. p. 895; idem, *Averroes' Three Short Commentaries on Aristotle's "Topics," "Rhetoric," and "Poetics,"* ed. and trans. C. E. Butterworth (Albany, 1977).

126. Butterworth, "Averroes: Politics and Opinion," p. 895; and see *Short Commentary on "Topics,"* pars. 6–8.

toricians they do not hit the mark.[127] In this context he remarks that poetics are directed to the masses and that poetics motivate people to believe or withhold belief by means of poetic examples. The Qur'ān, he adds, is the best known poetic creation.[128]

The main advantage of dialectic, then, is to serve as a defensive weapon that is capable of saving both philosophy and religion.[129] It is a weapon that should be kept in the hands of the sages and philosophers. It should not be in the hands of the Mutakallimūn, who have distorted it. In the ideal regime ("the best city") the Sages will direct everything. Dialectic will be useful for preparing those who aspire to belong to the category of the Sages, and it will provide explanations for the few who succeed in transcending the level of the masses without, however, reaching the level of the Sages.

Charles Butterworth suggests that Ibn Rushd's principal works (*al-Ḍamīma, Faṣl al-maqāl, Kashf manāhij al-adilla, Tahāfut al-tahāfut*) are dialectical in character.[130] He notes, for instance, the fact that these works were all written for a specific person (an addressee) and that the discussion goes step by step in a style akin to question and answer. These works are intended to save philosophy from the stigma that adhered to it as a result of religious and political considerations.

In the light of the preceding, it may be argued, in my opinion, that the *Guide of the Perplexed* is a work that is mainly dialectical. To be sure, Maimonides disdained the Mutakallimūn and their methods. But this does not mean that he forsook dialectic. The *Guide* is a dialectical work deliberately directed to an addressee and those like him. One of the purposes of the work is to prepare this category of potential philosophers for philosophy, to arouse them to understand its hidden treasures. The book is intended for those special individuals who have not as yet attained a philosophical level. It is also aimed at the masses whom it intends to educate by means of dialectical arguments, that is, opinions well known among a certain people and opinions accepted by human beings in general.[131]

Tel Aviv University

127. Butterworth, "Averroes: Politics and Opinion," pp. 896–97.
128. Ibid., p. 897; *Short Commentary on "Topics,"* pars. 1, 4.
129. Butterworth, "Averroes: Politics and Opinion," p. 900.
130. Ibid., p. 899.
131. This is apparently the meaning of the quotation from Proverbs 8:4 which appears at the beginning of the introduction to the first part of the *Guide:* "Unto you, O men, I call, And my voice is to the sons of men." According to medieval commentators (e.g., Shem Tov Ben Shem Tov and Ephodi), Maimonides is suggesting that the *Guide* is directed to the intellectual elite and to the common people.

5 Humility as a Virtue: A Maimonidean Critique of Aristotle's Ethics

DANIEL H. FRANK

I. INTRODUCTION

It is doubtless true that on a general level Maimonides follows Aristotle closely in his moral theory. He adopts Aristotle's doctrine of the mean[1] and his distinction between the intellectual and the moral virtues.[2] Furthermore, as I have argued elsewhere, Maimonides, like his Greek predecessor, distinguishes between the life of moral virtue and the contemplative life, with the latter's taking precedence over the former.[3] However, within this broad general agreement there are many particular points of difference between Maimonides and Aristotle on ethical matters. This essay will concern itself with one such difference, a difference which I believe amounts to a critique of Aristotle by Maimonides.

In *Hilkhot De'ot* II, 3, Maimonides asserts that "[t]here are some dispositions in regard to which a man is forbidden to accustom himself to the mean. They must be shunned to the extreme. Such a disposition is pride (*govah lāv*). The right way in this regard is not to be merely humble (*anav*), but to be humble-minded (*shfal ruaḥ*) and lowly of spirit to the utmost." Although the general point made here, that in some cases one must not follow the mean, is not un-Aristotelian,[4] the high

1. *Shemonah Perakim* IV, *Hilkhot De'ot* I, 2–4.
2. *Shemonah Perakim* II, *Guide of the Perplexed* III, 54.
3. *Guide* III, 27, 54. For my interpretation of the contemplative life, the summum bonum, according to Maimonides, see "The End of the *Guide*: Maimonides on the Best Life for Man," *Judaism* 34, no. 4 (1985); see also Alexander Altmann, "Maimonides's 'Four Perfections'," in *Essays in Jewish Intellectual History* (Hanover, New Hampshire, 1981), p. 73.
4. *Nicomachean Ethics* (*NE*) II, 6 (1107a8–15): "But not every action nor every passion admits of a mean; for some have names that already imply badness, e.g. spite, shamelessness, envy, and in the case of actions, adultery, theft, murder; for all of these and suchlike things imply by their names that they are themselves bad, and not the excesses or deficiencies of them. It is not possible, then, ever to be right with regard to them; one must always be wrong."

value which Maimonides places upon humility, lowliness of spirit, is manifestly un-Aristotelian. In fact, it is more than un-Aristotelian; it is anti-Aristotelian. As I shall show, for Maimonides, humility is a—perhaps even *the*—virtue; for Aristotle, it is not.

So much, then, for preliminaries. Now we must turn to the relevant texts in Aristotle and Maimonides to ground our claims.

II. ARISTOTLE ON THE VIRTUE OF PRIDE

Having laid out in Books II and III, 1–5, of his *Nicomachean Ethics* a general schema for understanding moral virtue and vice, a discussion which includes, among other topics, his celebrated doctrine of the mean (II, 6) and an intricate analysis of moral responsibility (III, 1–5), Aristotle turns in III, 6–V to a discussion of particular virtues. In these chapters he analyzes virtues such as courage, temperance, liberality, good temper, and friendliness, according to the doctrine of the mean. He also discusses the virtue of pride (*megalopsychia,* literally "great-souledness"). And it is the discussion of this virtue in IV, 3, which is of interest to us, for it is in this discussion that Aristotle presents his most considered views about humility (*mikropsychia,* literally "small-souledness").

Pride, like most of the other virtues, falls in a mean state between extremes. On either end are the vices or, more accurately, errors[5] of vanity and humility. The proud man, unlike the vain or humble man, both deems himself worthy of great things, not just anything, and is indeed worthy of them.[6] Opposed to the proud man are both the vain (*chaunos*) man and the humble (*mikropsychos*) man. Like the proud man, the vain man deems himself worthy of great things, but, unlike him, he is in fact not worthy of them. And finally, at the other extreme, the proud man is to be distinguished from the humble man; this is a man who is worthy of great things, like the proud man, but who, unlike him, deems himself worthy of less than his true worth. The proud man, thus, makes claims and has expectations for himself in accordance with his actual merit, while the vain or humble man exceeds or falls short in his rightful claims.[7] In sum, the proud man claims much, and he is worthy of it.

But what is it that the proud man claims as his (rightful) due? In a

5. *NE* IV, 3 (1125a19).

6. The proud man also differs from the temperate man, who in the present context is only worthy of little things and views himself in like manner, a manner commensurate with his (little) worth (*NE* IV, 3 [1123b5–6]).

7. *NE* IV, 3 (1123b13–15).

word, *timē*—honor.[8] A full discussion of *timē* would be nothing less than a discussion of the entire aristocratic bias of Greek ethics from Homer on, from the wrath of Achilles to the character before us. Suffice it to say, "*timē*," as the most recent commentator on the *Nicomachean Ethics,* Terence Irwin, has noted, "reflects other people's judgment of someone's worth . . . Honor suggests primarily the attitude of esteem and admiration."[9] The proud man justifiably claims and expects his share of the admiration and esteem of others. By contrast, the humble man is deficient in self-respect; he has no, or too little, opinion of his own merits and achievements and consequently claims too little for himself.

A word of caution is necessary at this point. For Aristotle, the proud man is not a pompous man. He is to be distinguished, as will be recalled, from the vain man who claims more than his due. Unlike the vain man, the proud man has merit in his claim. And the grounds for his claim to honor are based explicitly upon his goodness, his virtue (*aretē*).[10] The proud man is courageous, liberal, temperate, and so forth. And since he is such, he has a rightful claim[11] and thus makes his claim to the admiration and esteem of others.

At this point we may well wonder whether being virtuous is desired for the sake of honor. Is virtue an end in itself for Aristotle? Or is the autonomy of virtue compromised, given the honor which the virtuous man thinks is his due? It is clear that for Aristotle the former is the case. There are numerous passages in which he is explicit about the autonomy of virtuous action.[12] Virtuous action is an end in itself. Given this, it is incorrect to suppose that virtuous actions are performed for the sake of honor, for the sake of what other people will think. No, the good man is good for its own sake, for the sake of

8. *NE* IV, 3 (1123b21–24).

9. Terence Irwin (tr.), *Aristotle: Nicomachean Ethics* (Indianapolis, 1985), pp. 408–9 (s.v. *honour*).

10. *NE* I, 5 (1095b26–31), IV, 3 (1123b26–30).

11. Unlike the vain man who bases his (misguided) claim to honor on the wrong sort of thing, namely natural goods such as wealth and good birth (*NE* IV, 3 [1124a26–b2]).

12. *NE* VI, 5 (1140b6–7), X, 6 (1176b8–9); cf. also *NE* II, 4 (1105a28–33). On this point, the autonomy of virtuous action for Aristotle, Marvin Fox is in error when he asserts that for Aristotle "moral virtue is only a propaedeutic to intellectual virtue and thus to the life of ultimate felicity" ("The Doctrine of the Mean in Aristotle and Maimonides: A Comparative Study," in S. Stein and R. Loewe [eds.], *Studies in Jewish Religious and Intellectual History* [University, Ala., 1979], p. 116). Julius Guttman is closer to the truth when he writes: "For Aristotle, metaphysical knowledge is the highest of all, but he ascribes to the other fields of knowledge independent value" (in his abridged edition of the *Guide* [tr. C. Rabin, London, 1952], p. 225, n. 89).

virtue,[13] and as a result of this he expects the esteem of others. Honor is the prize (*to athlon,* 1123b35) for virtue, not its consciously sought-after goal.

Viewed in this way, pride is, as Aristotle suggests, the "crown," the *kosmos* (1124a1–2), of the virtues.[14] This second-order virtue depends upon antecedent virtue and provides the final manifestation of the virtue and goodness of a man. "Pride, then, seems to be a sort of crown of the virtues; for it makes them greater, and it is not found without them. Therefore it is hard to be truly proud; for it is impossible without nobility and goodness of character" (1124a1–4).

Passages such as the one we have just quoted have convinced Troels Engberg-Pedersen that "Aristotle should be seen as having taken the whole step away from an 'archaic' conception of high-mindedness [pride] . . . to a more 'moral' outlook."[15] By this Engberg-Pedersen means that honor is now to be awarded for moral virtue, and not for natural goods such as wealth and good birth. And Engberg-Pedersen is right.[16] Yet, before we succumb to the picture of Aristotle the anti-aristocrat we should notice that to a large extent those very virtues which will be recognized for esteem and admiration by the proud man's peers are those able to be exercised well only by the aristocrat. Certainly the virtues concerned with money, namely liberality and munificence (*NE* IV, 1–2), require money with which to be liberal and munificent.[17] If Aristotle should really be seen "as having taken the whole step away from an 'archaic' conception of high-mindedness . . . to a more 'moral' outlook," then he should not make the exercise of the moral virtues dependent in any way upon wealth and birth. In sum, for all that Aristotle does say about virtuous action, and not wealth or birth, as providing the grounds for honor and esteem, his

13. Cf. Maimonides, *Sefer ha-Madda* (=*Mishneh Torah* I), *Repentence* X, 2: "Whoever serves God out of love, occupies himself with the study of the Law and the fulfillment of commandments and walks in the paths of wisdom, impelled by no external motive whatsoever, moved neither by fear of calamity nor by desire to obtain material benefits—such a man does what is truly right because it is truly right, and ultimately, happiness comes to him as a result of his conduct" (tr. M. Hyamson).

14. Sc. the *moral* virtues, not all the virtues, moral and intellectual. The proud, magnanimous man is not ipso facto a philosopher, as Gauthier imagines (R. Gauthier, *Magnanimité* [Paris, 1951], p. 106). W. F. R. Hardie makes the necessary correction of Gauthier on this point in "'Magnanimity' in Aristotle's Ethics" (*Phronesis* 23 [1978]), pp. 68–69.

15. Troels Engberg-Pedersen, *Aristotle's Theory of Moral Insight* (Oxford, 1983), pp. 76, 78.

16. *NE* IV, 3 (1124a26–b2); cf. n. 10 and 11.

17. *NE* X, 8 (1178a28–31): "The liberal man will need money for the doing of his liberal deeds, and the just man too will need it for the returning of services (for wishes are hard to discern, and even people who are not just pretend to wish to act justly)."

prior discussion of the virtues themselves undercuts his moral, anti-aristocratic, outlook.[18]

Although not a vain man, the proud man disdains many. Not only does he disdain those wealthy who base their claim to honor upon their wealth, but he is also contemptuous of "commoners"(*hoi tuchontes* [1124a10], literally, "whomever one may meet") who because of lack of wealth cannot partake of virtuous action. Aristotle asserts: "One ought to be dignified (*megan*, 1124b19) toward people who enjoy high position and good fortune, but unassuming (*metrion*, 1124b20) towards those of the middle class (*hoi mesoi*, ibid.); for it is a difficult and lofty thing to be superior to the former, but easy to be so to the latter, and an august bearing over the former is no mark of ill-breeding, but among lowly people it is as vulgar as a display of strength against the weak" (1124b18–23). Aristotle's point here should not be missed. Given who he is and what he has done, for the proud man to show dignity to the common man is most "unseemly." And this is a cardinal sin for the proud aristocrat.

A clear picture is beginning to emerge of Aristotelian *megalopsychos*. He is the paradigmatically virtuous man, in fact, the *phronimos* upon whom the whole of Aristotle's ethical theory is based.[19] Opposed to him, even more than the vain man, is the humble man.[20] This is a man who is actually virtuous and thus worthy of great honor, but who robs himself of what he deserves.[21] By placing too little value upon his virtue the humble man deems himself unworthy of his merited honor. For Aristotle, this man is *ignorant* (*agnoein*, 1125a22) of himself. Indeed, this gives a peculiar twist to the Delphic Maxim *Gnothi sauton* ("Know thyself"). In the present context to know oneself is to know what one has a right to expect. Given that the humble man, like the proud man, is virtuous, he has a right to the esteem of his peers. But it is just this that the humble man is unaware of. Retiring (*oknēros*, 1125a24) in nature, this virtuous man underestimates the value of his virtue and thus is ignorant of the prize for his virtue—honor and esteem from his peers. For this, the humble man is culpable according to Aristotle.

Let this suffice for our discussion of the Aristotelian virtue of pride. Although Aristotle highlights the virtuous nature of the proud man,

18. I find further confirmation of Aristotle's aristocratic, anti-democratic outlook in his *Politics*; see my "Aristotle on Freedom in the *Politics*," *Prudentia* 15, no. 2 (1983).
19. *NE* VI, 13 (1144b30–32).
20. *NE* IV, 3 (1125a32–33).
21. *NE* IV, 3 (1125a19–21).

we must not overlook the importance which he likewise attaches to the prize for virtue: honor. If honor were of no importance, humility would be no vice.

III. MAIMONIDES ON THE VIRTUE OF HUMILITY

Now let us turn to Maimonides. Our discussion will focus upon one, but perhaps the most important, work in which Maimonides discusses humility—what for Aristotle was a vice. As I asserted at the outset, Maimonides will be seen to disagree with Aristotle on the value of humility and the importance of honor, and in such a way that one may view his disagreement as actually constituting a critique of Aristotle. In fact, this disagreement can be seen to underlie the utterly different conception of humanity and human nature which Maimonides has from Aristotle. Again, given Maimonides' view of humanity and man's status in the cosmic order, humility will be seen to be the crown of the virtues, much as pride, its opposite, was for Aristotle.

The passages for discussion are to be found in *Hilkhot De'ot* I, 4–5, and II, 3. In I, 4, Maimonides, in good Aristotelian fashion, asserts that "the right path is the mean."[22] For example, a man should neither be irascible nor should he be unable to feel anger; he should neither be niggardly nor should he squander his wealth; he should be neither a buffoon nor a melancholic.[23] Maimonides concludes this paragraph of the chapter by asserting that the wise man (the *ḥakham*) is one whose character traits lie in the mean.[24]

But a dramatic difference awaits us when we read more in the *Hilkhot De'ot.* In I, 5, we learn that there is a man, the *ḥasid* (the pious man), whose life and characteristic activities go beyond that of the *ḥakham.* The actions of the *ḥasid* do not all lie in the mean. Maimonides asserts: "Whoever is exceedingly scrupulous with himself and moves a little toward one side or the other, away from the mean, is a pious man (a *ḥasid*)." And Maimonides gives the following example which we should note well: "Whoever moves away from haughtiness to the opposite extreme so that he is exceedingly humble is called a pious

22. Cf. *Shemonah Perakim* IV.

23. Note that, as for Aristotle, a mean is to be found both in feelings and emotions (anger, melancholy) as well as types of actions (niggardly actions); cf. *NE* II, 6 (1106b16–18).

24. As a result of Maimonides' discussion here it seems reasonable to conclude that the *ḥakham* is Aristotle's *phronimos*, the man of outstanding moral virtue. Furthermore, I would suggest that in the last chapter of the *Guide* (III, 54) the penultimate human perfection, moral perfection, is the life here characterized as that of the *ḥakham*. On this last point see my "The End of the *Guide* . . . ," n. 24 and 33.

man (a *ḥasid*); this is the standard of piety.[25] If he moves only to the mean and is humble, he is called a wise man (a *ḥakham*); this is the standard of wisdom."

Before we pause to consider the ramifications of these remarks, let us turn to II, 3. Reiterating his remarks of I, 5, Maimonides states "[t]here are some dispositions in regard to which a man is forbidden to accustom himself to the mean. They must be shunned to the extreme. Such a disposition is pride. The right way in this regard is not to be merely humble, but to be humble-minded and lowly of spirit to the utmost. Therefore, it was said of Moses, our master, that he was "very humble" [Numbers 12:3] and not merely humble. And therefore the wise men[26] commanded: "Be exceedingly humble in spirit" [*Avot* IV, 4]. Moreover, they said that anyone who makes his heart haughty denies the existence of God. As it is said: "And your heart shall be proud, and you shall forget the Lord your God" [Deuteronomy 8:14].

We now have sufficient evidence before us to make a number of comments. As I said at the beginning of this essay, the general point made here, that in some cases one must not follow the mean, is not un-Aristotelian. Aristotle asserts that there is no mean of spite or shamelessness or envy (among emotions); nor is there a mean in adultery, murder, or theft. All these are bad per se, and the virtuous man must avoid them to the extreme, at all costs. It is important to point out this similarity between Aristotle and Maimonides so that one will not be tempted to adopt the view, put forth most strongly by Steven Schwarzschild, that Aristotle and Maimonides differ dramatically, to the extent that the former offers us an ethics of (in Schwarzschild's words) "moderation," whereas the latter ultimately offers us an ethics of "moral radicalism."[27] This is an overstatement as far as the evidence

---

25. Cf. *Avot* IV, 4: "Rabbi Levitas of Yavneh said: 'Be exceedingly humble in spirit. . . .'" In his commentary on this passage Maimonides writes: "[W]ith regard to this attribute alone [!] among all the rest, meaning to say, with regard to pride, the rabbis tended all the way to the extreme of deficiency; that is, they inclined completely to humbleness of spirit in order that they would not leave any room for pride in their souls" (*Commentary on the Mishnah, Avot* IV, 4 [tr. Arthur David]) [my emphasis].

26. Presumably Rabbi Levitas and his school; see n. 25.

27. Steven S. Schwarzschild, "Moral Radicalism and 'Middlingness' in the Ethics of Maimonides," *Studies in Medieval Culture* 11 (1978): 65–94. The very title of Schwarzschild's paper hints at his view. And on p. 82 he writes: "Maimonides teaches an ethic of Aristotelian moderateness only as an initial and lower stage of ethics. This is still an ethic derived from and thus bound to existing society. From this he goes on to a higher and ultimate stage of moral radicalism, which is determined by *imitatio Dei*." The only truth to this bold statement is that at the highest stage of moral development morality "is determined by *imitatio Dei*" (cf. *Guide* III, 54). But this theocentric morality is not ipso facto "radical" in the way which Schwarzschild suggests. As we shall presently see, median ethics defines the actions of both the *ḥakham* (the wise man) and the *ḥasid* (the

goes. As we have just seen, Aristotle is prepared to dismiss certain emotions and actions as beyond the pale of civilized (Greek) society. He is "radical," in Schwarzschild's terms, in his condemnation of spite, envy, and so forth. And on the other hand, Maimonides clearly indicates that only some virtues are defined by extreme behavior, extreme humility being the example which we have noted.[28] The other virtues are defined by the mean between extremes;[29] for that matter, moderate humility is not a vice or any other kind of shortcoming, but is in fact a virtue, albeit a virtue of the *ḥakham,* not the *ḥasid* (I, 5). Again, quite generally, the moderate activity of the *ḥakham* constitutes a bona fide moral life according to Maimonides, and he approves of it. In sum, Aristotle can be (*pace* Schwarzschild) "radical" and Maimonides can be "moderate."

This may seem somewhat disingenuous. It is true that Aristotle and Maimonides agree that some virtues are to be defined by reference to a mean while other virtues are to be defined by reference to an extreme. It is also true that Maimonides' extremism as regards humility is merely a particular point of difference from Aristotle. Nevertheless, the fact that an individual, because of his extremism with regard to a particular virtue—humility—is promoted to a higher level of morality—that of piety—should make us pause to consider how similar the views of Aristotle and Maimonides really are. Aristotle has no distinction that I am aware of between two different levels of morality. He has no category corresponding to Maimonides' category of piety.[30]

---

pious man), save for the virtues of extreme humility and absolute patience (that is, lack of anger; see *Hilkhot De'ot* II, 3).

28. The avoidance of anger is another; see n. 27.

29. For (implicit) confirmation of this, note the *proscription* of asceticism in *Hilkhot De'ot* III, 1: "Perhaps a man will say: 'Since desire, honor, and the like constitute a bad way and remove a man from the world [*Avot* IV, 27], I shall completely separate myself from them and go to the other extreme.' So he does not eat meat, nor drink wine, nor take a wife, nor live in a decent dwelling, nor wear decent clothing, but sackcloth, coarse wool, and so on, like the priests of Edom [Christian monks]. This, too, is a bad way and it is forbidden to follow it. Whoever follows this way is called a sinner. Indeed He [God] says about the Nazirite: "He [the priest] shall make atonement for him because he sinned against the soul" [Numbers 6:11]."

The point I am making is simply this: If asceticism is proscribed, moderation (save for the explicit exceptions we have noted) is the norm for everyone.

30. A parallel is not to be found in *NE* II, 4 (1105b5–9), where Aristotle distinguishes between (a) the man who performs just and temperate acts and (b) the man who performs such acts as just and temperate men do. For Aristotle, only the latter is (truly) virtuous; the former is just and temperate in name only. On the other hand, Maimonides does admit two genuine levels of morality, that of the *ḥakham* (which I would equate with the activities of [b]) (see also n. 24) and that of the *ḥasid* (an utterly un-Aristotelian category).

Indeed, Aristotle distinguishes between the man of moral virtue and the contemplative, with the latter taking pride of place.[31] But, as I have argued elsewhere,[32] the contemplative is by his very nature amoral and apolitical. Not so for Maimonides.[33] For him, the pious contemplative is to be squarely placed within the moral and political sphere, but indeed on a plane above the *ḥakham.*

How does the *ḥasid* differ from the *ḥakham*? For all that Maimonides tells us in the passages at which we have looked, the *ḥasid* differs from the *ḥakham* by his extreme behavior on some occasions, in some spheres of moral activity. In the sphere of humility the *ḥasid* goes to the extreme. His excessive humility betokens an utter lack of regard for worldly honor[34] (as well as an utterly un-Aristotelian conception of the self in the cosmic order, as will be seen). The excessively humble man cares not a whit for what the human, all-too-human, world takes as significant.

How unlike Aristotle: for Aristotle, worldly honor and man's proper appreciation of it are of importance. If this were not so, Aristotle's condemnation of humility would collapse. Although honor is not the consciously sought-after goal for the sake of which all virtuous action is done, nevertheless, when virtue is manifest, then the virtuous man expects recognition, and from the right people. Not so for Maimonides. Indeed, the *ḥakham* is humble, and like the proud Aristotelian *megalopsychos* pursues a mean between haughtiness and abasement,[35] but the *ḥasid,* Maimonides' moral exemplar, is quite radical in his denial of the praise of other men. For the *ḥasid*—and this point is obvious but nonetheless important—the ultimate ground for morality is God. "Anyone who makes his heart haughty denies the existence of God," said the rabbis of *Avot,* thinking of Deuteronomy 8:14, a passage which we have seen Maimonides' quoting with approval. To take an interest in worldly honor is to forget God, to live and to act as if God did not exist. It is to place the mundane above the divine, and in so doing to deny the latter's all-encompassing (moral) significance.

What we see then is that a particular point of contrast between Aristotle and Maimonides ramifies into a manifestation of an utterly different ethical outlook. In this way Schwarzschild has raised an im-

31. *NE* VI, 7 (1141a20–22); X, 7 (1177a12–18, 1178a5–8); X, 8 (1178a9).
32. "The End of the *Guide* . . . ," pp. 485–87.
33. *Guide* III, 54.
34. To this effect Maimonides quotes with approval *Avot* IV, 27: "Envy, desire, and honor remove a man from the world" (quoted at *Hilkhot De'ot* II, 7).
35. *Shemonah Perakim* IV.

portant point. Although his general claim that "[o]ne could lay down the general rule: look for the evaluations of honor and humility, and you will find the fundamental rift between Greek and Jewish ethics down through the ages"[36] is perhaps too strong, it does seem to be true as regards Aristotle and Maimonides. Although Maimonides is not (*pace* Schwarzschild) invariably "radical" in his ethical theorizing, the one case which we have been considering, humility,[37] manifests nothing less than his anti-Aristotelian theocentric morality.

This last point may be strengthened by considering Moses—for Maimonides the paradigm of what man may achieve in this earthly life. Moses achieved knowledge of God as no other had.[38] For him, God, not man, is the author of the moral law, and as a result of this ethical theocentrism the Mosaic stance toward God was one of extreme humility,[39] but toward secular honor, the Aristotelian reward for virtue, was utter disdain. Moses, the *ḥasid*, stands revealed as the polar opposite of the Aristotelian *megalopsychos*.

This latter contrast is clarified when we recall the close connection which Aristotle draws between lack of concern for honor (that is, humility) and ignorance of self (*NE* 1125a19–23). For Aristotle, the humble man's ignorance of self and lack of self-worth are manifested by his robbing himself of the honor that he rightfully deserved, given his (antecedent) virtue. In no small measure desire for honor is a function of worth. Contrarily, for Maimonides, disdain for worldly honor is compatible with awareness, not ignorance, of self and a strong sense of self-worth. In the case of Moses, the paradigmatic *ḥasid*, extreme humility and disdain for worldly honor necessarily follow from the knowledge that God is the author of the moral law and that man's ultimate felicity depends upon obedience to this (divine) law, and to nothing else.

In sum, then, we shall see that Maimonides, like his Biblical namesake, denies the centrality of worldly honor and replaces it with a transcendent value, God. As a result of this displacement he radically alters the Aristotelian concept of humility. Aristotle's vice becomes Maimonides' outstanding virtue. No longer bound by the norms of a secular society and a secular morality,[40] Maimonides presents humility as a, maybe even *the*, virtue becoming a pious man, a man of God.

36. Schwarzschild, "Moral Radicalism," p. 68.
37. See n. 28.
38. *Guide* I, 54.
39. Numbers 12:3: "Moses was a very humble man, more so than any other man on earth," a passage which Maimonides lays emphasis upon (at *Hilkhot De'ot* II.3).
40. Cf. Schwarzschild, "Moral Radicalism," p. 75.

IV. CONCLUSION

By way of conclusion, we might note that both Aristotle and Maimonides were disdainful men. But the objects of their disdain are instructively different. For Aristotle, the proud man is contemptuous of honors offered by the wrong people, both those people who claim honor solely on account of wealth and birth and those who, because of lack of wealth, cannot partake of virtue. He is contemptuous, thus, of the idle rich as well as of the common man. In this way, Aristotle's aristocratic sensibility shows through; although wealth does not provide the grounds for honor and esteem, it is a prerequisite for virtue.[41] Maimonides also had his strong dislikes. In his contempt for worldly honor, however, Maimonides' dislikes, unlike Aristotle's, were not so much a function of what he was, but rather of what he, or any other human, could not be.

University of Kentucky

41. *NE* X, 8 (1178a28–31); see n. 17.

6 Medieval Biblical Commentary and Philosophical Inquiry as Exemplified in the Thought of Moses Maimonides and St. Thomas Aquinas

IDIT DOBBS-WEINSTEIN

I. INTRODUCTION

In a recent article, "Maimonides, Aquinas and Gersonides on Providence and Evil,"[1] David Burrell implicitly outlines the reasons for the relative paucity of philosophical inquiry into the concept of providence within the monotheistic traditions. He considers this silence to manifest

> collective prudent counsel, for the history of each tradition records, one after another, the shipwrecks of those who essayed it, as well as bitter aftermaths in their respective religious communities. The more bitter [he believes], as certain stages of this inquiry lead one to dilemmas so harsh that atheism alone could offer plausible rest to the spirit.[2]

Prudence counsels greater caution when comparing the treatment of an issue as thorny as providence in two traditions which are distinct both culturally and linguistically.

In addition to the general difficulties inherent in the present inquiry, a philosophical study of Biblical exegesis, and especially one focusing on the *Book of Job*, presents further problems which perhaps should discourage the prudent. Nevertheless, our understanding of both Maimonides and Aquinas will remain piecemeal unless and until we resolve the question concerning the relation between philosopphy and revelation in their thought. Since, as M.-D. Chenu states, the *lectio divina* was the bread and butter of the medieval scholar,[3] the medieval philosopher could not shed his theologian's mantle.

1. David Burrell, "Maimonides, Aquinas and Gersonides on Providence and Evil," *Religious Studies* 20, no. 3 (1984): 335–51.
2. Burrell, "Maimonides, Aquinas and Gersonides," p. 335.
3. M.-D. Chenu, O.P., *Introduction à l'Étude de Saint Thomas d'Aquin* (Paris, 1954);

Apart from the evident advantage offered by the fact that Job is the single Biblical book upon which both Maimonides and Aquinas commented systematically and at some length,[4] it is also one of the few Biblical texts shared by both traditions that fully addresses a philosophical question from outside the framework of revelation, namely, man's natural capacity for perfection. Moreover, since the text raises the question of the relations between rational cognition and knowledge through faith, it presents a unique occasion for an examination of the harmony between philosophy and revelation, as understood by Maimonides and Aquinas, respectively, from within the boundaries of both disciplines.

Before outlining the questions comprising the present study, I wish to delimit its scope with respect to two main problems, the first methodological, the second substantial.

1. Apart from drawing attention to the facts that, properly speaking, Maimonides and Aquinas possessed different texts;[5] that we do not know what Bible Aquinas used;[6] and that the language and style of Job present unique difficulties which still occupy grammarians and philologists,[7] my concern here is not with literary criticism but rather with textual criticism.[8] That is, rather than question the linguistic and

---

English ed. *Toward Understanding St. Thomas,* trans. A. M. Landry, O.P., and D. Hughes, O.P. (Chicago, 1964). See in particular chap. 7, "The Commentaries on the Bible," pp. 233–63.

4. Although Maimonides never wrote a Biblical exposition as such, some Biblical texts are addressed by him systematically as exemplary treatments of philosophical subjects in the *Guide;* of these Job is the only text commented upon by Aquinas. Moses Maimonides, *Guide of the Perplexed,* trans. Shlomo Pines (Chicago, 1974). For the Judeo-Arabic text, see J. Joel, *Dalālat al-Hā'irīn,* rev. ed. based upon the Arabic ed. of S. Munk (Jerusalem, 1929). All English references will use Pines's translation. St. Thomas Aquinas, *Expositio super Iob ad litteram* (Rome: Editio Leonina, 1965).

5. Maimonides' and Aquinas's Bible differs not only in language but also in that the Latin text of Job, following the Septuagint, is at times a paraphrase rather than a translation and at times omits lines, and so forth. See Marvin Pope's summary outline of the problems in Marvin Pope (trans.), Introduction, *The Anchor Bible: Job* (New York, 1965), pp. xxxix–xlii, and Walter E. Aufrecht (ed.), *Studies in Job,* SR Supplements, vol. 16 (Ottawa, 1985).

6. See editor's preface to the *Expositio* 20–25; and editor's preface to the *Expositio super Isaiam ad litteram* (Rome: Editio Leonina, 1974), pp. 43–47.

7. "In addition to the textual difficulties already mentioned, the *Book of Job* also presents formidable linguistic and philological problems. Sometimes it is hard to say whether the difficulty of a given passage is more a philological than a textual problem. There are more *hapax legomena* (. . .) and rare words in Job than in any other Biblical book." Pope, Introduction, *The Anchor Bible,* p. xlii.

8. The designations for differing approaches to interpretation vary between disciplines and periods. Since I understand literary criticism to refer to the approach of students of language and of literature, I reluctantly choose the other common designation. Perhaps "text criticism" would be more appropriate for my purpose. My general

stylistic origins, the possible authorship, and the historical dating of the text, I focus upon the medieval tradition of Job, and Maimonides' and Aquinas's interpretation of it. At this introductory point, suffice it to point out that since for the medieval man the entire Bible was the word of God, transmitted to mankind through the prophets, its origin and authenticity were beyond questioning. As Gregory the Great states in his preface to the *Moralia*, it is folly to inquire what pen was used to express the words of the Holy Spirit.[9]

2. Regarding providence as the substantial topic of my study, I focus upon God as *providens* rather than *praevidens*,[10] and man as a potential participant in divine government. The importance of this delimitation becomes evident as soon as the secondary literature on providence in Maimonides and Aquinas is surveyed. It is my studied opinion that the shipwrecks of history mentioned by Burrell are primarily those unable to reconcile God's eternal knowledge with human free choice, and especially those attempting to respond to metaphysical questions by means of demonstration alone. The restriction of certain knowledge to demonstrative reasoning is at the center of most controversies surrounding both Maimonidean and Thomistic scholarship.

Following an examination of the respective exegetical traditions inherited by Maimonides and Aquinas, first, the present paper will outline their general methods of interpretation and the difficulties inherent in interpreting their work, and then will focus upon their application of these methods to resolving the question of the nature of Job's transgression.

II. MEANING AND METHOD

> *It is not by chance that we use the words "meaning" and "purpose" interchangeably, for it is mainly purpose which constitutes meaning for us.*
>
> Karl Löwith, *Meaning in History*

The concept of providence is a relevant category of human self-understanding in those discourses of both philosophy and revelation wherein man's ontological status is explored. For both Judaism and Christianity, the concepts which are meaningful to human existence

---

approach to interpretation is indebted to Hans-Georg Gadamer and to Paul Ricoeur, whose pertinent works are cited in n. 43–46.

9. St. Gregory the Great, *Moralia in Iob* [Corpus Christianorum Series Latina CXLIII–LIV (1979)].

10. This distinction is developed by J. P. Rock in "Divine Providence in St. Thomas Aquinas," *Boston College Studies in Philosophy* 1 (1966): 67–103.

are thus constituted through their relations to the purpose of human existence. The threefold relation among language, meaning, and purpose in the context of revelation gains special importance due to a heightened awareness of the potentially disjunctive distance between the divine and the human, between the incorporeal silence of eternity and the historically determined, embodied language of time.[11]

Both Maimonides and Aquinas are heirs to traditions which understand the Torah to possess many faces and to speak in the language of the sons of men, and hence hold interpretation to be the very stuff of human existence.[12] Although there is as much divergence between Jewish and Christian exegesis as there is similarity, interpretation as an ongoing historical process is a shared concern involving the Biblical exegete in a game not only played in earnest and delimited by rules,[13] but also played for the highest possible stakes, the salvation of human souls.

Whereas Christianity gained from Augustine a unified philosophy of Biblical study,[14] Judaism did not develop a single systematic approach to exegesis until the latter half of the thirteenth century.[15] Nevertheless, although until Maimonides most Jewish Biblical exegesis was neither philosophical nor systematic, it was not anti-intellectual. On the contrary, knowledge and perfection were closely linked as early as the pre-Macchabean period.[16] The multifaceted nature of the Torah not only became an early commonplace of Jewish thought but also led directly to the concomitant truism regarding its hierarchical levels

11. Discourse about revelation consists of three moments, namely, revelation about the Divine, revelation by the Divine, and the prophet's translation of the received knowledge into a corporeal language which is entirely incommensurate with the reality of the concepts. Whereas the language of analogy and metaphor can almost solve the difficulties inherent in the second and third moments, the very use of language already falsifies the reality of the first, which is necessarily immediate. The problem is not merely one of the relative merits of positive or negative theology since both of these approaches recognize the difficulty that, by definition, attribution is a limiting condition. In this sense, language is a manifestation of the limitations of rational discourse about, although not of knowledge of, the Divine. Indeed, silence is the most profound praise man can give God.

12. For the comprehensive analysis of the medieval tradition of Jewish exegesis and its divergence from the Christian tradition, see Frank Talmage, "Apples of Gold: The Inner Meaning of Sacred Texts in Medieval Judaism," Arthur Green (ed.), *Jewish Spirituality* (New York, 1985), pp. 313–55.

13. Talmage, "Apples of Gold," pp. 344–45.

14. Beryl Smalley, *The Study of the Bible in the Middle Ages* (Terre Haute, Indiana, 1964), pp. 22–24.

15. Talmage, "Apples of Gold," p. 319.

16. Georges Vajda, *L'Amour de Dieu dans la théologie juive du moyen âge* (Paris, 1957). In part I, Vajda outlines the early emphasis in the Jewish tradition on the relation between disinterested study of the Torah and love of God, the manifestation of human perfection.

of meaning, accessible to progressive degrees of knowledge.[17] Moreover, despite later attempts to separate radically the letter of the Torah from its more profound layers of meaning and to legitimize this practice by reference to the revered scholars of tradition, the various levels of meaning are understood to be interrelated until the thirteenth century. In fact, the more speculatively inclined the interpreter seemed to be, the more concerned he was with establishing a relation between the external and the internal levels of meaning, rather than with invalidating the former. Saadia Gaon, the tenth-century Iraqi Jewish thinker, not only established principles of interpretation, but also wrote a philological study seeking to explain ninety of the unique and rare words in the Bible on the basis of cognates.[18] Abraham Ibn Ezra, whose thought is considered often to approach pantheism,[19] was a cautious Biblical interpreter who as an exegete commented on his text verse by verse and

> limited his horizon to the text or to the immediate context, especially if his intention was, at least in principle, to make his text express what in his opinion it signified literally.[20]

Consequently, apart from the strictly legal teachings of the Torah and the Talmud which are to be observed literally, Maimonides inherits an exegetical tradition which is neither systematic nor dogmatic, but rather can be characterized as an attitude of open reverence to the text as a living historical *traditio.* In his systematic explanations of Jewish teachings, both legal and philosophical, Maimonides' main concern is to establish the truth contained in the Torah through a clearer articulation, rather than to adhere reverentially to a word which is seemingly unfitting and hence may lead to perplexity. Just as the Sages openly and vigorously disagreed with one another in seeking the truth,[21] so Maimonides disagrees with authorities both past and present, when he deems it necessary.

Christian Biblical exegesis can be said to originate with Christ's rebuke of Jewish literalism. The distinction between the law of the heart

17. Irrespective of the typology, rabbinic or philosophical, all systems of Biblical interpretation are rooted in the prior understanding that "the Torah has many faces." See Talmage, "Apples of Gold," passim.

18. For details of Saadia's life and works, see Henry Malter, *Saadia Gaon: His Life and Works* (Philadelphia, 1921).

19. Julius Guttmann, *Philosophies of Judaism* (New York, 1973), pp. 134–36.

20. "Quand il commente un texte scripturaire verset par verset, l'exégète est porté a limiter son horizon au texte ou au contexte immédiat, surtout si don dessein est, du moins en principe, de faire dire à son texte ce que, à son avis, il signifie littéralement." Vajda, p. 113, n. 1. Unless noted otherwise, translations into English are my own.

21. Ephrain E. Urbach, *The Sages: Their Concepts and Beliefs* (Jerusalem, 1982).

and the law of the members, which is repeated often in the New Testament[22] and which is reinforced by the understanding of the Old Testament as a prefiguration of the New, led to a heightened interest in interpretation and necessitated its systematization, especially when faced with the Jewish denial of the validity of the new teachings. The supersession of the law of the members by the law of the heart became the first principle of Christian exegesis, in which, initially, two layers of meaning were distinguished, the literal-carnal and the figurative-spiritual. Although the letter was rarely discarded completely, its importance became evident progressively as Christian exegesis developed its own synthesis of rabbinic and philosophic (Philonic) interpretation.[23] This development culminated with St. Augustine, who

> gave the letter a concrete chronological reality which it had never had before . . . Augustine accepted the historical truth of the letter more wholeheartedly than St. Jerome. We must believe in the fact; then and then only may we seek its spiritual meaning.[24]

The fact, however, must be understood in its historical context. When the context is changed (as is the case with customs), or when the letter seems to conflict with charity, the literal meaning must be discarded.[25] Augustine's sensitivity to the nature of language, to the distinction between sign, signifier, and signified, led to a keen awareness of the immanent possibility of error and hence to a development of a language theory and a hermeneutic that not only dominated the Middle Ages, but also did not meet its equal until the twentieth century. In *De Doctrina Christiana,* Augustine clearly designated four levels of meaning, literal, allegorical, moral, and anagogical; he outlined the causes of error, he enumerated tools for their remedy; and finally, he set norms for instruction. For all that, Augustine's sensitivity to language and his openness to non-Christian traditions did not extend to the Hebrew language of the Old Testament, to which he preferred the Greek Septuagint.[26] It is noteworthy that Augustine's instruction concerning the Hebrew language is the only one completely disregarded by later Christian exegetes.[27]

22. Smalley, *Study of the Bible,* c. 1, i, pp. 1–26; Talmage, "Apples of Gold," p. 313.
23. Smalley, *Study of the Bible,* ibid.
24. Smalley, *Study of the Bible,* p. 23.
25. St. Augustine, *De Doctrina Christiana* [Corpus Christianorum Series Latina XXXII (1962)], Bk. III.
26. *De Doctrina,* Bk. II, x–xv.
27. Charles Homer Haskins, *The Renaissance of the Twelfth Century* (Cambridge, Mass., 1927), c. 9; Marie-Therese d'Alverny, "Translations and Translators," in Robert L. Benson and Giles Constable (eds.), *Renaissance and Renewal in the Twelfth Century* with Carol D. Lanham (Cambridge, Mass., 1982), pp. 421–62; Smalley, *Study of the Bible,* passim.

While St. Gregory's exegesis embodied the teachings of Augustine, his emphasis on the moral and spiritual senses of the Bible set these as the focus for succeeding exegetes until the thirteenth century.[28] With the rediscovery of Aristotle, however, Christian exegesis was becoming more systematically philosophical and the letter of Scripture was reunited with its spirit.[29]

Although Aquinas is heir to a tradition of interpretation more systematic and more defined than Maimonides', Beryl Smalley's *The Study of the Bible in the Middle Ages* makes abundantly clear that it is not a rigidly fixed tradition. Consequently, like Maimonides, Aquinas heeds the letter of the tradition only when he deems it to be the best and clearest expression of the truth contained in the Bible. Rather than a dogmatic adherence to authority, Aquinas' exegesis is reverential to its spirit, that is, to the pursuit of truth.[30]

III. MAIMONIDES AND AQUINAS AS INTERPRETERS

The voice is Plato's voice, but the hands are the hands of Aristotle.

My paraphrase of Genesis 27:22 is an analogical abbreviation meant to demonstrate both the method and the substance of Maimonides' and Aquinas's exegesis. Since truth is one and error the cause of multiplicity,[31] since language and comprehension are historically conditioned, and since the correspondence of sign, signifier, and signified is neither simple nor perfect, it is both fitting and desirable to combine whatever tools are available in order better to understand the truth. Consequently, both Maimonides and Aquinas perceive a harmony of ends, that is, an essential harmony, not only between Plato and Aristotle, but also between philosophy and revelation.

Whereas Smalley understood the Aristotelian influence on Biblical

28. Smalley, *Study of the Bible*, pp. 33 and 281–92.

29. Smalley, *Study of the Bible*, pp. 292–328.

30. On the relations between the *intentio auctoris* and the commentator, see M.-D. Chenu, *La Théologie au douzième siècle* (Paris, 1957); English trans., Jerome Taylor and Lester K. Little, *Nature, Man and Society in the Twelfth Century* (Chicago, 1968), c. 9, pp. 310–30; and *Toward Understanding*, passim. Whereas Chenu maintains that the medieval expositor often appropriates the text as his own (*Toward Understanding*, pp. 207–8), the opposite opinion is put forth by P. O'Reilly, "Expositio super librum Boetii 'De Hebdomadibus': An Edition and Study," diss. University of Toronto, 1960, pp. 387–88.

31. Although this specific articulation is taken from Aquinas's *In librum Beati Dionysii De Divinis Nominibus Expositio* (Rome: Marietti, 1950), IV, 4, the same understanding is common to the Western philosophical tradition which identifies univocity with God and hence with simplicity and truth and degrees of multiplicity with progressive distance from God and truth.

study and its consequent recognition of theology as a speculative science to have resulted in a desirable liberation of theology from exegesis, and vice versa,[32] it seems to me that this recognition changed these disciplines and modified their relations rather than radically separated them. Maimonides and Aquinas are examples par excellence of medieval philosophical exegesis, combining the best tools of the exegete, the philosopher, and the theologian.[33]

The importance of the intimate relation between the correct method of interpretation and understanding for both Maimonides and Aquinas cannot be exaggerated. Both thinkers preface every single work with a statement designating its purpose, audience, and above all, proper procedure; both preface new subjects within each work; and each dedicates a section of his magnum opus to hermeneutics.[34] Had certain of their interpreters been as careful when reading them, many controversies would not have seen the light of day.

Likewise, as will become clearer in the brief discussion of Job later, closer attention to their "letter" can resolve many seeming disagreements, both of method and of substance, between Maimonides and Aquinas and so may facilitate comparative studies of their thought.[35]

Two major closely related questions merit closer scrutiny in this context: the nature of individual expositions and the relations between distinct works. With respect to Maimonides, the general tendency is to distinguish radically his "legalistic exoteric" works from the "esoteric" *Guide of the Perplexed*[36] and, in the latter work, the exoteric from the esoteric layers of meaning (or those subjects designated by him as secrets of the Torah).[37] In contradistinction, Maimonides describes the

32. Smalley, *Study of the Bible*, p. 293.

33. Examples abound. To name but a few: William of Auvergne, Roland of Cremona, Albertus Magnus, in the Christian tradition; Saadia Gaon, Abraham Ibn Ezra, Samuel Ibn Tibbon in the Jewish tradition.

34. *Guide*, see the [Epistle Dedicatory], the general introduction to part I, the introduction to proofs of the existence of God (I, 71–73), and so on; *Expositio*, see the *praefatio*, and the statements of preceding a change of interlocutors; *Summa Theologiae* (Ottawa, 1941), Ia Pars, *prologus*, Q.1, esp. aa. 9–10, and the statements preceding each question in the work.

35. The paucity of comparative studies of their thought is *in se* an indication of an implicit judgment concerning an incompatibility between Maimonides and Aquinas, given the stature and historical proximity of the two thinkers, and given the numerous references to Maimonides by Aquinas. Apart from a very small number of articles, such as Burrell's, the majority of comparative studies have been partisan, in my opinion.

36. In the following section, I will discuss Maimonides' interpreters in greater detail.

37. It should be noted that in addition to the two main secrets of the Torah, the Account of the Beginning and The Account of the Chariot, all the prophetic books contain secrets, the elaboration of which requires great caution: "and I saw that you are one worthy to have the secrets of the prophetic books revealed to you so that you

relation between the two levels of interpretation as that of an apple of gold to its silver filigreed casing. Moreover, a brief look at the "Book of Knowledge," the preface to his most legalistic (hence "exoteric") *Mishneh Torah,*[38] either should dissipate such a radical distinction, or lead to perplexity indeed. Under principles of the Torah, Maimonides discusses not only the unity, simplicity, and incorporeality of God, but also composition, the four elements, the soul as the form of man, the spheres, and the relation between the Account of Creation and the Account of the Chariot. Admittedly, the discussion of each topic is brief; nevertheless, no subject is concealed, whatever its difficulties.

A similar tendency can be observed in Thomistic scholarship, although the terms used are different. That is, the *Summa Theologiae,* especially Ia Pars and Ia IIa, the commentaries on Aristotle, are the preferred reading of the philosophers, whereas the Biblical commentaries are the domain of the theologians.[39] Given this tendency to divide the works and like divisions of the sciences, Thomistic scholars can be distinguished into "natural scientists" and "metaphysicians," or Aristotelians and Neoplatonists. In contradistinction, Aquinas recalls his Biblical commentaries in the *Summa* as often as he refers to the Philosopher, the *platonici,* and so on.[40]

It is striking that the restraint in combining traditions, which can be found in the works of either thinker, is shared by both and also can be explained by the context of the discussion and by Maimonides' and Aquinas's method. In those works addressed to the less learned within their respective communities, direct references to the pagan philosophers and to other thinkers who are not members of their specific religious communities are rare, since both Maimonides and Aquinas held that the study of the Bible, at least in its first phase, should precede divine science, the study of physics, metaphysics.[41] Moreover, since those ignorant of philosophy could despise it out of

would consider in them that which perfect men ought to consider. Thereupon I began to let you see certain flashes and to give you certain indications." *Guide* III. See also the introduction to part I, 5–20.

38. *Mishneh Torah, Sefer ha-Mada'* (Jerusalem: Mosad ha-Rav Kook, 1961).

39. In fact, a review of Thomistic bibliographies reveals a paucity in studies of Aquinas's Biblical commentaries which is rather surprising given the wealth of other studies.

40. I understand Aquinas's constant references to Biblical passages in the *Summa,* esp. in the *sed contra* and the *respondeo,* to indicate his instruction to the reader to consult his treatment of a given subject elsewhere. For an outline of all direct references to the *platonici* see R. J. Henle, *St. Thomas and Platonism: A Study of Plato and the Platonici* (The Hague, 1956).

41. *Guide* [Epistle Dedicatory] and Introduction, I, 3–2; Bruno Decker, ed., *Expositio super librum Boethii De Trinitate* (Leiden, 1956), Qs. V–VI.

ignorance, proper procedure was requisite for eradicating prejudice. The procedure which counsels the proper division of the sciences reflects the pedagogical prudence common to both philosophy and the tradition.[42]

As interpreters, Maimonides and Aquinas seem quite modern insofar as they satisfy the demands of the better contemporary hermeneuticists.[43] Both avoid the control of method over the subject matter; they are thereby able to question the method's legitimacy and define its limitations.[44] Both maintain a balance between the historicity of the narration and its claim to universal truth.[45] And by understanding the dialectical nature of discourse, both make manifest the overlap between explanation and understanding.[46] As interpreters, both Maimonides and Aquinas undertake to actualize a shared sphere of meaning by unfolding the multiplicity of intermediate terms between understanding and explanation, the historically specific and the universally true. The recognition that the Torah speaks the language of the sons of men manifests the necessity both for unfolding the range of meaning and for translating the terms in which universal truths were expressed into contemporary idiom. Upholding the unity of truth, both Maimonides and Aquinas strive to represent it through all the intermediate transformations and disciplinary variants of its expression.[47]

42. Rather than referring to the particular curricula used at their time, I am repeating Maimonides' and Aquinas's own recommendations. Whereas both are faithful to the spirit of their traditions, they are also critical of the manner and methods of teaching.

43. As noted, my general approach to hermeneutics is influenced primarily by Hans-Georg Gadamer and Paul Ricoeur. For a comperehensive general introduction to hermeneutics and hermeneuticists, see Richard E. Palmer, *Hermeneutics: Interpretation Theory in Schleiermacher, Dilthey, Heidegger, and Gadamer* (Evanston, Ill., 1969).

44. Hans-Georg Gadamer, *Truth and Method* (New York, 1975), pp. 274–341; and "Hermeneutics as Practical Philosophy," and "Hermeneutics as Theoretical and Practical Task," in: *Reason in the Age of Science* (Cambridge, Mass., 1981), pp. 88–138.

45. *Truth and Method*, pp. 274–78; 305–41; and 378–87.

46. Paul Ricoeur, "Explanation and Understanding," *Interpretation Theory: Discourse and the Surplus of Meaning* (Fort Worth, Tx., 1976), pp. 71–88.

47. Understanding and explanation require taking account both of the historical changes in linguistic usages of terms and of the evolution of human consciousness, hence the means of expression, as well as variations in use of the same terms by different disciplines. Differences due to the latter condition are ahistorical and arise from the differences among the possible audiences to whom works are addressed and from distinctions in *foci* while treating a single topic, e.g., God, the cause of causes of the Philosopher, the Creator of the Biblical tradition.

IV. MAIMONIDES, AQUINAS AND THEIR INTERPRETERS

Maimonidean scholarship spans a spectrum whose polarized extremes seem to discuss two different thinkers. At one end are those scholars who, themselves unable to harmonize faith and reason, project their perplexity onto Maimonides and read him as a prudent dissimulator of his true opinions.[48] Those maintaining this position often read Maimonides as an Aristotelian philosopher in all realms except political philosophy, where he is understood to follow al-Fārābī's Plato.[49] Consequently, they do not consider any of his works to be properly philosophical, apart from *The Treatise on the Art of Logic*.[50] At the other end are scholars so respectful to the Master as to diminish difficulties in Maimonides' writings, most often by justifying a problematic position as consistent with a traditional interpretation.[51] The graduated middle is occupied primarily by mitigated versions of the preceding positions and by scholars evaluating Maimonides' thought by means of post-Enlightenment standards,[52] with the notable exception of those attempting to read Maimonides with as little modern "prejudice" as possible.[53] It is not surprising that both polarized positions often agree that there are two Maimonides, a theologian and a philosopher: the former Maimonides represents the "we" position of the tradition, the latter upholds the "I" position of the philosopher, which is expressed rarely, and always in a veiled form, precisely because it often contradicts the "we" position.[54] Nor is it surprising that

48. The best known advocates of this reading are Leo Strauss and his students; cf. "The Literary Character of the *Guide for the Perplexed*," *Persecution and the Art of Writing* (Westport, Conn., 1952), pp. 38–94; introductory essay to Pines's translation of the *Guide*, xi–lvi, reprinted in Leo Strauss, *Liberalism Ancient and Modern* (New York, 1968), pp. 140–84.

49. Cf. Lawrence Berman, "Maimonides the Disciple of Alfarabi," *Israel Oriental Studies* 4 (1974): 154–78.

50. Berman, "Maimonides the Disciple," p. 163.

51. Cf. Marvin Fox, "Maimonides and Aquinas on Natural Law," *Diné Israel* 3 (1972): 5–36.

52. Cf. Norbert M. Samuelson, "The Problem of Free Will in Maimonides, Gersonides, and Aquinas," *CCARJ* 17 (1970): 3–13. Clearly, the approach of contemporary analytic philosophy is foreign to Maimonides and other medieval thinkers. Consequently, a methodological investigation of the applicability of the methods of analytic philosophy to interpreting medieval works must precede their use.

53. Cf. Charles Touati, "Les deux théories de Maimonide sur la providence," in: S. Stein and R. Loewe (eds.), *Studies in Jewish Religious and Intellectual History* (presented to Alexander Altmann), (Alabama University, 1979), pp. 331–41; Georges Vajda, "La pensée religieuse de Moise Maimonide: unité ou dualité?," *Cahiers de Civilisation Médiévale* 9 (1966): 29–49.

54. Cf. Charles Raffel, "Maimonides' Theory of Providence," diss. Brandeis University, 1983.

those scholars attempting to withhold preconceptions see Maimonides' works as complementary rather than contradictory, although, at times, "falling short" of the philosophical consistency and rigor which he promises.[55]

The diversity of readings encapsulated here is neither unwarranted nor readily resolvable. The most controverted subjects, those designated by Maimonides as secrets of the Torah, are also those which, according to him, exceed demonstrative reasoning.[56] Moreover, Maimonides does not elaborate a systematic epistemology by means of which the interpreter can develop a comprehensive account adequate for bridging knowledge by abstraction and revealed knowledge, without engaging in extensive interpretation. Consequently, the interpreter's philosophical "bias" cannot be left out of the interpretation entirely. Even so, by heeding Maimonides' letter, by attempting to understand and uphold the *intentio auctoris*, and by granting a coherence to the latter, if not to the former, it is possible to develop a theory of knowledge consistent with Maimonides' thought which can reconcile seeming contradictions—and, in fact, two modes of cognition. As will become evident, it seems to me that Maimonides' account of providence affords the starting point for such an attempt.

The problem central to understanding Aquinas's Biblical commentary, both in relation to his other works and in relation to the works of others, is the place of the literal exposition. The focus of the question is whether Aquinas's own thought is ever evident in a commentary,[57] or whether he does de facto "overstep the explanation of the work of God" for spiritual purposes, despite his insistence "that the literal sense alone be adhered to."[58] The resolution of this problem can be found both in the *Summa* and in the testimony of one of Aquinas's students. Both in *Quodlibet* VII and in the *Summa*, Aquinas states clearly that the three senses distinct from the literal are all contained

55. Cf. Alfred L. Ivry, "Maimonides on Possibility," in : J. Reinharz and D. Swetchinski (eds.), *Mystics, Philosophers, and Politicians: Essays in Jewish Intellectual History in Honor of Alexander Altmann* (Durham, N.C., 1982), pp. 67–84. Ivry's conclusion that Maimonides is not "a mystic in any formal or traditional sense" and that he "attempts to work within that rational and scientific framework which he regards as both necessary and inevitable for man" (pp. 83–84) can be developed further if mystical and philosophical knowledge are distinguished, respectively, as the negation and the affirmation of reason. Thus, Maimonides' affirmation of an apprehension which exceeds demonstrative reasoning only seems to fall short of the philosophical rigor promised by him.

56. Cf. Maimonides' discussion of the indemonstrability of either the creation or the eternity of the world, *Guide* II, 15–17; Maimonides' explanation of how he arrived at his own knowledge of providence, *Guide* III, 17, 471, a part of which is quoted in n. 75.

57. O'Reilly, "Expositio super librum,." pp. 387–88.

58. Chenu, *Théologie au douzième siècle*, p. 257.

within the literal sense and are dependent upon it.[59] Moreover, he maintains that the literal sense does not manifest a correspondence between the sign and the object signified, but rather is a signifier of the latter's substance,

> [f]or when Scripture designates the arm of God, the literal sense is not that there is a corporeal member of this kind in God, but that which is signified by this member, namely, the operative power.[60]

The testimony of Guillaume de Tocco, repeated by Bernard Gui in the *Vitae Sancti Thomae de Aquino,* brings Aquinas's understanding into the sharpest focus. "He wrote . . . on Job 'ad litteram' which no doctor had attempted to explain literally on account of the profundity of the literal sense which no one was able to discover."[61] Both the text quoted from the *Summa* and Aquinas's witnesses suffice to overcome the gulf between the previously mentioned positions. The inadequacy of language for representing incorporeal concepts and objects necessitates the explanation of the full range of meanings contained in the letter of the Bible.[62]

V. THE BOOK OF JOB

Whereas the Old Testament book of Job is central to Maimonides' discussions of providence and Maimonidean scholarly investigations of providence cannot ignore it, most Thomistic scholars do not treat Aquinas's commentary on Job as an essential part of his explanation of providence. In fact, as a glance at Thomistic bibliographies makes evident, only Yaffe and Manzanedo address this commentary specifi-

59. "Dicendum, quod varietas sensuum, quorum unus ab alio non procedit, facit multiplicitatem locutionis; sed sensus spiritualis semper fundatur super litteralem, et procedit ex eo," *Quaestiones Quodlibetales* (Rome: Marietti, 1956), VII, A. 6, a. 1, ad 1m. (Marietti's divisions depart from earlier editions designating this section of Q. VII as a. 14). Cf. *Summa,* Ia Pars, Q. 1, aa. 9–10.

60. "Non enim cum Scriptura nominat Dei brachium, est litteralis sensus quod in Deo sit memberum huiusmodi corporale, sed id quod per hoc membrum significatur, scilicet virtus operative," *Summa,* Ia Pars, a. 10, ad 3m.

61. "Scripsit . . . super Job ad litteram, quem nullus Doctor litteraliter tentavit exponere propter profunditatem sensus literae, ad quem nullus potuit invenire." Guillelmus de Tocco, "Vita S. Thomae Aquinatis," *Fontes Vitae S. Thomae Aquinatis,* D. Prümmer, O.P. (ed.) (Tolosa: Privat, Bibliopolam, 1912–37), p. 88. Cf. "Scripsit quoque super Job ad litteram, quem nullus doctor litteraliter sic sicut ipse exponere attemptavit." Bernardus Guidonis, "Vita S. Thomae Aquinatis," *Fontes,* p. 219.

62. Biblical exegesis exhibits only one aspect of the limits of linguistic expression. These are manifest most fully in Divine Science since therein the limitations of human knowledge, and especially of demonstrative reasoning, are brought into the sharpest focus. Cf. *In librum Beati Dionysii De Divinis Nominibus Expositio* (Rome: Marietti, 1950); *De Trinitate.*

cally, and only the former also attempts to compare Maimonides' exposition to Aquinas's.[63] Moreover, both Burrell and Samuelson, the only scholars who compare Maimonides' and Aquinas's views on providence, address the subject indirectly. That is, rather than asking what providence is, they question the possibility of affirming the freedom of the human will in the light of divine (fore)knowledge.[64] But divine knowledge is distinct from divine providence. Indeed, there is a relation among divine knowledge, providence, and human free will, but it is a complex relation which is far from self-evident.

Given the one-sided tendency in Thomistic scholarship in general, and in comparative works in particular, I center my inquiry on Maimonides' and Aquinas's commentaries on Job since its central question deals with the relation between free will and providence rather than divine knowledge, or God as *providens* rather than *praevidens*. My focus is chosen not only in order to balance the scales somewhat, but especially because it seems to me that understanding the ontological and noetic aspects constituting man's relation to providence is a prerequisite to understanding the relation between the human will and divine knowledge.

At first glance, there seems to be no basis for comparing Maimonides' and Aquinas's expositions on Job. Properly speaking, Maimonides never wrote an exposition on Job nor on any other Biblical text. Rather, the text is explained in two of the chapters comprising the general discussion of providence,[65] and it is said to be a parable, possessing no historical reality. On the other hand, Aquinas comments on the text verse by verse, *ad litteram*, and insists on the historical veracity of the story. Nevertheless, despite this disparity and numerous other dissimilarities between their respective accounts,[66] the conclusions reached by both Maimonides and Aquinas are strikingly similar, in my opinion, both with respect to the nature of Job's transgression and with respect to the relation between divine providence and human

63. Marcos F. Mazanedo, O.P., "La antropologia filosfica en el comentario tomista al libro de Job," *Angelicum* 62 (1985): 419–71; Martin D. Yaffe, "Providence in Medieval Aristotelianism: Moses Maimonides and Thomas Aquinas on the Book of Job," *Hebrew Studies* 20–21 (1979–80): 62–74.

64. Henceforth knowledge, since foreknowledge implies time whereas divine knowledge is eternal. In my opinion, the application of the prefix *fore-* to divine knowledge has produced much of the confusion about its relation to the freedom of choice.

65. *Guide* III, 22–23.

66. The most notable, substantial dissimilarity between Maimonides and Aquinas is their interpretation of Elihu's speech. Whereas Maimonides considers Elihu's opinion to represent a profound truth exceeding Job's preprophetic understanding, Aquinas considers his understanding superior to the other interlocutors', but inferior to Job's. See *Expositio* XXXVIII–XLII.

action. It should be emphasized, however, that I limit my assertion concerning the similarity of their respective interpretations to providence as it pertains to rational creatures, rather than to its relation to the entire sublunar realm.[67]

The only other study comparing Maimonides' and Aquinas's expositions on Job (*Providence in Medieval Aristotelianism: Moses Maimonides and Thomas Aquinas on the Book of Job*) is at variance with my conclusion and argues that despite their shared Aristotelian philosophy and Biblical tradition of interpretation, Maimonides and Aquinas take radically opposed positions on Job: this, because they use the text to address specifically different and urgent concerns within their respective communities. With regard to the shared traditions, the philosophic is seen as a strength as a result of its proper procedure of scientific inquiry, whereas the Biblical is seen as certain a hermeneutic encumbrance imposed upon the unity and coherence of the book by rabbinic and ecclesiastical doctrines. Since I have already discussed the nature of their relation to their respective traditions, I will forgo repeating my conclusions. It is interesting to note in passing that Yaffe's view is the mirror image of that of Chenu, who emphasizes the integrity of the scholastic method of Biblical exegesis.[68]

In insisting on the "protreptic" intention and propaedeutic nature of their procedure and in stressing that the full scope of Aristotelian science includes metaphysics, Yaffe demonstrates both Maimonides' and Aquinas's debt to Aristotle. However, his designation of either thinker as Aristotelian can be maintained only if Aristotle is understood to be the first Neoplatonist. This disagreement is not purely semantic. Rather, the designation of Maimonides and Aquinas as Aristotelian provides Yaffe with the opportunity to offer "an 'Averroistic' account of their meaning"[69] which is based upon the separation of reason and revelation, physics and metaphysics, and in this context leads to a radical juxtaposition of Maimonides' and Aquinas's accounts.

The difference postulated by Yaffe between Maimonides' and Aquinas's interpretations of Job can be summarized as follows: whereas Maimonides understands Job to be perfectly just but unwise, Aquinas understands him to be perfectly wise but unjust. Consequently, Mai-

67. The operations of divine providence with respect to the irrational creatures composing the sublunar realm belong to a discussion of the nature of divine knowledge, and especially of God's knowledge of singulars, which is beyond the intention and scope of this paper.

68. Chenu, *Théologie au douzième siècle*, pp. 233–63.

69. Yaffe, "Providence in medieval Aristotelianism," p. 62.

monides is seen to use the text for teaching the rabbinic student that wisdom ought to be the object of his temporal quest since his reader is religiously intolerant of philosophic wisdom. Aquinas, on the other hand, perceiving his reader's shortcoming to stem from an overemphasis on theoretical reason, is understood to use Job as the example of the doctor's failure to communicate his wisdom to those untrained in the subtleties of philosophy. Despite its compact symmetry and its attempt at contextual grounding, this interpretation cannot be textually supported both because it is based upon an a priori assumption that reason and revelation are irreconcilable and because it identifies the readers of both Maimonides and Aquinas incorrectly. These two elements are not independent of one another, but rather one serves to reinforce the other. That is, the assumption that reason and revelation necessarily conflict leads to the separation of theoretical and practical reason to such an extent that these seem to belong to two different faculties of the soul. Consequently, it can be assumed that either wisdom or justice can be possessed in perfect independence of one another.

With respect to the audience of the *Guide,* Maimonides' introduction seems unambiguous in its designation. Rather than the rabbinic student who is dogmatically complacent in his knowledge, the text is addressed to one who has progressed beyond the tradition to philosophy and is perplexed because he is unable to harmonize their teachings.[70] Neither the perplexed student nor Job possessed wisdom or justice perfectly (few do!). In like manner, Yaffe mistakes the audience of Aquinas's Biblical commentary. For even if we assume that the *Exposition on Job* was addressed to students advanced in Biblical studies, it is far from evident that they were perfectly wise. On the contrary, given Aquinas's judgment, in the Prologue to Ia Pars of the *Summa,* concerning the impediments to knowledge in the path of its readers, it is doubtful that he would have considered the reader of the exposition wise.[71]

Although Maimonides identifies the opinions of Eliphaz, Bildad and Zophar with the opinion of the Torah, the Muʿtazila, and the Ashʿarīya doctrines, respectively, and Aquinas does not, both clearly differentiate their views from Elihu's and Job's. What characterizes the three opinions in both expositions is so radical a disproportion between human and divine knowledge as to lead either to blind pietism or to despair—not dissimilar to Burrell's shipwrecks. In fact, both

70. *Guide,* Epistle Dedicatory, 3–4.

71. Note also that in the *prologus* Aquinas refers to the readers of the *Summa* as *incipientes.*

Maimonides and Aquinas seem to divide the five opinions into either those based upon rational consent or those originating in nonrational, blind obedience. Moreover, although both are rather contemptuous of blind obedience, both also view a narrowly rational understanding of providence as erroneous and dangerous. The narrow domain of unaided natural reason is the symbolic realm of Satan and (unfortunately) of Aristotle,[72] where theoretical and practical reason are radically separated, as are divine knowledge, will and justice.

In contradistinction to Yaffe, it seems to me that their accounts of Job exemplify Maimonides' and Aquinas's view that wisdom and justice are fully interrelated. In fact, I consider the designations wisdom and justice as corresponding, respectively, to theoretical and practical reason erroneous, since the term "wisdom" (*sophia* or *sapientia*) subsumes both theoretical and practical reason (*episteme* and *phronesis*).

Since both Maimonides and Aquinas emphasize the fact that Satan is denied dominion over Job's soul and since both explain the term soul as immortality,[73] it seems to me that neither considered Job *perfectly* just or wise, given that his status in the world-to-come is still in question. Rather, Job is their occasion for elaborating an epistemological account of wisdom as the ultimate perfection which overcomes the Aristotelian separation between the theoretical and practical reason on the basis of principles known through revelation. Overcoming this separation is a prerequisite for the soul's permanence. Although these principles are not attainable by means of natural reason and, hence, are not possessed by the philosopher qua natural scientist, nevertheless, they are held with the same degree of certainty and function in the same way, as (and in cooperation with) the primary principles of theoretical reason.

In conclusion, and in order to demonstrate my claim, I turn to the *Guide*, III, 22–23 and to the *Expositio* XXXVIII–XLII, where the fundamental agreement between Maimonides and Aquinas regarding the nature of Job's transgression can be seen. After drawing attention to the fact that the Book of Job aims at explaining divine providence in the sublunar realm, a concept which has caused great perplexities, Maimonides states that "[t]he opinion attributed to Job is in keeping with the opinion of Aristotle." Job's, or the opinion of Aristotle, is reproved by Elihu for its ignorance "because of his having manifested

72. The former designation is Aquinas's, the latter Maimonides'.

73. *Guide* III, 22, 488; "*pro anima sua,* idest pro vita sua conservand" and ff. *Expositio* II, 95–99. It is noteworthy that although many Christian commentators on Job, apart from Aquinas, comment on this verse, neither Albertus Magnus nor any commentator in the *Glossa Ordinaria* explains the term *soul.*

his self-esteem. . . . For he had expatiated at length on the goodness of his actions."[74] In his rebuke of Job, Elihu differs from the other companions and from Job in maintaining that an ill man requires the intercession of an angel, any angel, to be "saved and restored to the best of states."[75] In referring to prophecy and describing its quiddity in relation to providence, Elihu also makes evident that he is the only friend who understands that there is an essential relation between prophetic knowledge and correct understanding of the content of prophecy. According to Maimonides, both Elihu's explanation of providence and Job's subsequent prophetic revelation do not go beyond explanation of natural matters:

> for our intellects do not reach the point of apprehending *how* these natural things that exist in the world of generation and corruption are produced in time and conceiving *how* the existence of the natural force within them has originated them.[76]

Given the weakness of the human intellect with respect to natural subjects, Maimonides asks, How can we wish to explain divine providence and government as similar to our own?

The correct understanding of the dissimilarity between us and God is the guarantee that misfortunes will be borne lightly by man, will not lead to doubt about God, and, above all, will increase love. In III, 17, Maimonides maintains that although he has not reached his conclusions about providence by means of demonstration, nevertheless his opinion "is less disgraceful than the preceding opinions and *nearer than they to intellectual reasoning*."[77] It seems clear to me that Job's transgression is intellectual hubris.

Although Aquinas's method of exposition differs from Maimonides', and although they disagree about many specific details, their conclusions are strikingly similar. Chapters XXXVIII–XLI of the *Expositio* consist of lengthy explanation about the insufficiency of the natural power of reason for *understanding* divine providence and about the relation between human ills and pride, the figurative symbol of which is Satan.

At first, Aquinas's interpretation of God's response to Job seems to differ substantially from Maimonides', insofar as it seems to limit God's rebuke of Job to his improper manner of expressing a correct understanding. A closer study of the opening statement discloses that

74. *Guide* III, 23, 494.
75. *Guide* III, 23, 495.
76. *Guide* III, 23, 496. My emphasis.
77. *Guide* III, 17, 471. My emphasis.

Aquinas is drawing a nuanced distinction between comprehension and unexamined opinion (which may be true) upon which the remaining discussion is based:

[B]ut since human wisdom does not suffice for *comprehending* the truth of divine providence, it was necessary that the aforementioned disputation be determined by divine authority. But since Job has *thought* correctly concerning divine providence, but has transgressed to the extent that thereby an offense arose in the hearts of the others so long as they thought that he was not displaying due reverence to God; therefore the Lord, as an arbitrator of the question, reproved both Job's friends concerning what they have thought incorrectly, and Job concerning the disordered mode of speaking, and Elihu concerning the unfitting conclusion.[78]

God's response, according to Aquinas, can be interpreted metaphorically as an interior divine inspiration to Job, that is, as prophetic revelation. In addition, Aquinas maintains that in this life, because of "a certain obscuring of sensible similitude,"[79] we cannot perceive divine inspiration clearly. The interrogative form of God's response and especially the focus on the sensible world is aimed at demonstrating to man the extent of his ignorance, rather than at teaching him. Consequently, although Job held a correct opinion about divine providence, his disordered speech reflects not only the limitations of human reason, but also a lack of understanding and of acknowledgment of such a limitation. Job's opinion may have been correct, but it was an unexamined opinion, and thus neither was it assented to rationally, nor could it realize the limitations of human reason.[80]

Prior to explaining Job's restoration to well-being, Aquinas summarizes Job as follows:

it ought to be considered that God began to manifest his operation which He employs against evil men, in relation to the proud, and ends the narration

78. "[S]ed quia humana sapientia non sufficit ad veritatem divinae providentiae *comprehendendam*, necessarium fuit ut praedicta disputatio divina auctoritate determinaretur; sed quia Iob circa divinam providentiam recte *sentiebat*, in modo autem loquendi excesserat intantum quod in aliorum cordibus exinde scandalum proveniret dum putabant eum Deo debitam reverentiam non exhibere, ideo Dominus, tamquam quaestionis determinator, et amicos Iob redarguit de hoc quod non recte sentiebant, et ipsum Iob de inordinato modo loquendi, et Eliud de inconvenienti determinatione." *Expositio* XXXVIII, 5–17. My emphasis.

79. "quia scilicet divinam inspirationem in hac vita non possumus clare percipere sed cum quadam obumbratione sensibilium similitudinum." *Expositio* XXXVIII, 31–34. Note reference to Dionysius in this passage, and cf. n. 60.

80. It should be noted that according to Aquinas, an opinion can be said to be held by faith only when it succeeds an intellectual apprehension and that faith precedes hope and charity in the temporal order of the theological virtues. "Per fidem autem apprehendit intellectus ea quae sperat et amat. Unde oportet quod ordine generationis fides praecedat spem et caritatem." *Summa* Ia IIae, Q. 62, a. 4.

with the proud, in order to show that Job should have feared this especially, lest the devil who had sought to tempt him would attempt to lead him especially to pride, so that thus he could be transferred to his realm, and therefore he should have guarded against the disposition and the words which may savour of pride.[81]

According to both Maimonides and Aquinas, it is knowledge which guards against intellectual pride, a wisdom (*sapientia*) possessed by those who acknowledge the natural limitations of human reason (*scientia*) and which manifests man's provident participation in divine providence and government.

Vanderbilt University

81. "Ubi considerandum est quod Dominus operationem suam quam exercet in malos circa superbos manifestare incepit et in superbis narrationem terminat, ut ostendat hoc praecipue Iob fuisse timendum ne diabolus, qui eum expetierat ad tentandum, praecipue eum ad superbiam inducere conaretur ut sic transferretur in regnum ipsius, et ideo cavere debebat affectum et verba quae superbiam saperent." *Expositio* XLI, 448–57.

7 "What Can We Know and When Can We Know It?" Maimonides on the Active Intelligence and Human Cognition

BARRY S. KOGAN

Maimonides' views on epistemology and particularly on the psychology of knowing have long been recognized as central to the interpretation of his thought. For if human well-being, both individual and political, depends significantly upon what he calls intellectual perfection, it becomes crucial for us to identify what he thinks human beings can know and under what circumstances such knowledge can be attained. But upon investigation, it is not altogether surprising to find that the evidence he provides for answering these questions in the *Guide of the Perplexed* and elsewhere turns out to be elusive, ambiguous, and at times inconsistent.

Whether the ambiguities apparent in Maimonides' treatment of human cognition arise from what he calls "the necessity of teaching and making someone understand" or from a need "in speaking about very obscure matters . . . to conceal some parts and to disclose others,"[1] or even from both together, is not immediately evident. Certainly none of these possibilities can be totally excluded. But there is, in addition, another possibility that deserves consideration. Maimonides tells us at the beginning of his discussion of the spheres, the separate Intelli-

1. Moses Maimonides, *The Guide of the Perplexed,* trans. Shlomo Pines (Chicago, 1963), I: Introduction, pp. 17–18 (pp. 10a–10b). The Pines translation is based upon the Judeo-Arabic text established by Salomon Munk, *Le Guide des Égarés,* 3 vols. (Paris, 1856–66), and edited with variant readings by Issachar Joel, *Dalālat al-ḥa'irin* (Jerusalem, 5691 [1930–31]). Subsequent references to the Pines translation will be abbreviated as *Guide* and followed by references to the first, second, or third part; the chapter number; and the page number. Reference to the corresponding page in Munk's Judeo-Arabic text follows immediately in parenthesis: thus, for example, *Guide* I, 54, p. 123 (p. 64a). An earlier version of this paper was presented to the Eighth World Congress of Jewish Studies, in Jerusalem, in August 1981.

gences, and related topics, that his purpose is not "to compose something on natural science or to make an epitome of notions pertaining to divine science. . . . For the books composed on these matters are adequate."[2] Indeed, he adds that the correctness of most of their expositions has been demonstrated; and, where this is not so, Maimonides modestly suggests that his own remarks "will not be superior" to what his predecessors have said.[3] His aim is not originality, but clarification of hidden matters in the Law, and thus his epitomes of these subjects are designed to be simply a means to that end.

Maimonides here alerts us to the fact that his discussion of the separate Intelligences, including the Active Intelligence, with all its importance for human cognition, relies on a variety of sources, most of whose contents he regards as demonstrated, but not all. If this is the case, it may be that, on this subject at least, many of the ambiguities in the *Guide* reflect his attempt to synthesize and epitomize what he himself regarded as either demonstrated or probable truths in each of the various texts he used. The result would be a composite teaching containing elements from all or most of his sources, but not all of which would necessarily accord well with the others. Consequently, the task for interpreting Maimonides on human cognition would be first of all to determine whose position, against the spectrum of views available, Maimonides' composite teaching most closely resembles. Only then would we be in a position to trace the implications of that teaching with regard to the possible scope and limits of human cognition and the status of the theoretical life vis-à-vis the practical life. Accordingly, I would like to focus our attention more on which philosophers he actually uses and how he draws from them than on which ones he recommends and why. For the purposes of this presentation, let us consider al-Fārābī (d. ca. 950), Avicenna (d. 1037), and Ibn Bājja (d. 1138) as our main paradigms and briefly summarize their views on the Active Intelligence in relation to cognition before turning to Maimonides.

For al-Fārābī, the existence of the Active Intelligence is established by the fact that the transition from potential to actual human thinking cannot be explained without it.[4] Its function is to actualize our innate

2. *Guide* II, 2, p. 253 (pp. 11a–11b).

3. Ibid.

4. Abū Naṣr al-Fārābī, *Ārā' al-ahl al-madīnah al-fāḍilah*, ed. Dieterici (Leiden, 1895), pp. 44. See also *al-Siyāsah al-madanīyah*, ed. F. Najjar (Beirut, 1964), pp. 32, 71–72; a full translation with notes of *The Political Regime* has been published by Thérèse-Anne Druart (Washington, D.C.: Georgetown University, 1981, catalogue reference A-30-50d). *Falsafat Arisṭūṭālīs*, ed. M. Mahdi (Beirut, 1961), pp. 121, 125–29. For a compre-

disposition for thought, which he calls the potential intellect, by overflowing with a lightlike emanation that illuminates the universal characteristics of material objects which we perceive, imagine, or remember.[5] In effect, the Active Intelligence enables us to abstract universal concepts from the forms inherent in concrete particulars by focusing our attention on their common features. What it does not do, however, is to present us with intelligible forms flowing toward us from itself. While its illuminative operation is continuous, al-Fārābī maintains that its effects are evident only at the beginning and at the end of the learning process.

In the beginning, it enables us to grasp the first principles of thought, such as the laws of identity and noncontradiction, as well as the first principles of the individual sciences we study. Once we have grasped them, we must then proceed independently to construct our knowledge of whatever can be known.[6] If and when we perfect our intellects by understanding all or most intelligible thoughts, our minds then reach their highest stage, that of acquired intellect.[7] At this stage, according to al-Fārābī, our intellects are still "related to *hyle* and matter," but they are "united" (*muttaḥidah*) or "conjoined" (*ittaṣala*) with the Active Intelligence as matter is united with form in the composite.[8] Here the totality of our knowledge is illuminated by the Active Intelligence, but there is no unqualified identification of the intellect with it.[9] While some men may reach this stage through instruction by others, the prophet is self-taught and reaches it by himself.[10] But upon doing so, neither one produces or acquires any new theoretical knowledge, since possession of an acquired intellect presupposes the mastery of all the sciences.[11] Finally, it is only at this stage, according to most of al-Fārābī's works, that we can know the incorporeal beings, and even this occurs by a kind of unexpected encounter (*muṣādafah*)

---

hensive and penetrating discussion of the Active Intelligence in these and other works of al-Fārābī, see Herbert Davidson, "Alfarabi and Avicenna on Active Intellect," *Viator: Medieval and Renaissance Studies* 3 (1972): 109–178.

5. *al-Madīnah al-faḍilah*, p. 45, and *al-Siyāsah al-madanīyah*, pp. 35, 71–72; al-Fārābī, *al-Risālah fi'l-ʿaql*, ed. M. Bouyges (Beirut, 1938), p. 27.

6. *al-Madīnah al-fāḍilah*, p. 45, and *al-Siyāsah al-madanīyah*, pp. 60ff., 71–72, 74–75. On the analogy between the indirect influence of the Active Intelligence on potential knowers and that of the celestial bodies on sublunar particulars, see also Davidson, "Alfarabi and Avicenna," p. 139.

7. *al-Madīnah al-fāḍilah*, pp. 57–58, and *al-Risālah fi'l-ʿaql*, pp. 20–22.

8. *al-Madīnah al-fāḍilah*, pp. 58–59; *al-Siyāsah al-madanīyah*, p. 79; *al-Risālah fi'l-ʿaql*, pp. 22–24. See also F. Rahman, *Prophecy in Islam* (London, 1958), pp. 12, 23, n. 8; p. 29, n. 34, 35.

9. *al-Madīnah al-fāḍilah*, p. 46. See Rahman, *Prophecy in Islam*, p. 66, n. 7.

10. *al-Madīnah al-fāḍilah*, pp. 50–51. See Rahman, *Prophecy in Islam*, pp. 30–31.

11. *al-Madīnah al-fāḍilah*, pp. 57–58, and *al-Risālah fi'l-ʿaql*, pp. 20–22.

rather than by union.[12] But, as is well known, he reportedly denies even this possibility in his lost commentary on the *Nicomachean Ethics,* although even there he evidently retains the view that the Active Intelligence is the efficient cause of our knowledge.[13] In sum, the role of the Active Intelligence for al-Fārābī is to illuminate the abstract and universal features of things we perceive, at the beginning and end of our learning, but it provides us with no new knowledge as such.

Avicenna accepts al-Fārābī's account of the Active Intelligence's illuminative role in actualizing human thought, but he nonetheless differs with him in several important respects.[14] First and foremost, he denies that the universal can be abstracted from images and impressions that derive from sense experience or memory. That is because the universal does not reside there, either potentially or actually. For there is simply no finite number of particular images that is capable of producing a universal concept or judgment, since the latter is necessarily applicable to an infinity of instances.[15] As an intelligible form, a universal resides only in an intellect, in this case, the Active Intelligence, and abstraction only prepares the mind for its reception. When our minds are suitably prepared, the Active Intelligence overflows with the intelligible forms themselves and projects them into us directly. This is why Avicenna speaks of the Active Intelligence as "the Giver of forms."[16] We in turn apprehend them through direct intuition, and we do so throughout the learning process, not just at the beginning and the end.[17] To use his standard example of learning to

12. *al-Risālah fi'l-ʿaql,* pp. 20–22. See Davidson, "Alfarabi and Avicenna," p. 151.

13. Ibn Bājja refers to this position of al-Fārābī's in a short treatise preserved in the Bodleian collection, MS Pococke 206, fols. 206a–208a. Averroes also speaks of it in the *Commentarium Magnum in Aristotelis De Anima Libros,* ed. F. Stuart Crawford (Cambridge, Mass.: Medieval Academy of America, 1953), pp. 433, 485–86. See also Shlomo Pines, "The Limitations of Human Knowledge According to Al-Fārābī, Ibn Bājjah, and Maimonides," *Studies in Medieval Jewish Literature,* ed. I. Twersky (Cambridge, Mass., 1979), pp. 82–85; "La philosophie dans l'économie du genre humain selon Averroès: une réponse à al-Farabi?" *Multiple Averroès* (Paris, 1978), pp. 189–207; Alexander Altmann, "Ibn Bajja on Ultimate Felicity," *Studies in Religious Philosophy and Mysticism* (Ithaca, N.Y., 1969), pp. 74–75; Davidson, "Alfarabi and Avicenna," pp. 152–54.

14. Avicenna, *al-Shifā': De Anima,* ed. F. Rahman (London, 1959), pp. 234–35; *Kitāb fī ithbāt al-Nubuwwāt,* ed. M. Marmura (Beirut: 1968), p. 44; *Kitab al-najāh,* ed. M. S. Kurdī, 2nd edition (Cairo, 1938), pp. 192, 193.

15. S. Landauer, "Die Psychologie des Ibn Sina," *Zeitschrift der deutschen morgenländischen Gesellschaft* 29 (1876), pp. 370–71. Cf. Davidson, "Alfarabi and Avicenna," p. 162.

16. *al-Shifā': al-Ilāhīyāt,* ed. G. C. Anawati et al. (Cairo, 1960), p. 413; *al-Najāh,* pp. 192–93, 283; *al-Shifā': De Anima,* pp. 235–36; F. Rahman, *Avicenna's Psychology* (Oxford, 1952), pp. 68–69, 116–17. See Davidson, "Alfarabi and Avicenna," pp. 156, 163–64.

17. *al-Shifā': De Anima,* pp. 235–36, 261; *al-Najāh,* pp. 192, 197; *al-Ishārāt wa'l-tanbīhāt,* ed. J. Forget (Leiden, 1892), pp. 126–27. Cf. Ibn Sina (Avicenne), *Livre des Directives et Remarques,* Traduction avec introduction et notes par A. M. Goichon (Paris, 1951), pp. 324–28.

write, the Active Intelligence gives us not only the ABCs of thought, but every intelligible conception that leads us to our becoming skillful scribes in action.[18] The highest stage is once again called "acquired intellect," but it no longer presupposes acquisition of all or most intelligible thoughts. We attain it whenever an intelligible form enters the mind and we actually think it.[19] Because the form overflows into us, acquired intellect turns out to be an aspect of the Active Intelligence projected into us.[20] As such, it is separate from matter. Conjunction with the Active Intelligence or with its overflow, therefore, consists simply in the familiar act of understanding something intelligible, and the scope of this conjunction can always be enlarged. Scientists and philosophers enlarge it discursively and in a limited way, but since the prophets possess an extraordinary power of intuition (*quwat al-ḥads*), they can grasp the middle terms and conclusions of syllogisms instantaneously and thus extend the range of theoretical knowledge far beyond that of most men.[21] When conjunction is at its fullest, one knows the Active Intelligence no longer by "surface contact" but by something akin to, although not the same as, real identification, for Avicenna claims that one is then imprinted with its likeness and "enters into its company."[22] In sum, understanding turns out to be a progressive act of conjunction with the Active Intelligence, that becomes ever deeper and more comprehensive as we exercise our cognitive faculties, and this conjunction can always produce new knowledge.

Finally, for Ibn Bājja, there appear to be two theories of cognition. According to the first, the human intellect grasps intelligible objects through a divine faculty of insight (*baṣīrah*) which emanates from the Active Intelligence but which is not identical with it. This faculty illuminates the images produced by perception and imagination and enables us to grasp their quiddities, the noblest being those of the celestial motions. As quiddities, they are presumably universals.[23]

18. *al-Shifā':De Anima*, pp. 48–50; *al-Ishārāt*, p. 126.

19. *al-Shifā': De Anima*, pp. 245–48; Rahman, *Avicenna's Psychology*, pp. 117–20; *al-Ishārāt wa'l-tanbīhāt*, p. 129. Cf. Goichon, *Livre des Directives*, pp. 330–33. See also Davidson, "Alfarabi and Avicenna," pp. 161, 163, 168–69.

20. *al-Najāh*, p. 166.

21. *al-Shifā': De Anima*, pp. 249–50; *al-Najāh*, p. 167; Rahman, *Avicenna's Psychology*, pp. 35–37, 93–95. Cf. Rahman, *Prophecy in Islam*, p. 31.

22. *al-Shifā': al-Ilāhīyāt*, p. 425; *al-Shifā': De Anima*, p. 240; *al-Najāh*, p. 293. See Goichon, *Livre des Directives*, p. 331, n. 5. See also Majid Fakhry, "The Contemplative Ideal in Islamic Philosophy," *Journal of the History of Philosophy* 14 (April 1976): 137–45, and Davidson, "Alfarabi and Avicenna," pp. 169–70, n. 391, 173, 176.

23. Ibn Bājja, MS Pococke 206, fols. 207a–208a. See also Pines, "The Limitations of Human Knowledge . . . ," pp. 85–86. I would like to record my thanks to Professor Pines for reviewing his translation of this important text with me.

The second theory distinguishes between two levels of intelligible objects. The first level represents the species and genera of material things abstracted from sense perception and imagination. They correspond to the intelligibles of al-Fārābī's acquired intellect and are known in the same way, by an illumination of the Active Intelligence. Above these, however, are the pure intelligibles, or the pure characteristics of things devoid of any reference to particularity or universality, and they are identical with the thought content of the Active Intelligence. Hence, they are separate from matter in every respect.[24] In cognition, we first apprehend material things in nature and the first intelligibles. If we reach the level of theory about natural things as physicists do, the Active Intelligence illuminates their universal features, as sunlight is reflected in a medium, for example, in water or on polished surfaces. At the highest level are the happy ones, for example, Aristotle and the prophets, who break virtually every connection with matter and grasp the pure intelligibles by becoming identical with them. They shine like the sun itself. While conjunction with the Active Intelligence occurs in every act of cognition, it is complete only here.[25] Thus, acquired intellect is totally separate from matter, both in its union with the Active Intelligence and in its having no connection with universals or particulars. Here, too, no evils assault the knower, nor does the bestial soul combat him.[26] In sum, the Active Intelligence facilitates insight into or abstraction of the quiddities of material things at various points in the process of understanding prior to the last stage. And if this last stage is eventually reached, it consists in union and not just conjunction or contact with the Active Intelligence.

Given this backdrop of divergent views on the Active Intelligence and human cognition, what does Maimonides say about the relevant issues? Which position or combination of positions do his views resemble most? He tells us first that "the existence of the Active Intelligence is indicated by the fact that our intellects pass from potentiality to actuality and that the forms of the existents subject to generation and corruption are actualized after they have been in matter only *in potentia*."[27] This formulation could reflect all three of our sources, but his explanation of how the Active Intelligence actualizes these poten-

24. Ibn Bājjah, *Risālah fi'l-ittiṣāl al-ʿaql bi'l-insān*, ed. M. Asin Palacios, *al-Andalus* 7 (1942): 35–39. See also Altmann, "Ibn Bajja," pp. 79–107, and Pines, "Limitations," pp. 86–89.

25. *al-Risālah fi'l-ittiṣāl* . . . , pp. 36–37. See also Altmann, "Ibn Bajja," pp. 79, 87–88.

26. *al-Risālah fi'l-ittiṣāl*, p. 38. See also Altmann, "Ibn Bajja," pp. 86–87.

27. *Guide* II, 4, pp. 257–58 (pp. 14a–14b).

tials is distinctly Avicennian. It does not merely illuminate images in the mind. Rather, it gives the form to the mind and to any substratum prepared for it. "As for the things produced in time that we find are not consequent upon the mixture of the elements, namely *all the forms,* they also must *indubitably* have an agent—I mean the giver of the form, which giver is not a body."[28] Clearly, mental motions are among the things produced in time, and it is characteristic of Avicenna's view to speak of the *wāhib al-ṣuwar* or "Giver of forms" as conveying them to us. Lest there be any doubt, Maimonides states further that "the intellect *in actu* existing in us" is something "which derives from an overflow of the Active Intellect and through which we apprehend the Active Intellect."[29] The overflow, of course, is the distinctive act of that which is not a body, namely a separate substance or form, which insofar as it is separate from matter is like an intellect.

Maimonides again signals his acceptance of the notion of intelligible forms overflowing to the mind in his treatment of universals. For in the *Guide* III, 18, he speaks on this subject both emphatically and in his own name, "I say that it is known that no species exist outside the mind, but that the species and other universals are . . . mental notions and that every existent outside the mind is an individual or group of individuals." There is no qualification made here. Universals exist neither actually, potentially, nor in any other way outside the mind. But if that is so, they cannot be abstracted from material particulars by a lightlike illumination or anything else, as both al-Fārābī and Ibn Bājja maintain in all their theories, and the reason they cannot be abstracted from matter is that they do not lie there. Accordingly, if they exist only in the intellect as forms, they must come to our potential intellect from an actual intellect or Active Intelligence, just as Avicenna contends.

Maimonides suggests further in one of his explanations of the verse "In Thy light, do we see light" (Psalms 36:10) that the overflow of forms from the Active Intelligence into us occurs throughout the learning process, in contrast to al-Fārābī's illuminations at both ends and Ibn Bājja's overflow at the final end. Thus he states, "Through the overflow of the intellect that overflowed from Thee, we intellectually cognize, and consequently we receive correct guidance, we draw inferences, and we apprehend the intellect. Understand this."[30] Now Maimonides refers to this overflow extending to our minds as conjunctive. The consequence is that if there is conjunction whenever

28. *Guide* II, 12, p. 278 (p. 25a).
29. *Guide* II, 4, p. 258 (p. 14a).
30. *Guide* II, 12, p. 280 (p. 26b).

there is intellectual understanding, and our apprehension of, as opposed to union with, the Active Intelligence follows simply upon drawing inferences, he is again supporting a recognizably Avicennian view.

What then of the acquired intellect? Maimonides describes it by name in the *Guide* I, 72, as something that is "not a faculty in the body, but is truly separate from the organic body and overflows toward it."[31] He regards the proofs for this view as correct, but recondite. For that reason, he concedes that critics may well find things to cavil about. Nevertheless, his confidence in it seems clear. Whatever the obscurities of the doctrine he espouses here, however, it is clearly not that of al-Fārābī, for whom the acquired intellect was the highest of those things related to matter. Rather, the separateness of the acquired intellect and its emergence through overflow are consistent with the ideas of both Avicenna and Ibn Bājja. While there are grounds for thinking Maimonides preferred Ibn Bājja's account of the unity of acquired intellect vis-à-vis Avicenna's pluralist account of it, the absence of references to grasping pure intelligibles or to identifying with the Active Intelligence leaves the issue an open one. In general, however, Maimonides' proximity to the Avicennian epistemology seems clear.

These preliminary identifications of Maimonides' epistemological lineage are not only of historical interest; they help to clarify other passages that bear upon Maimonides' account of human cognition. Thus in describing how the truth flashes out to us like lightning on a very dark night,[32] he depicts those who see the lightning directly at whatever intervals, if any, as the prophets, whether the flashes are continuous enough to light up the whole sky, as in the case of Moses, or whether they occur only once, as in the case of the elders. Below them are those for whom the flashes appear only indirectly as reflections on polished bodies. They, however, are not identified. After listing both these groups, but before mentioning still a third, Maimonides tells us that "It is in accord with these states that the degrees of the perfect vary." Finally, there are those who see no flash whatever, despite the strength of its manifestation. They, of course, are the vulgar. The main source of the parable has been traced to Avicenna's *Ishārāt*, although Ibn Bājja's threefold classification of knowers is evident as well.[33] Taken by itself, the passage seems to suggest, as Professor Pines has argued, that "the cognition that can be achieved by the prophets is *different in kind* from that of all other men (including the philoso-

31. *Guide* I, 72, p. 193 (p. 104a).
32. *Guide* I, introduction, pp. 7–8 (pp. 4a–4b).
33. *Guide*, Translator's Introduction, "The Philosophic Sources of *The Guide of the Perplexed*," pp. ci, n. 72, civ–cv.

phers) and may be beyond their ken."[34] Philosophers and all other men are limited to mere reflections of truth abstracted from particular objects, but they have no direct connection with the separate Intelligences and no hope of ever apprehending them.

Still, we must ask whether this interpretation is as plausible after analyzing the parable of the lightning flashes as it appears before doing so. I would like to contend that it is not, for if we ask what makes the prophet's apprehension superior to that of the others mentioned, the Avicennian epistemology which we have already identified provides a perfectly good explanation. It is the prophet's unique power of intuition, the *quwat al-ḥads,* which enables him to grasp the truth more quickly and thus more comprehensively than others. Intermittent recourse to empirical data is here at a minimum. Maimonides himself endorses this view in part II, 38.[35] But the central point is that having this power of intuition does not make the prophet's knowledge different in kind from that of the philosopher because both grasp the middle terms and conclusions of syllogisms. The prophet does this instantaneously compared to the others, and thus he can learn comparatively more. But there is no barrier or distinction of kind between him and other men. In that respect, prophecy is a natural human perfection and as such is attainable at least in principle by any human being who fully satisfies the prerequisites.[36]

In addition, Maimonides' apparent exclusion of philosophers from the level of those who can apprehend theoretical truth and the Active Intelligence turns out, upon analysis, to be only apparent. First, he blurs the distinction between the two groups in the parable itself by including the philosopher-scientists with the prophets among "the degrees of the perfect."[37] Second, for Maimonides, in contrast even with Avicenna, the prophets must first become adept philosophers before they receive the prophetic overflow corresponding to their "speculative perfection."[38] This implies that all that ultimately distinguishes

34. Pines, "The Limitations of Human Knowledge," p. 90.

35. *Guide* II, 38, p. 377 (pp. 82b–83a). See also Pines, translator's introduction, p. ci, and generally pp. xciii–cii. There is also significant evidence of al-Fārābī's influence on Maimonides' theory of prophecy, especially on his requirement of extensive philosophical preparation prior to prophetic experience and his conception of the prophet-legislator. See Rahman, *Prophecy in Islam,* pp. 30–45; L. V. Berman, "Maimonides, The Disciple of Alfarabi," *Israel Oriental Studies* 4 (1974): 154–78, and "Maimonides on Political Leadership," *Kinship and Consent,* ed. Daniel Elazar (Philadelphia, Montreal, 1981), pp. 113–25; Miriam Galston, "Philosopher-King v. Prophet," *Israel Oriental Studies* 8 (1978): 204–18.

36. *Guide* II, 32, pp. 360–62 (pp. 72b–73b). See also Alvin J. Reines, *Maimonides and Abrabanel on Prophecy* (Cincinnati, 1970), pp. 1–27.

37. *Guide* I, Introduction, p. 7 (p. 4b). Cf. *Guide* II, 36, p. 372 (p. 79b).

38. *Guide* II, 36, p. 372 (p. 79b).

the prophets in kind from the most accomplished philosophers is their reliance upon the imaginative faculty in expressing what they know. But prophets do not necessarily differ from philosophers in the way they apprehend what they know. Third, and finally, Maimonides returns to the theme of the parable in part III, 51, when he explains how individuals who have already attained apprehension may still suffer misfortune. Providence, he says, withdraws from them when they are occupied with something other than apprehending God. At such times, they are like a skillful scribe when he is not writing, whereas those lacking intellectual cognition of God altogether are in darkness and have never seen the light.[39] Maimonides then adds an unexpected but important identification: Those from whom providence is withdrawn when they are distracted from apprehending God include "all prophets *or* perfect and excellent men whom one of the evils of this world befell."[40] Now Avicenna's example of the scribe when he is not writing dealt with the levels of intellection only, and it allowed for the still higher level of actual writing, which signifies conjunction with the Active Intelligence. Presumably those who would attain it would be mystics and prophets whose cognitive powers exceed ordinary intellection. But Maimonides goes on to add perfect or excellent men who are not prophets. And the only perfect and excellent men who have already apprehended true reality, but who are not prophets, must be philosophers. Hence, insofar as Maimonides includes them with various prophets in his identification of those who are like a skillful scribe who is not writing, there is again no reason to suppose that they, any more than the prophets, are excluded from apprehending incorporeal entities like the Active Intelligence or God, so far as this is possible.

Closer attention to the progressive character of conjunction with the Active Intelligence in Avicenna's epistemology also helps to resolve some puzzling aspects of Maimonides' discussion of divine attributes. The problems are well known: If the point of the negative theology is that God is unknowable, either per se or in relation to the human intellect alone, why does Maimonides insist on the value of knowing the negative attributes in their detailed variety? If it is just to avoid making misplaced references to God's essence, Maimonides' requirement of mastering one science after another to negate individual attributes hardly seems necessary.[41] A careful reading of the relevant chapters of the *Guide* would probably suffice. Again, it is widely held that the negative theology is manifestly inconsistent with the theory

39. *Guide* III, 51, p. 625 (p. 127b).
40. Ibid.
41. *Guide* I, 59, 60, pp. 138, 144 (pp. 72b, 75b–76a).

of God as the self-thinking intelligence or form of the universe. The former seems to rule out any positive characterization of God, since it would liken Him to things in nature, while the latter gives a positive characterization of God's very essence and likens it to the human intellect.

These difficulties, however, can be overcome if we recall that in Avicenna's theory of knowledge, conjunction with the Active Intelligence occurs progressively whenever actual knowing occurs, but it is not complete until, one step after another, all intelligibles are actually known. Only then can one contemplate the formal contents of one's mind without further recourse to empirical data. Knowing the natures of things in this universal way parallels God's self-thinking knowledge, except for our own limited intellectual capacity and for the fact that our knowledge is caused whereas God's knowledge is not. To apprehend God, therefore, as Maimonides would have us do, we must come to know the intelligibles actually and actively and realize the differences between God and all other entities in as much detail as is possible for us.

Maimonides evidently regards the negative theology in just this programmatic way. He states several times that the negative attributes "*conduct* the mind toward the utmost reach that man may attain in the apprehension of Him."[42] Clearly, the procedure of negating or excluding from God specific attributes possessed by things in nature must presuppose detailed knowledge of these attributes as they occur in nature. That is why complete sciences may have to be mastered in order to negate a single attribute with respect to God. For even though one begins with specific and familiar characteristics of natural things—material objects, animals, human beings, and even spheres—and denies that they are applicable to God, only growth in knowledge of the sciences and their systematic relations enables one to make such a denial in an informed way.[43] By thus learning more and more about the forms or rational patterns of things in nature and using Maimonides' procedure of negation, one will be able to grasp, indirectly but progressively, what is meant by the notion of God as a self-thinking "form of forms." And that is because one will have become a "form of forms" oneself, that is, an actual knowing mind. And one achieves this through ever-broader acts of conjunction with the Active Intelligence.

Again, if there is a contradiction between the negative theology and

42. *Guide* I, 58, p. 135 (pp. 70b–71a).
43. *Guide* I, 58, 59, pp. 134–37, 143–47 (pp. 70a–72a, 75a–77b).

the teaching of part I, 68–69, namely, that God is at once the intellectually cognizing subject, the intellectually cognized object, and the activity of intellectual cognition, in short, the form of all forms in the universe, it is surely too obvious to belong to the seventh type of contradiction, in which a secret teaching must be guarded and the contradiction itself concealed from the masses. It would have to belong instead to the fifth type of contradiction, in which an apparent inconsistency arises from the requirements of instruction. Here, recognition that the negative theology represents a program for inquiry and analysis, combined with its proper use, eventually dissolves the problem. For if we follow this theological problem to its conclusion, we will presumably find that the radically incorporeal Deity of whom Maimonides speaks must be, for that very reason, a separate form or intelligence. And "form of forms" is simply one of Aristotle's ways of referring to any actualized mind or Intelligence. What is more, we will also find that the notion of "form of forms" does not strictly liken God to anything in nature, not even the actualized human mind.[44] For nothing whatever in nature is a self-thinking form of forms as God is. Consequently, the theory of negative attributes is not at odds with Maimonides' final teaching about theology in part I, 68–69. Rather, it is a necessary condition, or really a method, for understanding his final teaching about the nature of the Divine.

Finally, we come to the difficult question of the status of the theoretical or contemplative life vis-à-vis the practical life in the closing chapter of the *Guide*. Interpreters have tended to suppose that for Maimonides either one or the other must be ultimate, but surely not both, because placing two patently different ways of life on the same level of a value hierarchy violates our conception of what a hierarchy is. It becomes, as it were, top-heavy.

I believe, however, that a careful examination of the texts will not bear out either line of interpretation. In part III, chapter 54, of the *Guide*, Maimonides outlines the four human perfections taught by the philosophers in a hierarchical fashion and discusses the character and

44. *Guide* I, 1, 58, 69, pp. 23, 135, 168–69 (pp. 13a, 71a, 89b–90a). See also Aristotle, *De Anima* III, 4, 429b 5–10; Averroes, *In Aristotelis De Anima Librum Tertium*, ed. F. S. Crawford (Cambridge, Mass.: Medieval Academy of America, 1953), t.c. 8, p. 420; Richard Norman, "Aristotle's Philosopher-God," *Phronesis* 14–15 (1970): 63–74, and Barry S. Kogan, *Averroes and the Metaphysics of Causation* (Albany, 1985), pp. 229–48. It should be recalled that Maimonides' student, Joseph ibn Judah ibn Sha'mun, for whom the *Guide* was written, knew little about the natural sciences, but needed to master these disciplines before entering metaphysics. The negative theology, as Maimonides develops it, clearly requires study and mastery of the natural sciences if one is to identify negative attributes of God in an informed and illuminating way.

worth of each one. Perfection of possessions is subordinate to perfection of bodily constitution and shape, which is itself subordinate to perfection of the moral virtues, and perfection of the moral virtues is subordinate to "the true human perfection," which consists in acquisition and exercise of the rational virtues.[45] Immediately afterward, he attempts to show that both the prophets and the rabbinic Sages have taught the very same doctrine. That is the point of his citing the famous verses from Jeremiah 9:22–23:

> Thus saith the Lord: Let not the wise man glory in his wisdom, let not the mighty man glory in his might, let not the rich man glory in his riches, but let him that glorieth glory in this, that he understandeth and knoweth Me, that I am the Lord who exercises loving-kindness, judgment, and righteousness in the earth. For in these things I delight, saith the Lord.

Showing that the rabbis taught the same doctrine is also his purpose in presenting a midrashic exposition of the text from *Genesis Rabbah* XXXV, where again wisdom, in the unrestricted sense he identifies with apprehension of God, is superior to both the possession of treasures and the performance of actions prescribed by the Law.[46]

At the conclusion of this exposition, however, Maimonides makes a very illuminating observation. He says, "Consider how concise is this saying [namely, the rabbinic exposition of the four perfections], how perfect is he who said it, and how he left out nothing of all we have mentioned and that we have interpreted and led up to at length."[47]

45. *Guide* III, 54, p. 637 (p. 134b). See also Alexander Altmann, "Maimonides' 'Four Perfections,'" *Israel Oriental Studies* 2 (1972): 15–24.

46. *Guide* III, 54, pp. 636–37 (p. 134b). "It is said there: One scriptural dictum says: And all things desirable are not to be compared unto her. Another scriptural dictum says: And all things thou canst desire are not to be compared unto her. The expression, things desirable, refers to the commandments and good actions; while, things thou canst desire, refers to precious stones and pearls. Neither things desirable nor things thou canst desire are to be compared to her, but let him that glorieth glory in this, that he understandeth and knoweth Me."

47. *Guide* III, 54, p. 637 (p. 134b). Just what is and what is not included in the fourth and highest perfection, and specifically what relation, if any, it may have to moral/political activity is an unresolved question. Recent discussions of the issue include those of David Hartman, *Maimonides: Torah and Philosophic Quest* (Philadelphia, 1976), pp. 187–214; Warren Zev Harvey, "Political Philosophy and Halakhah in Maimonides," *Iyyun* 29 (July 1980): 198–212; Shlomo Pines, "The Limitations of Human Knowledge . . . ," pp. 82–109; L. V. Berman, "The Ethical Views of Maimonides Within the Context of Islamicate Civilization" (unpublished lecture delivered at the Tel Aviv University Colloquium "Maimonides in Egypt," June 1982), pp. 1–24; Aviezer Ravitzki, "'According to Human Capacity'—Maimonides on the Days of the Messiah," *Messianism and Eschatology* (Heb.), ed. Zvi Baras (Jerusalem: Merkaz Zalman Shazar, 1985), pp. 191–220; Norman Roth, "Attaining 'Happiness' (*Eudaimonia*) in Medieval Muslim and Jewish Philosophy," *Centerpoint: City University of New York* 4 (1981): 21–32; Daniel H. Frank, "The End of the *Guide:* Maimonides on the Best Life for Man," *Judaism: A*

Thereafter he goes on to summarize what he has mentioned and to "complete the exposition of what it includes." What is important about Maimonides' laudatory remark here is that it indicates that his subsequent discussion of the fourth perfection, which completes the exposition of what it includes, is to be taken as part of his earlier discussion. And what he now says the fourth perfection qua perfection includes is both a specific kind of theoretical apprehension and conduct that accords with it. The conduct he has in mind is not merely the by-product of the fourth perfection, but part of it. This becomes more evident from Maimonides' final statement about man's ultimate end and what it includes.

It is clear that the perfection of man that may truly be gloried in is the one acquired by him who has achieved, in a measure corresponding to his capacity, apprehension of Him, may He be exalted, and who knows His providence extending over His creatures *as manifested in the act of bringing them into being and in their governance as it is. The way of life of such an individual will always have in view loving-kindness, righteousness and judgment, through assimilation to His actions,* may He be exalted, just as we have explained several times in this Treatise.[48] (emphasis added)

Quarterly Review 34, no. 4 (Fall 1985): 485–95. Barry S. Kogan, "Maimonides' Conception of the Human Ideal," *Shlomo Pines Jubilee Volume*, ed. Moshe Idel et al. (forthcoming).

48. *Guide* III, 54, p. 638 (p. 135b). It might be argued that Maimonides explicitly contradicts the claim that the fourth and ultimate perfection includes both a specific kind of theoretical apprehension and conduct conforming to it, in a passage appearing earlier in the *Guide* (III, 27, p. 511 [p. 60a]). "His ultimate perfection is to become rational *in actu*, I mean to have an intellect *in actu;* this would consist in his knowing everything concerning all the beings that it is within the capacity of man to know in accordance with his ultimate perfection. It is clear that to this ultimate perfection there do not belong either actions or moral qualities and that it consists only of opinions toward which speculation has led and that investigation has rendered compulsory." Assuming that the contradiction is real and not just apparent, it must be either of the fifth or the seventh variety (Cf. *Guide* I, introduction, pp. 17–18 [pp. 10a–10b]). I would argue that it is not a contradiction of type seven but of type five. Type seven contradictions deal with "very obscure matters" with regard to which "the vulgar must in no way be aware of the contradiction; the author accordingly uses some device to conceal it by all means." The contradiction over whether the highest human perfection embraces actions and moral dispositions is hardly obscure or remote, even if controversial. It deals with something close at hand and familiar. Also, this contradiction is too explicit and obvious to belong to the seventh type. Accordingly it properly belongs to the fifth type of contradiction in which pedagogical necessity dictates divergent accounts of the same facts. In *Guide* III, 27, Maimonides contrasts perfection of the soul with perfection of the body and body politic, which presupposes it in nature and time. The actions and moral dispositions in question pertain to conventional morality as taught by the apparent sense of the Torah. In *Guide* III, 54, however, Maimonides examines what is contained in the fourth perfection, in contrast to the other three, and behavior with a view to loving-kindness, judgment and righteousness reflects the philosophic-political morality expounded in the previous chapter (*Guide* III, 53) rather than the conventional morality alluded to by the third perfection. So understood, the fourth perfection embraces both apprehension and action without difficulty.

The final end is thus to be a certain kind of person. It is to be one who both apprehends God and His ways in nature and who conducts himself in ways that conform to this apprehension. Contrary to certain appearances, the final end is not to be identified either exclusively or primarily with the life of apprehension alone, not because such a life is not possible but because, as Maimonides himself points out, such a life is incomplete. It brings about the true human perfection, to be sure, but it belongs to its possessor alone and perfects him alone. A perfection is greater, however, when it does something more—when it overflows and perfects others.[49] And the imitation of God clearly requires this additional measure, because God's apprehension is so comprehensive and abundant that it overflows beyond itself and enables others to be perfected.

Recognition of this fact explains why the text of Jeremiah does not stop with the words "But let him that glorieth glory in this, that he knows and understands Me . . ." but immediately adds "that I am the Lord who practices loving-kindness, judgment, and righteousness in the earth."[50] Hence, those who would be perfect must have these attributes in view so as to act in accordance with what they apprehend, namely, God as the self-thinking form of all forms whose own outward acts conform to His wisdom and will and constitute "loving-kindness, judgment, and righteousness in the earth."[51]

By the same token, however, the final end cannot be identified either exclusively or primarily with the practical life of performing acts of loving-kindness, judgment, and righteousness. Still less does it presuppose one's ever "ceasing to be a philosopher."[52] For Maimonides emphasizes in the same chapter that one who wearies and troubles himself for the sake of others, neglecting to care for his own soul, has succumbed to the domination of his corporeal faculties. All such

49. *Guide* II, 37, pp. 374–75 (pp. 81a–81b).

50. *Guide* III, 54, p. 637 (p. 135a).

51. *Guide* III, 52, pp. 630–32 (pp. 131a–131b). See also Eliezer Goldman, "The Worship Peculiar to Those Who Have Apprehended True Reality," *Sefer Hashanah shel Universitat Bar Ilan* 6 (1968): 287–313 [in Hebrew].

52. S. Pines, "The Limitations of Human Knowledge . . . ," p. 100. By contrast, Maimonides depicts those who have attained the level of apprehending true reality and who remain in "a permanent state of extreme perfection" as having their minds entirely focused upon God while attending to mundane matters with their limbs. "And there may be a human individual, who through his apprehension of the true realities and his joy in what he has apprehended, achieves a state in which he talks with people and and is occupied with his bodily necessities, while his intellect is wholly turned toward Him, may He be exalted, so that his heart is always in His presence, may He be exalted, while outwardly he is with people." *Guide* III, 51, pp. 623–24 (pp. 126b–127a). Maimonides asserts that Moses, Abraham, Isaac, and Jacob attained this state.

preoccupation with the realm of the "necessary," with the *bios praktikos* as an end in its own right, is a distraction from intellectual cognition, which separates the individual from God and leaves him "a target for every evil that may happen to befall him."[53] That is hardly an optimistic prospect for effective political governance as Maimonides envisions it.

Rather, the final end embraces both apprehension and conduct conforming to it as a unity, because it is meant, after all, to be an imitation of God's own unified activity. The requisite apprehension consists in a detailed recognition of God as the cause of all causes and the form of all forms, who is separate from matter. To achieve this, however, is at the same time to know that He is an Intelligence whose act of cognition by its very nature overflows. It does so because form in Maimonides' metaphysics is always essentially active, while matter is essentially passive. In God, it is one and the same activity or dynamism that expresses itself as contemplation and as overflow. Merely to approximate this kind of activity, we have to extricate ourselves from preoccupation with material things as well as with phantasies of the imagination and strive instead to actualize our intellectual capacities as extensively as possible. But to imitate God's ways in the fullest sense requires our progressive apprehension, in detail, of the forms of things in nature and of the way they are sustained, an apprehension that naturally and constantly overflows in our conduct with a view toward loving-kindness, righteousness, and judgment, properly conceived.[54] All this can occur if, and only if, we ourselves actively become like God, an active form of forms, separate from matter and its concomitants, which is to say, from passivity, from instability, and from submission to pain and suffering insofar as we are able.[55]

On this analysis, the final end of the perfect ones gives primacy neither to the theoretical life nor to the practical life as such, because it no longer treats them as intrinsically separate. They are, as far as it is possible for our twofold nature, integrated into a single, active life. Intellectual apprehension continues, as it must, lest the bond between us and God be broken; nevertheless, it overflows into conduct and confers benefits on others, not because that is its purpose, but because, as Maimonides points out, it is the nature of generous and superior individuals to do so, for "*this* is to become like Deity, may His name be exalted."[56] (emphasis added)

53. *Guide* III, 51, p. 625 (p. 128a).
54. *Guide* III, 54, pp. 637–38 (pp. 135a–135b). Goldman, "Worship Peculiar," pp. 306–13.
55. *Guide* I, 47, p. 104 (pp. 53a–53b).
56. *Guide* I, 72, p. 192 (p. 103b). Cf. II, 11, p. 275 (pp. 23b–24a).

As the final end, this conception of the unified active life sets a very high standard indeed, and surely Maimonides had no illusions about how much effort would be required to achieve it. Yet in itself, this standard accords well with the thrust of the *Guide* as a whole. For the book is organized so as to move the reader from perplexity and imagining to wisdom and *imitatio dei,* from the inner conflicts felt by those who resemble Joseph to the unified active life known by those who resemble God. The same standard seems equally well suited to Maimonides the man, whose life and work provide ample testimony to the fact that the unified active life can indeed be achieved.

Hebrew Union College

8 Freedom and Determinism in Maimonides' Philosophy

JEROME GELLMAN

The issue of human freedom and determinism has engaged the attention of philosophers throughout the history of philosophy. In general terms, we can distinguish three positions philosophers have adopted with regard to this problem:

(a) *Strong determinism*: human actions are determined, and not free.
(b) *Strong libertarianism*: human actions are free, and not determined.
(c) *Compatibilism*: human actions are determined and also free.

Strong determinism might endorse *ancestral determinism,* which holds that human actions are determined by a causal chain reaching back to creation, or as far back as you care to go, if there was no creation.[1] Or it might endorse what we can label *inner determinism,* the view that a person's actions are determined by his present character and motives, whether these can be traced back ancestrally or not. When an ancestral or inner determinist argues the negation of human freedom, he is being a strong determinist. Strong determinism is perhaps the position of at least some contemporary scientistic philosophers.

Strong libertarianism might hold what we can call an "agent theory" of human actions. This maintains that while it may be true that every event, including a human action, has a cause, it is false that a cause must always be another event. Some events, namely human actions, are not caused by prior events, but by agents. The cause of a human action is the human agent who brings it about, initiating a cause and effect chain, whose beginning is not an event. Thus, that every event, including a human action, has a cause does not entail either ancestral or inner determinism. And the strong libertarian maintains that indeed human action is free, and determinism is false. The agency view

1. The term *ancestral determinism* is borrowed from Roderick M. Chisholm, "Freedom of Action," in Keith Lehrer, ed., *Freedom and Determinism* (New York, 1966).

was the position of Thomas Reid in *Essays on the Active Powers of Man*, and more recently of Roderick Chisholm and Richard Taylor.[2]

Compatibilism distinguishes inner causes from external compulsion or constraint. To the compatibilist, to say a human action is free, is to say that it is unfettered by anything external, or, as Hobbes put it, there are no "impediments to action that are not contained in the nature and intrinsical quality of the agent." The compatibilist can therefore embrace inner determinism, or even ancestral determinism that determines the nature and "intrinsical quality" of the inner life, and still maintain that human actions are free. This was the view of Hobbes and of Hume; in Jewish thought it was the view (or close to the view) of Abner of Burgos and Hasdai Crescas.[3]

In what follows I will show that Maimonides was a strong libertarian, although he perceived the issues in theological terms, as opposed to the contemporary strong libertarian, who might not be likely to do so. More specifically, Maimonides held the following three propositions:

(1) There are no external "Hobbesian" constraints which override our freedom by coercing or influencing us to choose one way rather than another.
(2) There is no inner compulsion of character or of motive in human behavior. Inner determinism is false.
(3) Human actions are not determined by an ancestral determinism originating in the will of God at the onset of creation.

One can logically affirm (1), yet deny (2), as well as (3). Also, one can affirm (2) and deny (3). This is possible by affirming, for example, that character can be changed or motives overridden by "strength of will," this being tantamount to the affirmation of (2); yet go on to say that whatever change of character there be or overriding act of the will there be has itself been determined all along ancestrally, this being the denial of (3). (1) through (3) are thus presented in the Talmudic order of "not only this, but even this."

Recently, Shlomo Pines and Alexander Altmann have argued independently that Maimonides was what I have termed a strong lib-

2. See, Chisholm, "Freedom of Action," and "Responsibility and Avoidability," in Sidney Hook, ed., *Determinism and Freedom in the Age of Modern Science* (New York, 1958); Richard Taylor, "Determinism and the Theory of Agency," in Hook, *Determinism and Freedom*, pp. 211–218. Chisholm attributes the agent theory to Aristotle in *Eudemian Ethics* II, c. 6, and in *Nicomachean Ethics* III, c. 1–5.

3. See Thomas Hobbes, *On Human Nature*, and a selection of Hobbes's writings, *Body, Man and Citizen* (New York, 1962); David Hume, *Enquiry Concerning Human Understanding*, Section 8; Abner of Burgos, *Sefer Minhat Kenaot* (Hebrew exerpts) *Tarbiz* XI, 188–206; Hasdai Crescas, *Or Adonai*.

ertarian only in his "popular" works.[4] In the *Guide of the Perplexed,* they argue, he had a different position. There, it is alleged, Maimonides reveals himself as denying the strong libertarian point of view. This constitutes in their eyes Maimonides' real, esoteric belief concerning human freedom. In this essay I counterargue that Maimonides has no esoteric teaching on freedom and is a strong libertarian in all his works, including the *Guide.*

Section I is a documentation of propositions (1) through (3) in Maimonides' works other than the *Guide.* Section II is an examination of the Pines-Altmann thesis that in the *Guide* Maimonides rejected strong libertarianism.[5]

I

The Denial of External Constraints or Compulsions

In the *Commentary to the Mishnah,* Maimonides elucidates his understanding of free will in the introduction to the tractate of *Avot,* this introduction popularly known as *Shimone P'rakim.* In the eighth chapter Maimonides writes:

> There is no doubt that a person's actions are up to him, if he so wishes, he acts, and if he so wishes, he does not act, there being no necessity or compulsion upon him.[6]

From the context it is clear that external necessity and compulsion are being rejected. In particular, Maimonides addresses astrological compulsion:

> [The astrologers] believe that the constellation at the time of one's birth causes him to have a virtue or a vice, and that therefore he is forced to do what he does. However, it is agreed upon by our Torah and Greek philosophy . . . that all actions of a person are up to him, there being no external force inclining him to virtue or vice.[7]

4. Shlomo Pines, "Studies in Abul-Barakat al-Baghdadi's Poetics and Metaphysics," in "Excursus," in *Studies in Philosophy, Scripta Hierosolymitana* 6 (1960): 195–198; Alexander Altmann, "The Religion of the Thinkers: Free Will and Predestination in Saadia, Bahya, and Maimonides," in S. D. Goitein, ed., *Religion in a Religious Age* (Cambridge, 1974), reprinted in Altmann, ed., *Essays in Jewish Intellectual History* (Hanover, N.H., and London, 1981). Citations in this essay are from the former.

5. I do not discuss here the problem of free will and omniscience in Maimonides. I have discussed that issue in my "The Philosophical *Hassagot* of Rabad on Maimonides' *Mishneh Torah,*" *The New Scholasticism,* 58 (1984): 145–169.

6. *Commentary to the Mishnah,* translated into Hebrew by D. Kapach (Jerusalem, 1968), p. 261 (Hereafter: *CM*). All translations into English in this essay are mine unless otherwise noted.

7. loc. cit.

In the *Mishneh Torah,* the same themes are sounded. Chapter 5 of the *Laws of T'shuvah* opens with a statement of free will:

Every person has free will. If he wishes to turn himself in a good direction and be righteous, he is free to do so, and if he wishes to turn himself in an evil direction and be wicked, he is free to do so.[8]

In particular, nothing exerts external compulsion upon a person: "Nothing compels him or decrees upon him or influences him in one of two paths, rather he himself turns to whichever path he wishes."[9]

In particular, God also does not influence our decisions, even our decisions for good.[10] We do not stand in need of intervention by Divine Grace on our behalf in order to do good. Divine assistance is given, rather, in the form of providing the conditions necessary for our choosing the good:

He has sent His prophets to make known the ways of God, and to bring people to repent. Also He had provided the ability to learn and to understand, for every person is such that, when he follows the paths of wisdom and righteousness, he finds himself with a desire [for those paths] and the pursuit [of wisdom and righteousness]. And this was the intention of the Rabbis, may their memory be a blessing, when they said, "He who comes to be purified, is assisted," that is to say, he finds himself assisted in the matter.[11]

God does not intervene so as to compel or even influence our decisions. He assists us by having provided the conditions which enable us to choose the good and to succeed in carrying out our intentions.

Finally, Maimonides reiterates this position in his *Letter on Astrology*:

It is one of the roots of the religion of Moses our Master . . . that every action of human beings is left to them and that there is nothing to constrain or draw them. . . . There is no influence or constellation under which one is born that will draw him in any manner toward any one of these ways.[12]

Thus, the denial of external determinism is Maimonides' consistent position. As noted, the affirmation of (1) does not entail (2) or (3). That Maimonides held these latter two must be further documented.

The Denial of Inner Determinism of Character or Motive

In the *Mishnah* commentary, Maimonides recognizes that people have natural propensities, but maintains that these are not determining: "It is possible a person be born with a natural disposition for a

8. *Mishneh Torah, T'shuvah* 5:1.
9. *T'shuvah* 5:2.
10. loc. cit.
11. *T'shuvah* 6:5.
12. "Letter on Astrology," translated by Ralph Lerner, in R. Lerner and M. Maher, eds., *Medieval Political Philosophy* (New York, 1963), p. 233.

virtue or a vice so that some actions be easier for him than others. But it is not possible that he be born with a virtue or a vice."[13] He goes on to claim that anyone who neglects to train his natural disposition will not acquire the corresponding virtue or vice; and that anyone lacking the appropriate natural disposition can "without doubt" still acquire the corresponding virtue or vice, it only being difficult for him to do so. The implication is clear: there is no inner determinism that overrides human choice.

In the *Mishneh Torah,* Maimonides reiterates his rejection of inner determinism. In Chapter 5 of *T'shuvah* he affirms a radical form of inner libertarianism: "Every person can be as saintly as Moses our teacher, or as wicked as Jeroboam; or, wise or ignorant; or, merciful or cruel; or, stingy or magnanimous, and likewise for other human traits."[14]

Inner freedom is a condition of *t'shuvah* (repentance), and so: "Just as a person must repent from [sinful actions] so must he examine the evil traits he has, and repent from anger, hatred, jealousy, mockery, avarice, honor, gluttony, and the like. From them all must he repent."[15]

There is, then, no inner determinism of character or motive, for a person can radically change his character and motivation. If he fails to do so, that is his choice. If he does so, of him Maimonides writes: "Yesterday he was separated from God, the God of Israel. . . . And today he clings to the Divine Presence."[16]

The affirmation of (2) does not entail the denial of ancestral determinism. It can be maintained that all changes of character and motive are determined by a concatenation of causes and effects reaching back to the Divine Will that set the world into motion. (3), then, must be separately documented.

The Denial of Ancestral Determinism

It must now be shown that for Maimonides a human action is not an event for which there exists a sufficient cause or complex of causes determining it, which cause or complex of causes in turn has a sufficient cause, and so on, all the way back to the cause of all causes, determining the human action through the causal chain. In both the *Mishnah* commentary and *Mishneh Torah,* this position appears. In the former, it is ancillary to a different point, but in the latter, more centrally stated.

In the *Mishnah* commentary, Maimonides is concerned to repudiate

13. *CM,* p. 261.
14. *T'shuvah* 5:2.
15. *T'shuvah* 7:3.
16. *T'shuvah* 7:7.

the Kalām view that there is a new Divine Will at every moment, making each moment of existence discrete and independent of every other. This brings him to explain in what sense it can be said that "the standing and sitting of a person are done by God's will":

In the following sense it is said of a person who stood up or sat down that he stood or sat by God's will: that it was inherent in his nature from the start that he stand or sit by his own choice. Not that God wills that he stand, when he stands, or sit, when he sits. . . . But, just as God willed that man walk upright, and have a broad chest and fingers, so he willed that man move and rest of his own accord, and act of his own free will.[17]

In denying the Kalām view, Maimonides asserts that man acts in accordance with God's original will and not God's renewed, momentary will. What is the original will of God? We may answer by distinguishing between

(4) God wills that a man, stand or sit,

and

(5) God wills that a man stand or wills that a man sit.

Maimonides endorses (4). But (4) does not entail (5), and he explicitly rejects (5). Therefore, for Maimonides, if a person stands, or sits, not only is there not a present divine will now determining that he stand or determining that he sit, but also there never was a divine will ancestrally determining that he now stand or determining that he now sit. A person, we may say, is determined to *choose* to stand or sit, while not being determined to stand, nor to sit.

In *Mishneh Torah* a similar point is made, but directly about ancestral determinism, and not in the context of an anti-Kalām statement:

Know that everything is in accordance with the Divine Will, even though we have freedom of the will. How? Just as the creator wills that fire and air ascend, and water and earth descend, . . . so He wills that man be free and his actions be up to him, that there be no necessity or pull upon him, but that he himself, of his own, with his mind that God gave him, do all that a person can do. Therefore he is judged by his actions, if he does good, he is rewarded, if he does evil, he is punished.[18]

From this passage it is clear that Maimonides rejected ancestral determinism and deemed it incompatible with freedom. This concludes the documentation of (1) through (3) and confirms the claim that in works other than the *Guide,* Maimonides is a strong libertarian, holding that human actions are free and not determined.

17. *CM,* p. 262.

18. *T'shuvah* 5:4.

II

Shlomo Pines has argued that it was not Maimonides' real opinion that the human will is free. Instead, says Pines, Maimonides really believed that "volition and choice are no less subject to causation than natural phenomena, and do not form . . . a domain governed by different laws or by no laws at all."[19] For Pines, Maimonides was a strong determinist. Alexander Altmann, arguing essentially from the same sources, concludes that "Maimonides tacitly replaces the view expressed in his theological works by a deterministic theory that must be considered to represent his esoteric doctrine."[20] Unlike Pines, though, Altmann speaks of the "deterministic character of Maimonides' notion of free choice," suggesting that in his eyes Maimonides was really a compatibilist.[21] But Pines and Altmann concur in ascribing to Maimonides the view I have called "ancestral determinism," where Pines takes the latter to be incompatible with libertarianism, but Altmann does not.

Leaving aside for now the question of strong determinism or compatibilism, let us examine the Pines-Altmann thesis that Maimonides secretly affirmed ancestral determinism.[22] Both Pines and Altmann build their strongest case on *Guide* II, 48, a chapter to which Maimonides exhorts the reader to pay particular attention, an attention exceeding that due other chapters of the *Guide*: a sure signal that herein lies an important teaching. For Pines and Altmann that teaching is ancestral determinism.

The chapter opens by stating that everything produced in time has a proximate cause, which in turn has a cause, and so forth, until the series ends on reaching God's will, the First Cause. It then proceeds to explain that the prophets typically ignore the proximate and intermediate causes and ascribe events directly to divine agency. This is what they mean when they say God did something, said it, or commanded it. God, however, is really the remote, and not the proximate, cause of those events. Maimonides then applies this principle to three classes of events: natural, voluntary, and accidental or fortuitous. The "voluntary" includes both "the free choice of a man" as well as "the volition of an animal."[23] "Maimonides," says Pines, "appears to put on

19. Pines, "Studies in Abul-Barakat," p. 198.
20. Altmann, *Essays in Jewish Intellectual History*, p. 41.
21. Altmann, *Essays in Jewish Intellectual History*, p. 43.
22. Neither Pines nor Altmann uses this terminology.
23. *Guide of the Perplexed*, trans. by Shlomo Pines (Chicago, 1963), p. 410 (hereafter: *Guide*).

a par man's free choice and the volition of other animals, the former and the latter being caused by God."[24] Altmann concurs and asserts that the continuation of the chapter "fully corroborates" Pines's thesis.[25] Altmann quotes an excerpt also cited by Pines that follows in the *Guide*, as corroborating evidence:

This is the notion to which I wished to draw attention in this chapter. For inasmuch as the deity is . . . He who arouses a particular volition in the irrational animal and who has necessitated this particular free choice in the rational animal [that is, man] and who has made the natural things pursue their course . . . it follows necessarily from all this that it may be said with regard to what proceeds necessarily from these causes that God has commanded that something should be done in such and such a way or that He has said: Let this be thus.[26]

Altmann makes two points about this passage: (a) "[It] establishes a complete analogy between the necessities attending natural and volitional causes,"[27] and (b) "Certain results proceed necessarily from these causes, and the concatenation forming a causal series goes back to God's will, which justifies the prophetic manner of speech attributing all events directly to the First Cause."[28] Therefore, in the *Guide*, as opposed to elsewhere, Maimonides is an ancestral determinist. Thus the view of Pines and Altmann.

In reply, it should be noted that we have already established in Section I that Maimonides was a strong libertarian in his other works. Therefore, if II, 48, can be given a reading consistent with strong libertarianism that is at least as plausible as the Pines-Altmann reading, then prima facie the case will be in favor of strong libertarianism. I believe not only that such a reading exists, but that a close scrutiny of the chapter shows the Pines-Altmann thesis to be untenable.

As for (a), I find the reasoning unconvincing. That human free choice is necessitated need not imply that God's will determines *what* man chooses, but only *that* he choose. The Arabic *ikhtiyār* is ambiguous in this regard. This is almost certainly Maimonides' intention in *Guide* III, 17, where he writes: "It comes from His eternal volition in the eternity *a parte ante* that all animals move in virtue of their own will, and that man should have the ability to do whatever he wills or chooses."[29]

24. Pines, "Studies in Abul-Barakat," p. 197.
25. Altmann, *Essays in Jewish Intellectual History*, p. 43.
26. *Guide*, p. 410.
27. Altmann, *Essays in Jewish Intellectual History*, p. 43.
28. Altmann, *Essays in Jewish Intellectual History*, p. 44.
29. *Guide*, p. 469.

Here the Divine Will determines that man choose, not what he choose. If in III, 17, this could be said in the company of animals, so it could be said in II, 48, in their company, as well. I submit, therefore, that if a possible way of understanding II, 48, is that ancestral determinism is compatible with freedom, this is not because Maimonides is a compatibilist, in the sense explained at the outset of this essay, but only because the nature of the causal chain is such that it does not determine the events of man's choosing this rather than that, but only that he have the choice. What he chooses is his decision.[30]

With regard to (b), it will be best to consider first what appears a decisive reason in favor of the Pines-Altmann interpretation, that Maimonides illustrates his thesis about freedom and the Divine Will with a number of Biblical verses ascribing free human actions directly to God's doing or command. These include Genesis 45:8, where Joseph consoles his brothers by telling them, "It was not you that sent me hither, but God."[31] Now if I am right that II, 48, teaches strong libertarianism, then there is no ground for Maimonides' quoting this verse approvingly in this context. It contravenes strong libertarianism to say that God, and not I, is the cause of my action. The verse, however, supports Pines's claim that II, 48, rejects freedom in favor of divine ancestral determinism. It can also be made to conform, perhaps less successfully, with compatibilism: Joseph chooses to emphasize the deterministic nature of events over their libertarianist character. But the verse surely does not permit a strong libertarian reading.

Furthermore, if II, 48, were strongly libertarian, there would seem to be no esoteric teaching involved, and yet Maimonides seems to signal a secret doctrine. So, strong libertarianism would seem to be ruled out.

A closer look at the chapter, however, shows that Pines and Altmann have ignored a subtle shift that takes place in its central paragraph, quoted earlier. Let us review that paragraph. First, Maimonides calls for special attention to the chapter; next he writes that all of natural,

30. A similar interpretation is made by Seymour Feldman in a review of Altmann's *Essays in Jewish Intellectual History* (see n. 4), p. 14. However, Feldman defends this interpretation of the text in a way I cannot accept. He writes: "No wonder, Maimonides points out, that in these cases the Bible uses the language of "command" or "speak." . . . But after all, a commandment implies that the person to whom it is addressed *can* obey" (p. 14). Feldman thinks, then, that free will is intended in II, 48, since God only "commands." However, this cannot be correct for two reasons: (1) God is said to "command" as well natural events, where there is no free will, and, (2) in any case, in this chapter Maimonides says the prophets also speak of God's *doing*, in the same sense, so that if God does, it's done. There is no question of disobeying.

31. *Guide*, p. 411.

voluntary, and accidental causes are "ascribed to God"; and the prophets express this ascription in terms of God's doing, saying, and commanding. Then comes a second call for attention: "This is the notion to which I wished to draw attention," followed by: "For inasmuch as," and so on, intimating that the secret teaching follows.[32] Let us, then, requote the sentence that seems to contain that teaching:

> For inasmuch as the deity . . . arouses a particular volition in the irrational animal and . . . has necessitated this particular free choice in the rational animal and . . . has made the natural things pursue their course, . . . it follows necessarily . . . that it may be said *with regard to what proceeds necessarily from these causes* that God has commanded . . . or that He has said.[33] (my emphasis)

In what follows the second call for attention, there is no reference to the very act of choice, but only to what proceeds as a consequence of it, in the course that natural things pursue. This, then, is a separate point from the earlier one Maimonides makes. Earlier, the free choices of man are ascribed to God; here the consequences of those actions are so ascribed. It is strange that after the second "signal" Maimonides confines himself to the consequences of our choices, and not to our choices themselves. What can explain this, especially since what follows the second signal seems to be the essence of the secret? Indeed, if the secret teaching of the chapter were the determinism of human actions, why mention the consequences at all, especially at this critical point?

The answer I propose to these questions is that in Maimonides' mind there is a distinction to be made between the prophetic ascription to God of our *actions* and *consequences* of our actions. With regard to our actions themselves it cannot be maintained in any serious way that God has determined them, since God, I have already suggested, determines only that we choose, not what we choose. Our free acts are not elements in a causal chain ancestrally determined by God's initiating will. The ascription of them to God is "honorific," expressing, perhaps, the pious thought that we act freely only because God has created the world, has created us free, and has brought us to the choice. Only with regard to the ensuing consequences of our free acts can it be significantly said that God does them or commands them. That is because once we act, we give over the consequences of our acts to the natural order and chance. We, however, exercise no choice over the natural order or over chance. But God does. He wills the natural order which determines natural causes, and in accordance with which chance events transpire, as Maimonides says in this chapter

32. *Guide*, p. 410.
33. Ibid.

of the *Guide.* Since that natural order is, strictly speaking, willed by God, there is a significant sense in which the consequences of our acts are commanded by God. This is stronger than the merely honorific ascriptions to God of our actions themselves. The point about the consequences of our actions is not, as Altmann understands it, in (b), that the determining chain passes through us, as it were, toward the future and thus determines the consequences of these actions. Rather, the point is that only with regard to those consequences can it significantly be said that God commanded them. The person, as agent, initiates a causal chain that follows its course in accordance with God's "command."

That there is a distinction for Maimonides between the seriousness with which our actions can be said to be commanded by God and the consequences of our actions is borne out by his quotation from Genesis 45:8 where Joseph consoles his brothers. The larger context in Genesis 45 reads as follows:

> 4: and He said: I am Joseph your brother whom you sold to Egypt—
> 5: and now, be not grieved, nor be angry with yourselves, that you sold me hither; because to preserve life did God send me before you.
> 7: And God sent me before you . . .
> 8: So now, it was not you that sent me hither, but God . . .

In this passage Joseph attributes the very sale of him by his brothers to the brothers themselves. In verse 8, what is attributed to God is not the sale of Joseph to the Ishmaelites, but the subsequent descent of Joseph into Egypt. Verse 5 explicitly makes the contrast between the act, attributable to the brothers, and the chain of events sending Joseph to Egypt, attributed to God. Therefore, in quoting verse 8, it could not have been Maimonides' intention to offer a proof-text against strong libertarianism on the grounds that therein a human action is ascribed to God and not to man. For he and the reader both know that in verses 4 and 5, the sale of Joseph is attributed to the brothers, and in the entire passage only the coming to Egypt is ascribed to God. Indeed, Maimonides can cite verse 8 as an illustration of the point of this chapter of the *Guide* only if he recognizes a distinction between our actions and their consequences, only if, that is, he really believed that only with regard to their consequences is there a serious sense in which it can be said that God does it or commands them. His citing of verse 8, then, directs the reader to the subtle shift in the central paragraph. God does not determine our free actions—the brothers sold Joseph. The concatenation of events, following the natural order and chance: these are God's doing. God sent Joseph to Egypt.

If Pines and Altmann were right that Maimonides meant to affirm ancestral determinism of our actions, as well as of their consequences, there would be no way to make a distinction between the two, as regards their being done by God.

The truly "secret" doctrine of II, 48, then, is this: there is no divine initiation or direction of history. The prophetic language describing God as commanding human free actions does not imply a divine determining of these actions. God commands them only in an attenuated sense, namely, by granting us free will. History depends on us. If we choose to act in one way, it takes one course; if another, another course. God, as it were, waits for our decisions to be made. Only after we act can the Divine Will make history and then only by the long-determined natural order. The *Guide* teaches over and over again that God does not intervene in the natural order. The world follows its accustomed path. *Guide* II, 48, completes that teaching by affirming that neither is there a "built-in" divine direction or plan for history. There is no ancestral determinism of our actions, initiated by the Divine Will.

The Rambam's teachings on freedom and determinism are thus seen to be unitary in all his works, and *Guide* II, 48, far from being inconsistent with his teachings elsewhere, is a defense of strong libertarianism against the belief that God causes our actions. The topic of II, 48, is not free will, but the prophetic manner of speech.

Ben Gurion University of the Negev

9 Maimonides' Not-So-Secret Position on Creation

WILLIAM DUNPHY

INTRODUCTION

Several years ago, in a contribution to a festschrift for the noted Canadian philosopher Joseph Owens, I sought to demonstrate that all of the historians I had read who compare Maimonides and Aquinas on their respective positions on creation were dead wrong in their claims that Maimonides, unlike Aquinas, held that creation could not be demonstrated but most be accepted by faith alone.[1]

I then attempted to explain how these historians, including Gilson, Fakhry and Wolfson, went wrong. In the case of those historians who relied on modern translations of the *Guide of the Perplexed,* I was able to show that the Friedlander English version and the Munk version in French consistently equated creation with creation in time. One example will suffice: "the question whether the world is eternal or created" and "*cette question . . . si le monde est éternel ou créé.*" However, the Pines translation and a Latin version had, respectively, "this question—namely the eternity of the world or its temporal creation" and "*hujus quaestionis de novitate vel antiquitate mundi. . . .*"[2]

Thus, these historians were unable to discern the actual source in the text of Maimonides for the clear distinction made by Aquinas between the demonstrability of creation *ex nihilo* and the indemonstrability of creation *ab aeterno* or *de novo.*[3]

I analyzed the texts of the *Guide* toward the end of part I and the beginning of part II, where Maimonides criticizes the Mutakallimūn proofs for the existence of God and presents his version of proofs in

1. William Dunphy, "Maimonides and Aquinas on Creation: A Critique of Their Historians," *Graceful Reason: Essays in Ancient and Medieval Philosophy Presented to Joseph Owens, CSSR,* ed. Lloyd P. Gerson (Toronto, 1983), pp. 361–79.
2. Ibid., p. 372.
3. See, for example, Aquinas, *Summa contra gentiles* 2.38; *Summa Theologiae* I, 46, 2.

the Aristotelian tradition which, he claims, work whether the world be eternal in its duration or not.[4]

Thomas Aquinas recognized this point in his careful reading of the *Guide*. He followed Maimonides in arguing that, while the world can be demonstrated to be created *ex nihilo*, nevertheless, no valid demonstrations existed to prove either that the world be eternal or that it have a temporal beginning. The implications of this distinction, namely that the notion of an eternal creation *ex nihilo* was not self-contradictory, were as little understood by contemporaries of Aquinas as, apparently, historians of Maimonides. However, it explains the fact that when both thinkers present as valid proofs philosophical demonstrations for the existence of God, they each do so on the hypothesis of an eternal world, and each explicitly links the "unmoved mover" and the "necessary being," and so on, with the creating God of the Bible.[5]

But what of those contemporary interpreters of the *Guide* at home in both the Arabic and Hebrew languages? One figure who dominated twentieth-century historians of medieval Jewish thought was H. A. Wolfson. In one packed and magisterial article, "The Meaning of *Ex Nihilo* in the Church Fathers, Arabic and Hebrew Philosophy, and St. Thomas," he showed the close correspondence between Maimonides and Aquinas in delineating the different senses of "*ex nihilo*" in understanding creation. Wolfson also understood that "St. Thomas' *post non esse* is Maimonides' *post privationem* (in his Latin version), for *non esse* and *privatio* in these two statements mean the same thing and, in fact, the underlying Arabic term *maʿdūm* in Maimonides' statement means both 'privation' and 'non-existence.'" However, according to Wolfson, the meaning of *post,* for both Aquinas and Maimonides, had "to be purged of any implication of time, inasmuch as time came into existence only with the creation of time."[6] Yet even Wolfson tended to use the term *creation* and *creation ex nihilo* as almost the equivalent of *creation de novo*. One citation from many should suffice: "Though both Hallevi and Maimonides believe in creation *ex nihilo,* they admit that such a belief cannot be established by reason. Neither of them agrees with the Kalām, whether the Moslem or the Jewish Kalām, in believing that creation ex nihilo can be established by demonstrative reasoning."[7]

4. Dunphy, "Maimonides and Aquinas," pp. 366–71.
5. Ibid., p. 371.
6. Ibid., pp. 378–79. The Wolfson article is reprinted in the first volume of the two-volume *Studies in the History of Philosophy and Religion,* edited by I. Twersky and G. H. Williams (Cambridge, Mass., 1973). The citations are on pp. 215–17.
7. Wolfson, "The Platonic, Aristotelian and Stoic theories of Creation in Hallevi and Maimonides" as reprinted in *Studies* . . . I, p. 235.

I thought, therefore, that it might be useful to continue my analysis of the *Guide,* beginning after the first paragraph of chapter 2 of part II, immediately after Maimonides sets forth his own versions of proper ways to demonstrate the existence, incorporeality, and oneness of God, all the while accepting as an ungranted hypothesis that the world be eternal.

Now, however, Maimonides must deal with the question whether this demonstrated creation be eternal in duration (*ab aeterno*) or had a beginning (*de novo*). He had thoroughly rejected earlier the methods of the men of Kalām of the three monotheistic religions, Judaism, Christianity and Islam, who sought to preface their demonstrations of the existence, incorporeality and oneness of God by demonstrating that the world had a beginning in time (*de novo*). His revulsion for their methods, he tells us, was caused by their positing reality to be the way they think it ought to be in order to reach the conclusions they think necessary to preserve their religious beliefs about God and His creation.[8] His preference for the methods of the philosophers (read Aristotle and his later followers) was due to their beginning with reality as we can experience it, that is, the way that it actually exists, and seeking to establish what can be demonstrated about God from that foundation.[9] Maimonides, however, makes it quite clear that he does not grant the philosophers their position that the world be eternal. He will accept such a view as a hypothesis because it will provide him with a stronger, more unshakable proof that the Creator exists. He had stated in that place his own position:

> And everyone who engages in speculation, who is perceptive, and who has acquired true knowledge of reality and does not deceive himself, knows that with regard to this question—namely the eternity of the world or its temporal creation—no cogent demonstration can be reached and that it is a point before which the intellect stops.[10]

It is now Maimonides' task to refute the philosophers' proofs for an eternal world and to argue for his own position, consistent with his religious views, that creation is, in fact, *de novo.*

From that point in chapter 2, then, continuing to the beginning of chapter 32 and his treatment of prophecy, Maimonides has a consistent development of what he thinks can be understood of the secrets of The Account of the Beginning (*maʿaseh bereshith*) in keeping with the fundamental purpose of the *Guide* as stated in his Introduction to

8. Maimonides, *Guide of the Perplexed* I, 71, p. 178. This and all subsequent citations of the *Guide* are from the English translation by S. Pines (Chicago, 1963).

9. Ibid., p. 182.

10. Ibid., p. 180.

part I.[11] It is in these chapters that he sets forth his own arguments for the doctrine of creation *de novo*.

By way of contrast to my own analysis of this section of the *Guide*, I will make use of a classic treatment of this material by H. Davidson in his 1979 article, "Maimonides' Secret Position on Creation,"[12] in which he seeks to prove that Maimonides seriously contradicts himself on certain vital points regarding creation. I will attempt to show that this is not the case.

Ironically, I support one of the basic purposes of Davidson's article, namely his refutation of certain critics of Maimonides (labeled the "thoroughgoing esotericists") who interpret the medieval master as having cleverly hidden his own radical philosophical positions behind a smokescreen of traditional religious orthodoxy. In the instance, they claim to be able to discover, in the section we propose to analyze, a Maimonides who publicly "professed a belief in a God who is possessed of free will, while secretly believing in a God who has no free will,"[13] the necessary and eternal cause of an eternally existing world.

Davidson, however, thinks that he has discovered a number of contradictions in Maimonides' treatment of creation in this section of the *Guide*, which point to Maimonides' having secretly embraced a Platonic doctrine of "creation" from a preexistent matter, rather than, as the "thoroughgoing esotericists" would have us believe, holding a secret belief in an Aristotelian eternal world caused by a deity bereft of free will.[14]

In fact, Davidson concludes, we might be making too much of Maimonides' earlier remarks in his introduction to the *Guide* regarding an author's use of deliberate contradictions to hide from casual readers some hidden doctrines, and, when all is said and done, perhaps these contradictions in Maimonides' doctrine on creation might point to a Maimonides "less immune to error and carelessness than he and his readers through the centuries have imagined."[15]

Before I enter the lists with such distinguished Maimonidean scholars, armed as they are with all of the linguistic credentials so necessary to study the thought of a master who composed his *Guide of the Perplexed* in the Arabic language but written in Hebraic letters, I should make clear that my main interest in all of this is to determine the

11. Ibid., pp. 6–7.
12. In *Studies in Medieval Jewish History and Literature* (Cambridge, Mass., 1979), pp. 16–40.
13. Ibid., p. 18.
14. Ibid., p. 36.
15. Ibid.

nature and quality of Maimonidean influence on the history of Western philosophical thought. That influence (and it appears to me to have been considerable) was for many centuries exclusively accessible through Latin translations of Hebrew translations of the *Guide*. Thus, my use of this work of Maimonides is limited to the *Maimonides Latinus*, and, of course, to the corroborative and often corrective presence of the excellent translation from the Arabic original into English by Shlomo Pines.[16]

ANGELS AND OVERFLOW (PART II, CHAPTERS 2 TO 12)

After having completed his presentations of demonstrations proving the existence, incorporeality and oneness of God, demonstrations whose validity is independent of whether creation be *ab aeterno* or *de novo*, Maimonides proposes to complete (*perficere*) the topic by explaining the philosophers' proofs regarding the existence of separate intellects (*in esse intelligentiarum abstractarum*). He will do this, he states, before presenting his own arguments in favor of the view that creation is *de novo*.[17]

It is extremely important for us to note the reason Maimonides gives for observing this order. It is because "our strongest proofs for [creation *de novo*] are valid and can be made clear only after one knows that the separate intellects exist and after one knows how proofs for their existence may be adduced."[18]

Maimonides, however, sets forth strict limits to his exposition of matters pertaining to natural science and metaphysics (divine science). He is not interested in these philosophical matters for their own sake but rather "only to elucidate the difficult points of the Law and to make manifest the true realities of its hidden meanings."[19] He recalls his stated intention in the introduction that everything he has to say regarding philosophical matters "hinges on the explanation of what

16. The *Guide of the Perplexed* was written by Maimonides in Arabic. It was first translated into Hebrew by Samuel Ibn Tibbon in 1204. A second Hebrew translation, by Judah al'Harizi, followed shortly thereafter. It was from this second Hebrew translation that the first Latin translation was made sometime during the 1220s. (See W. Kluxen, "Literaturgeschichtliches zum lateinischen Moses Maimonides," *Recherches de Théologie Ancienne et Médiévale* 21 [1954], pp. 23–50.) Agostino Giustiniani prepared an edition of this translation from several manuscripts in 1520. It was published in Paris with the title *Rabi Mossei Aegyptii Dux seu Director dubitantium aut perplexorum*. Medieval Latin writers often referred to it as the *Dux neutrorum*. This edition is now available in a facsimile edition by Minerva (Frankfurt a. M., 1964).

17. *Guide* II, 2, pp. 252–53; fol. 41v. (The folio references throughout will be to the Latin edition of Giustiniani.)

18. Ibid.

19. Ibid.

can be understood in the Account of the Beginning and in the Account of the Chariot, and the clearing up of the difficulties attaching to prophecy and to the knowledge of the deity."[20]

The account of these limits is likened by Maimonides to "a lamp illuminating the hidden features of the whole of this Treatise," both of the chapters that precede it and of those that follow.[21] This is surely a text of capital importance for anyone claiming Maimonides to be a philosopher *tout court.*

Chapter 3 sharpens the focus on the content and purpose of what is to follow. After noting that what Aristotle had to say about the motions of the celestial spheres, on the basis of which he concluded the existence of separate intellects, were not at all demonstrations but rather only the most probable opinions on the matter (*licet non demonstrentur, sunt propinquae veritati*), Maimonides proposes to "cull from them what agrees with the Law and corresponds to the sayings of the Sages. . . ."[22]

Chapter 4, then, contains Maimonides' epitome of what Aristotle and later followers (especially Avicenna) said about the existence of the separate intellects, on the basis of their understanding of the movements of the various celestial spheres. Their exact number varied according to the individual philosopher's interpretations of celestial phenomena by means of the mathematics of their day. He allows that this science had not been brought to perfection in Aristotle's time and, thus, the calculation of the exact number of separate intellects had been improved in more recent times, as a result of increased and more accurate astronomical calculations based on an improved science of mathematics.[23]

Closely following Avicenna, Maimonides presents the philosophers' view of the universe as creatively derived from the "necessary of existence" (*necesse esse*) by way of an "overflow" that successively produces ten separate intellects. The first nine of these are the causes of their respective spheres and the following intellect and are also the causes of the perfect movements of their respective spheres by way of final causality, that is, by being apprehended and imitatively desired by their spheres. The tenth intellect, called the *agent* or *active intellect,* is the cause of all the passings from potentiality to actuality in this, our world. And this is true with respect to all physical or bodily changes, as well as human intellections. He explicitly uses the term *angel* to refer to these separate intellects, who act as "the intermediaries between God and all these bodies."[24]

20. Ibid., p. 254.
21. Ibid., p. 253.
22. Ibid., p. 254.
23. Ibid., pp. 255–59.
24. Ibid., pp. 258–59.

Beginning with chapter 5 Maimonides sets out to explain "what in our Law corresponds to these opinions and what in it differs from them." Texts from the Psalms and the Talmud are cited and discussed to show this correspondence regarding the spheres (*coeli*) as "living beings who obey their Lord and praise Him and extol Him greatly." To manifest this correspondence there are likewise texts regarding the view that the spheres consciously exercise governance over this lower sublunar world by means of an "overflow" to it of forces (*virtutes*) emanating from the spheres.[25]

That angels exist is manifestly clear from reading Torah and does not require a separate proof, Maimonides maintains in chapter 6. He notes, however, a difference in terminology between Torah and Aristotle, "for he speaks of separate intellects, and we speak of angels."[26]

After several remarkable pages, important for an understanding of Maimonides' notion of secondary causality, in which he concludes that "every force (*virtus*) charged by God, may He be exalted, with some business is an angel put in charge of that thing (*vocatur angelus missus super illa re*)," Maimonides carefully delineates the agreements and disagreements between Aristotle and the Law. This text is extremely important for our analysis and is worth citing in full:

> There is then nothing in what Aristotle for his part has said about this subject that is not in agreement with the Law. However, a point on which he disagrees with us in all this is constituted by his belief that all these things are eternal (*antiqua non nova neque creata*) and that they proceed necessarily from Him, may He be exalted, in that way. For we ourselves believe that all this has been created and that God has created the separate intellects and has put in the sphere the force of desire toward them, and that it was He who created the intellects and the spheres and put in them the governing forces. As to this (*in hoc ergo solo*) we do disagree with him. Later on you shall hear his opinion and the opinion of the true Law regarding the world's having been produced in time.[27]

In chapter 7, Maimonides admits that the term *angel* is an equivocal, referring as it does to all the forces (*virtutes*) serving as ministers in God's governance of His creation. Thus, the term includes all the active forces in nature, the animated celestial spheres, as well as the powerful separate intellects. But, Maimonides insists, there is a ranking among them, with the spheres superior to any force in nature and with the separate intellects at the highest level of creation, as a result of their possession of intellection and volition. He makes an important distinction between the superior kind of intellection, volition and governance exercised by these highest rank of angels and that exercised

25. *Guide* II, 5, pp. 259–61.
26. *Guide* II, 6, p. 262.
27. Ibid., p. 265; fol. 43v. Note that the two Latin phrases amplify the Pines version.

by humans, whereas "we sometimes do things that are more defective than other things, and our governance and our action are preceded by privations (*actiones vero nostrae sunt deficientes, et haec est privatio quae praecedit regimen nostrum et operationem*)."[28] "The separate intellects always do what is good and all that they have exists always in perfection and *in actu* since they have come into existence (*ab hora suae essentiae*)."[29]

A textual disagreement between Talmudic texts and Aristotle, on the question of the long-held belief by both some ancient philosophers and the general run of people that the motion of the spheres produces wondrous sounds, is resolved by Maimonides in chapter 8. After siding with the view of Aristotle that they produce no sound at all, he interprets a Talmudic text to the effect that, in those astronomical matters, they simply accepted the science of their day.[30]

In the following two chapters, 9 and 10, Maimonides builds upon a historic dispute among philosophical astronomers concerning the relationships of Mercury and Venus with respect to being below or above the Sun, to conclude that regardless of which view is correct, the number of spheres or groups of spheres that contain stars turns out to be four: that of the fixed stars, that of the group of five planets, that of the Sun, that of the Moon. He confides to his readers that meditating on this number, namely four, he was led to a most important philosophical conclusion that he had not found explicitly in any of the philosophers.[31] He devotes a long treatment in chapter 10 to the exposition of this new position, with support from both the philosophers and the religious Sages.

Before presenting his conclusions on this point, we would do well to recall the "obligatory preface" back in chapter 2 which Maimonides had likened to a lamp illuminating the entire *Guide*. He told us there that any presentation by him of a philosophical point was not philosophical in intent but rather had as its overriding purpose to elucidate some difficult point of the Law or to manifest one of its hidden meanings.[32] The point here is that this new philosophical speculation by Maimonides is a key to his notion of the divine "overflow" by which God creates, preserves and governs His universe. This, in turn, is the key to understanding Maimonides' own positions on creation *de novo*, prophecy and providence!

Thus, Maimonides proceeds to develop a view of the possible arrangement of the universe: the "spheres" are four; the elements

28. *Guide* II, 7, p. 266; fol. 44r.
29. Ibid.
30. *Guide* II, 8, p. 267.
31. *Guide* II, 9, pp. 268–69.
32. *Guide* II, 2, p. 253.

moved by the "spheres" are four, namely, earth, air, fire, water; and the forces "overflowing" from these spheres into that which exists in this sublunar world of ours are four, namely, the force causing the generation of minerals, the force of the vegetative soul, the force of the animal soul, and the force of the rational soul. Likewise the number four plays a role in explaining the causative activities of these animated spheres: their very shape or sphericity, their animating principle or soul, their cognizing power, and their respective separate intellect which, as loved by them, serves as the final cause of what they do. Maimonides then links all of this with a series of Talmudic and scriptural texts referring to four camps of angels, four angels seen by Jacob, four chariots interpreted by Zechariah as the four "airs" of the heavens which are, according to Maimonides, "the cause of everything that comes to pass in time."[33]

Maimonides here cautions his readers not to think that he has produced new astronomical demonstrations, as though this were even the purpose of astronomical science. That science rather seeks hypotheses that render possible accounts of the heavenly bodies that agree with what can be observed. He insists that his purpose in what has preceded was simply to number all of the forces observably operating in our world "without troubling to give a precise account of the true reality of the intellects and the spheres."[34] That numbering yielded the view that below the Creator there existed, in a decreasing order of perfection and importance, the realm of the separate intellects, the realm of the celestial spheres, and the realm of our sublunar world of generable and corruptible entities.

A further purpose in this, he tells us (and one most important for our analysis of Maimonides' position on creation *de novo*) was

> to show that governance overflows from the deity (*virtus autem regiminis diffunditur a creatore*), may He be exalted, to the intellects according to their rank; that from the benefits received by the intellects, good things and lights overflow to the bodies of the spheres (*similiter provenit ex largitate bonorum eis datorem, et ex splendore super corpora caelorum*); and that from the spheres—because of the greatness of the benefits they have received from their principles—forces and good things overflow to this body subject to generation and corruption."[35]

He concludes chapter 11 by proposing a chapter in which he will explain the true reality of the notion of "overflow" as the final preparatory step toward his long-promised treatment of the whole question of creation *de novo*.

33. *Guide* II, 10, pp. 271–73.
34. *Guide* II, 11, pp. 273–74.
35. Ibid., p. 275; fol. 45v.

Maimonides opens that chapter with an axiom from which he develops several arguments—indeed, demonstrations—drawn from natural science, all of which lead into his explanation of the notion of "overflow." He describes it as the mode of causality proper to certain kinds of efficient causes, namely the Creator and the separate intellects or angels.

That opening line of chapter 12 reads as follows: "It is clear that everything produced in time (*omne novum*) has of necessity an efficient cause that causes it to be produced after not having been existent (*quae fecit ipsum esse postquam non fuit*)."[36] From this he argues to the necessity of there being "something eternal and not produced in time that has caused that thing to be produced in time (*necesse est . . . ut perveniatur ad renovatorem antiquum qui non renovetur*)."[37]

Let us recall our earlier reference to Wolfson's remark that Maimonides' use of *after*, in the expression "after not having been existent," must "be purged of any implication of time." Indeed, Maimonides, after indicating that his presentation to this point has been based on what has been solidly demonstrated by the philosophers, notes that it prescinds from the question whether the world be eternal or produced in time (*utrum mundus sit antiquum an novum*).[38]

Maimonides then explains, regarding a world in which every new realization of form is due to an agent (*dator formae*) that is in no way a body or a force in a body, how such an incorporeal agent cannot act upon the world of bodies in the same way that one body acts upon another body, that is, by contact or at some particular distance. The action of such a separate agent or intellect "is always designated as an overflow (*nominant semper actionem separati in splendore*)."[39] Like a fountain of water that is constantly overflowing in all directions, the action of the separate intellect "is constant as long as something has been prepared so that it is receptive of the permanently existing action which has been interpreted as an overflow (*quae nominatur largitas*)."[40]

The case is the same with respect to the Creator, who has already been demonstrated to be incorporeal and the efficient cause of the universe. Maimonides notes that "it has been said that the world derives from the overflow of God (*quod mundus est ex largitate creatoris*), and that He has caused to overflow to it everything in it that is produced in time (*Ipse largitus est super ipsum quicquid renovatur in ipso*)."[41]

This term *overflow*, Maimonides says, has been applied to God in the Hebrew language by using the simile of a spring or fountain of water.

36. *Guide* II, 12, p. 277; fol. 45v.
37. Ibid.
38. Ibid.
39. Ibid., pp. 278–79; fol. 46r.
40. Ibid.
41. Ibid.

The reason for this use, he tells us, is the extreme difficulty, if not impossibility, of human knowledge—tied as it is to an imaginative faculty which can only represent to itself corporeal beings and actions—ever properly conceiving of an immaterial being or of its actions. Indeed, this simile is the most fitting in the circumstance.[42]

Maimonides makes two final points in this last of the preparatory chapters to his long-promised, personal treatment of creation, whether it be *ab aeterno* or *de novo*. The first is to note that although he has focused on the notion of "overflow" as used with respect to God and the separate intellects or angels precisely as incorporeal, the term can also be used with respect to the celestial spheres who are corporeal, in that they overflow toward that which exists in our sublunar world.[43]

The second point is to show how the term was figuratively applied in the books of the prophets to the actions of God. He cites Jeremiah 2:13, "the fountains of living waters," and Psalms 36:10, "For with Thee is the fountain of life." And then, in commenting on the rest of that verse, "In Thy light we see light," Maimonides sees a triple overflow from God to man: one results in our very existence, another in our ability to know intellectually; a third enables us to act virtuously.

> [this verse] has the self-same meaning as the overflow of being (*largitas esse*)—namely that through the overflow of the intellect that has overflowed from Thee, we intellectually cognize and consequently we receive correct guidance . . . (*eius expositio est, quod in largitate intellectus qui provenit a te, intelligemus et ambulabimus in via recta*).[44]

CREATION, AB AETERNO OR DE NOVO (PART II, CHAPTERS 13 TO 25)

As mentioned previously, my analysis of this section of the *Guide* will be accompanied by an attempt to refute the arguments of H. Davidson, who finds Maimonides guilty of contradicting himself there on two matters of major importance. The first of these involves Maimonides' treatment of Plato's position on creation in chapters 13 and 25. The second involves Maimonides' own arguments for creation. We

42. Ibid.

43. Ibid., p. 280.

44. Ibid.; fol. 46v. One may be forgiven for ruminating on the fact that, nearly eight centuries earlier, the great Christian doctor St. Augustine (of whom Maimonides was surely unaware) had used the metaphor of light and of a Divine Illumination to account for our very existence, our ability to know truly and to move toward God through loving righteous conduct. One text will suffice, in which Augustine is contrasting creaturely light with that light that is God: "hoc lumen non est lumen quod Deus est; hoc enim creatura est, Creator est ille; . . . et inde nobis initium existendi, ratio cognoscendi, lex amandi." *Contra Faustum Manichaeum* 20, 7, PL 42, col. 372.

will deal with each of these alleged contradictions at the appropriate place.

Maimonides is quite clear in chapter 13 that he is setting forth three different positions with regard to the eternity of the world or its production in time (*de antiquitate vel novitate mundi*) by those who admit the existence of God.

The first position is that of "all who believe in the Law of Moses our Master," and it holds that God, through His Will, brought the world as a whole into existence "after having been purely and absolutely non-existent," that is, by way of a creation that is both *ex nihilo* and *de novo*. For Maimonides, this is a foundation of the Law second only in importance to the proclamation of Abraham of the oneness of God.[45]

The second opinion is that of all the philosophers who say that "it is absurd that God would bring a thing into existence out of nothing"; indeed, it would be an impossibility in the class of, say, having a square whose diagonal is equal to its side. They believe, rather, that God, like a potter with his clay, produces in a matter coeternal with Him, whatever He wishes to make, as, for example, a heaven and an earth, which, in turn, can pass away. Maimonides says that this is the belief of Plato but insists that "he does not believe what we believe," as might be thought by one who "is not precise in speculation." The difference is simple but decisive: the heavens generated from an eternal matter, and our view that it "was generated out of nothing after a state of absolute non-existence (*post privationem absolutam*)."[46]

A third view is that of Aristotle, his followers, and the commentators of his books. It holds that all that exists in the state in which it is at present was not produced after a prior state of nonexistence (*post privationem*) and is made by God through His will, but a will that is incapable of change or variation.

It is in the concluding paragraph of this chapter 13 that Maimonides links the Platonic and the Aristotelian positions for strategic reasons. While, he says, there are obvious differences between the two positions (heavens generated and corruptible versus their being ungenerable and incorruptible), they both believe in the existence of something eternal other than God, whereas it is "the purpose of every follower of the Law of Moses and Abraham our Father . . . to believe that there is nothing eternal in any way at all existing simultaneously with God." A further crucial difference between a follower of the Law and both the Platonic and Aristotelian positions is that for the former, it is not

45. *Guide* II, 13, pp. 281–82.

46. Ibid., pp. 282–84; fol. 46v–47r.

an impossibility that God is able to create something *ex nihilo* (*post privationem*).[47]

Davidson's report of this important chapter is seriously flawed by what appears to be his inability to distinguish clearly between "creation" as equivalent to "creation *ex nihilo*" on the one hand, and "creation" as a kind of making *ex aliquo* on the other. A further difficulty with his report is the lack of any distinction between "creation" and "creation *de novo*," which is, after all, the very point at issue for Maimonides.

But this is not all. Davidson reports what he describes as Maimonides' formulation of the Biblical view of creation as follows: "during a period extending back through eternity nothing but God existed. Then, in the finitely distant past, God exercised "His Will," and by an act of will "brought the universe . . . into existence."[48] I find it difficult to understand how Davidson can represent the text of Maimonides in this fashion when the latter, in that very place, insists that although our language is tied to temporal imagery, it must be purged of all such imagery in this instance if we are to understand the matter at all:

> Accordingly one's saying: God "was" before He created the world—where the word "was" is indicative of time—and similarly all the thoughts that are carried along in the mind regarding the infinite duration of His existence before the creation of the world, are all of them due to a supposition regarding time or to an imagining of time and not due to the true reality of time.[49]

Further, while Davidson correctly sees that Maimonides contrasts the Aristotelian position with the scriptural one as between a view of God as an eternal, necessary, and unchanging cause of the world and one of a God who created the world through a free act of will, he nonetheless characterizes the latter view as one of creation *ex nihilo* rather than, as does Maimonides, one of creation *ex nihilo* and *de novo*. He also seems to deny that there is any volition involved in the Aristotelian God's causing of the world.[50]

At any event, Davidson claims to find the first major contradiction in that Maimonides lumps together the second and third positions on creation:

> Instead of declaring that "there is no difference" between the Platonic and Aristotelian positions, Maimonides should have said that the Platonic position

47. Ibid., p. 285.
48. Davidson, "Maimonides' Secret Position," p. 19.
49. *Guide* II, 13, p. 281.
50. Davidson, "Maimonides' Secret Position," p. 20.

lies between the scriptural and Aristotelian positions; and from a theological point of view, there is little difference between the Platonic and scriptural positions. The sole theological difference . . . is that the former rejects, while the latter recognizes, one specific type of miracle, the bringing of matter into existence out of nothing.[51]

And indeed, according to Davidson, in chapter 25 Maimonides:

acknowledges that in its theological implications the Platonic position is fully as acceptable as the scriptural position . . . Maimonides goes so far as to concede that the Platonic position can easily be harmonized with the text of the Bible, and that many passages in the Bible and in other authoritative branches of Jewish literature tend to support it.[52]

Why then, asks Davidson, does Maimonides still reject Plato's position? He answers his own question by noting that "Maimonides explains in a subdued voice that he rejected the Platonic position because creation *ex nihilo* seems more in harmony with the obvious sense of the Scripture."[53]

But what, in fact, does Maimonides say in this chapter? After having presented and then refuted nine arguments of the philosophers in favor of an eternal creation, Maimonides is eager to explain to his readers precisely why he was so opposed to the view that the world was eternal. It was not, he insists, because of a text in the Torah according to which the world has been produced in time. Indeed, there are as many texts on that score as there are texts indicating that God is corporeal. In the case of these latter texts, Maimonides notes that he had no problem in interpreting them figuratively.[54] Why then, he asks, can we not interpret the former texts figuratively and affirm as true the eternity of the world? There are two compelling reasons for not doing this, Maimonides tells us. First of all, we can demonstrate that God is not a body and therefore "it follows necessarily that everything that in its external meaning disagrees with this demonstration must be interpreted figuratively." But this is not the case with respect to the eternity of the world, which cannot be demonstrated.[55]

The second compelling reason is that whereas "our belief that the deity is not a body destroys for us none of the foundations of the Law and does not give the lie to the claims of any prophet," on the other

51. Ibid., p. 21.
52. Ibid.
53. Ibid.
54. *Guide* II, 25, pp. 327–28; Maimonides spent the better part of the first forty-nine chapters of the *Guide* in figuratively interpreting Biblical terms suggesting the corporeality of God.
55. Ibid.

hand, belief in the eternity of the world the way Aristotle sees it—that is, "the belief according to which the world exists in virtue of necessity, that no nature changes at all, and that the customary course of events cannot be modified with regard to anything—destroys the Law in its principle. . . ."[56]

It is precisely at this point in his discussion of the possibilities of figurative interpretations of texts in the Torah indicating a temporal beginning of the world that Maimonides notes a difference between the Platonic and Aristotelian positions. If one held, as is said of Plato, that the heavens came to be after not having been, that is, that they are subject to generation and corruption, "this opinion would not destroy the foundations of the Law and would be followed not by the lie being given to miracles."

However, for Maimonides, the only positive reasons for then figuratively interpreting those texts of the Torah indicating a temporal making of the world would be if this version of an eternal world were demonstrated. In short, the Platonic position, unlike the Aristotelian, escapes the second compelling reason against figurative interpretations of those creation texts in the Torah, but quite like the Aristotelian position, it does not avoid the first compelling reason against so doing.

In such a situation, Maimonides concludes, we shall take the texts according to their literal or external meaning and shall simply say, "the Law has given us knowledge of a matter the grasp of which is not within our power, and the miracle attests to the correctness of our claims (*Signa vero et mirabilia testificantur super veritate nostrae rationis*)."[57]

If my reading of the text is correct, I cannot understand how Davidson can construe Maimonides' position to be one of acknowledging "that the Platonic position is, from a theological point of view, virtually equivalent to the scriptural position."

In short, if my reading be correct, then the first of Davidson's serious contradictions vanishes.

Returning to our analysis of this section of the *Guide,* that is, to chapter 14, Maimonides promises to summarize the arguments put forth by Aristotle and his followers in favor of an eternal world. He indicates, however, that he will do so in the same way he had earlier presented the arguments of the men of Kalām, namely, in his own formulations but rigorously preserving their "intentions (*rationes*)." In this way, Maimonides presents a total of nine arguments for the world's eternity.

56. Ibid.

57. Ibid., p. 329; fol. 55v.

The first four are drawn from Aristotle, he tells us, and all begin from the world itself (*ex parte mundi per se*). In three of these, the ungenerability and incorruptibility of motion, time, first matter and the celestial spheres lead to the necessary inference that the world is eternal. In the fourth, the premise involves the necessity of there being a temporally prior substratum for the possibility of something produced in time which led Aristotle to conclude the perpetuity of circular motion and thus the perpetuity of the spheres.[58]

The next three start from the deity (*ex parte Creatoris*) and are based on what the followers of Aristotle derived from his philosophy. All three are based on the notion that the Creator is wholly actual in being, with no potency to change in any way, and that His actions are most perfect. This entails rejecting the production of the world "in time after its having been non-existent" and rejecting any "reason in respect of which He should act at one time and not act at another." And, finally, since the world flows from the perpetual and perfect wisdom of God, it too must be perpetual.[59]

To these seven, which Maimonides claims embrace all of the arguments that have been advanced by believers in the eternity of the world, he adds two others, less probative, based on the shameful attribution to God of idleness if the world were produced in time and based on the supposed general consensus of mankind in its eternity.[60]

In chapter 15 Maimonides introduces a strategic move designed to put his own subsequent arguments for a temporal creation on exactly the same footing as those of the Aristotelians, that is, as dialectical rather than fully demonstrative. He does so, he explains, because the majority of those who think themselves wise reject the view of the prophets on creation *de novo* and accept the philosophers' eternal world simply because the latter follow the method of science (*per viam disciplinae*) while the former simply accept God's revealed word (*per viam narrationis super creatore*).[61]

Maimonides here analyzes three texts of Aristotle regarding the eternity of the world (*Physics* VIII, 1; *De caelo* I, 10; *Topics* I, 11) and concludes that in spite of the declarations of later Aristotelians, Aristotle himself knew that his arguments for the eternity of the world were not demonstrations properly so called but rather dialectical; that is, they were "more correct than the opinions of those who disagree with him."[62]

In chapter 16, Maimonides clears the decks before beginning his

58. *Guide* II, 14, pp. 285–87.
59. Ibid., pp. 287–88.
60. Ibid., pp. 288–89.
61. *Guide* II, 15, p. 293; fol. 48v.
62. Ibid., pp. 290–91.

refutation of the seven main arguments of those affirming the eternity of the world, and of the presentation of his own dialectical arguments for its production in time. First of all, he reiterates his absolute rejection of the attempts of the men of Kalām to demonstrate the world's production in time. He also indicates his immediate intention to refute the arguments of the followers of Aristotle who claim to have demonstrations of the eternity of the world. "What I myself desire to make clear," says Maimonides, "is that the world, being created in time, according to the opinion of our Law . . . is not impossible." This being the case, this view should "be accepted without proof because of prophecy which explains things to which it is not in the power of speculation to accede." However, one can buttress this acceptance of divine revelation by arguments designed to make "prevail the assertion of creation in time over the assertion of eternity" (*praeeminentia fidei nostri in novitate mundi*).[63]

Maimonides uses a striking example of a young man raised on an isolated island with no women (or indeed females of any animal species) to make a crucial claim against the Aristotelians; and for Maimonides, this effectively undercuts the first four arguments for an eternal world. When that young man reaches maturity and asks questions about his origin, he cannot believe that he spent months enclosed within a human body. How could he eat or drink or breathe in such an environment? Starting from the situation in reality as he found it, such a young man would disbelieve, and indeed prove, that he had not come into being in the manner described to him. This is "exactly our position with regard to Aristotle," he argues. Starting from the state of perfected nature as it presently is constituted, Aristotle will draw certain necessary inferences that it has always been in that perfect state.[64]

However, Maimonides insists, we, the followers of Moses and Abraham, believe that this world came to be in its present state of completed perfection and actuality after a state of "absolute non-existence (*post privationem absolutam*)." The essential point of Maimonides is "that a being's state of perfection and completion furnishes no indication of the state of that being preceding its perfection," thus cutting the ground from under the four Aristotelian arguments.[65] In this manner, Maimonides can agree with the premises that first matter, motion, and time are ungenerable and and thus did not, and indeed cannot, begin

63. *Guide* II, 16, pp. 293–94; fol. 49r.

64. *Guide* II, 17, pp. 295–96. Aquinas uses this example of the boy in his *Commentary on the Sentences of Peter Lombard* to the same effect. See, *In II SS*, d. 1, q. 1, a. 5, c.

65. Ibid., pp. 297–98.

to be by way of generation. Creation *de novo,* however, is a different kind of production.[66]

Let us note that Maimonides is quite careful to insist that this does not establish as true the scriptural position of creation *de novo.* What it does do, however, is to establish that the Aristotelian arguments cannot demonstrate the impossibility of creation *de novo.*[67]

In similar fashion, in chapter 18, Maimonides makes certain claims that effectively nullify the probative character of the three arguments "taking the deity as their starting point." The first claim separates immaterial from material agents with the latter alone passing from potentiality to actuality in passing from nonacting to acting. The second claim likewise distinguishes will belonging to a material being from that of a being separate from matter. It is only with the former that there can be changes of will or impediments that prevent its execution. In fact, Maimonides goes so far as to claim that "actions" and "will" are equivocals when applied to material and immaterial beings. The final claim, to invalidate the third of these arguments, is that while "the universe is consequent upon His perpetual and inimitable wisdom," yet "we are completely ignorant of the rule of that wisdom," which, indeed, is identical with God's will.[68]

Maimonides now, in chapter 19, begins to advance speculative arguments to tip the scales in favor of the reasonableness (but not demonstrableness) of the scriptural position of creation *de novo.* The battle lines are carefully drawn between an Aristotelian world which "has proceeded from the Creator in virtue of a necessity" and therefore eternally, and a world freely willed to exist after not having existed by virtue of the purpose of one who purposed.[69] Once more, Maimonides explicitly distances his arguments from those of the men of Kalām. For although they wished to make the same point, their arguments destroy the nature of that which exists. Maimonides, however, proposes to begin, as did the philosophers, from the very nature of that which actually exists.[70]

One aspect of that which actually exists, agreed upon by both proponents of an eternal world and proponents of creation *de novo,* is that among things sharing a common matter that also differ from one another, the cause of that difference must be other than their common matter. Building on this premise, Maimonides poses to Aristotle a series of hypothetical questions regarding the sources of differences among individuals of the same sublunar species, among the four ele-

66. Ibid., pp. 296–97.
67. Ibid., p. 298.
68. *Guide* II, 18, pp. 299–302.
69. *Guide* II, 19, p. 303.
70. Ibid., pp. 303–4.

ments, between the matter of the heavens and that of the elements and, finally, among the velocities and directions of the motion of the spheres.[71]

Given that Aristotle, according to Maimonides, wished to give causal explanations for everything that could be observed so that all natural phenomena would be ordered in necessary patterns (thus eliminating the need for a volitional agent "purposing" or "particularizing"), how well did he do?

Maimonides' answer, which was given wide circulation in medieval Europe, is as follows: "all that he has explained to us regarding what is beneath the sphere of the moon follows an order conforming to that which exists, an order whose causes are clear," deriving necessarily from the motion and powers of that sphere. However, for the sphere and what is above it, "he has assigned no clear cause" and therefore no "order for which necessity can be claimed."[72]

Maimonides piles up astronomical examples which, he claims, Aristotle's theories cannot satisfactorily explain. He contrasts this difficulty with the greater ease by which the view of "those who affirm the production of the world in time" can account for and resolve these phenomena. "For we say that there is a being that has particularized, just as it willed, every sphere in regard to its motion and rapidity."[73]

Maimonides' first argument for creation *de novo*, then, comes down to this: Advocates of a creation *ab aeterno* are committed to a necessary causal explanation of all celestial phenomena, a task which they have not accomplished and which, indeed, never will be accomplished; advocates of a creation *de novo*, by a creator who freely wills and "purposes" that things be the way that they are, may not—indeed, cannot—fathom the wisdom and reason for this state of affairs, but at least their explanation preserves what can be observed.[74]

Davidson's analysis of this chapter reveals, for him, further contradictions. One of them lies, I believe, in a faulty translation compounded by his failure to understand the differences among "creation," "creation *ex nihilo*" and "creation *de novo*."

Thus, Davidson sees a contradiction between a reference in chapter 19 to "our position (*raʾy*) [that is to say, the position of] the advocates of the creation of the world" and the statement of "the position of the Jewish Law as creation *ex nihilo*" in chapter 13.[75] The translation of these passages by Pines is, respectively, "our opinion, that is, the opinion of the community of those who affirm the production of world in

71. Ibid., pp. 304–6.
72. Ibid., p. 307.
73. Ibid., p. 308.
74. Ibid., pp. 308–11.
75. Davidson, "Maimonides' Secret Position," pp. 27–28.

time" and (God) "through His Will and His volition . . . brought into existence out of nothing all the beings as they are . . . [such that all that is moved] is itself created in time and come to be after not having been." If Pines is correct (and the Latin translation bears him out), then this contradiction vanishes.[76]

Further, Davidson claims that in chapter 19 Maimonides' argument for creation *de novo* "has nothing to say about the creation or eternity of the matter from which the world is constituted."[77]

Davidson does not seem to realize that, for Maimonides, the philosophers have demonstrated creation *ex nihilo* (see II, 1). What he is arguing here—and it is his sole purpose in this chapter—is that the philosophers' view of this creation *ex nihilo* is in terms of a necessary causal nexus, which view does not give satisfactory answers to questions regarding what we can, in fact, observe regarding the heavens. For the purpose of Maimonides' dialectical procedure, the view of a creation *ex nihilo* proceeding by way of purpose (*per electionem*) answers these same questions much more easily and, indeed, more satisfactorily. Granted, Maimonides admits the religious position could give rise to another question: why did God create things in this way rather than another? But he makes no claims to be able to answer that question since it lies buried in the inscrutable Wisdom and Will of God.[78] In chapter 20, Maimonides credits Aristotle with proposing a volitional creation, except that his First Cause necessarily wills that which necessarily flows from it. In chapter 21, he dismisses the view of latter-day Aristotelians who speak of God as having chosen and "purposed" His creation, on the grounds that they are misusing these terms.

Davidson describes the second argument of Maimonides "for creation" as coming to him from the men of Kalām (John Philoponus and al-Ghazālī) and again concludes that it "does not in any way address the question whether the matter of the world is created."[79] The text analyzed is from chapter 22, which chapter Maimonides described as the one in which he would commence to set forth his own arguments "in favor of the world's having been produced in time according to our opinion" (*Incipiam autem modo dicere probationes meas ad praeponendum novitatem mundi antiquitati ipsius secundum fidem nostram*).[80]

76. *Guide* II, 19, p. 308; II, 13, p. 281. The Latin texts are, respectively, "secundum fidem nostram qui credimus novitatem mundi" (fol. 52r.) and "fecit esse omnia entia secundum quod sunt cum voluntate sua . . . est novum et creatum et est postquam non fuit" (fol. 46v.).

77. Davidson, "Maimonides' Secret Position," p. 30.

78. Recall "the universe is consequent upon His perpetual and immutable wisdom. But we are completely ignorant of the rule of that wisdom": *Guide* II, 18, pp. 301–302.

79. Davidson, "Maimonides' Secret Position," p. 31.

80. *Guide* II, 21, p. 317; fol. 53v.

In his recapitulation of the "first two" arguments, Davidson, not surprisingly, finds more contradiction:

the arguments we have examined purport to "tip the scales" in favor of what Maimonides calls "our position"; and in summarizing the first argument Maimonides asserts that the argument did prove his position. But in fact the two arguments establish only creation, not creation *ex nihilo.* If Maimonides' position can be proved by arguments that establish only creation, then his position must be just creation and not creation *ex nihilo.* And yet he earlier defined his position and the position of the Jewish Law specifically as creation *ex nihilo.* He has therefore contradicted himself here also.[81]

The third Maimonidean argument "for creation," according to Davidson, is directed against a theory of necessary emanation. To his surprise, Davidson admits, Maimonides inexplicably endeavors to prove not just creation but creation *ex nihilo.* This creates some ambiguity in Davidson's attempt to discover an esoteric Maimonidean position lying behind the contradictions in his texts on creation, and to proffer as one of two possible interpretations that perhaps Maimonides was guilty of some inadvertence and carelessness and that the contradictions were not deliberate after all.[82]

In my own reading of these texts of Maimonides, however, I find no contradictions. From as far back as part I, chapter 71 of the *Guide,* Maimonides begins his careful analysis of the Account of the Beginning in the light of what can be known by philosophical reasoning. From there to part II, chapter 31, we find an exegesis on the opening verse of Genesis, "In the beginning God created heaven and earth."

If my reading—and incidentally that by Thomas Aquinas—of Maimonides is correct, he carefully disengages the question of creation (understood as *ex nihilo*) from the question whether it be *ab aeterno* or *de novo.* The latter question for Maimonides, as for Aquinas, is not susceptible of rational demonstration, notwithstanding the men of Kalām and the Aristotelians. In the end, it must be accepted on the strength of Divine Revelation. This acceptance, however, is far from passive. The methods and premises of the men of Kalām must and can be refuted as sophistical, that is, as fallacious.

For both Maimonides and Aquinas, such Kalāmic arguments for creation *de novo,* although they seek to buttress the religious position, in fact are dangerous to the cause of religion. Believers who know the difference between true demonstrations and fallacious ones may lose their confidence in religion, thinking it rests on such a shakable foundation.[83]

81. Davidson, "Maimonides' Secret Position," p. 32.
82. Ibid., p. 36.
83. Cf. *Guide* I, 71; Aquinas, *Summa theologiae* I, q. 46, a. 2.

The arguments of the philosophers who purport to possess demonstrations that creation is *ab aeterno* do so in terms of a creator who necessarily wills that He must will, thereby giving the lie to every miracle and destroying the Law in its principle.

Fortunately, says Maimonides, all such purported demonstrations of an eternal creation "have a certain point through which they may be invalidated and the inference drawn from them against us shown to be incorrect."

As he had indicated earlier, "the utmost power of one who adheres to a Law and who has acquired knowledge of true reality consists, in my opinion, in his refuting the proofs of the philosophers bearing on the eternity of the world."[84]

In the last analysis, Maimonides concludes in II, chapter 22,

> we have explained the doubts attaching to each of the opinions and have shown to you that the opinion favoring the eternity of the world is the one that raises more doubts and is more harmful for the belief that ought to be held with regard to the deity. And this in addition to the fact that the world's being produced in time is the opinion of Abraham our Father and our prophet Moses, may peace be on both of them.[85]

St. Michael's College, University of Toronto

84. *Guide* I, 71, p. 180.

85. *Guide* II, 22, p. 320.

Select Bibliography

Altmann, Alexander. *Essays in Jewish Intellectual History* (Hanover, N.H.: University Press of New England, 1981).

Baron, Salo Wittmayer (ed.). *Essays on Maimonides: An Octocentennial Volume* (New York: AMS Press, 1966).

Berman, L. V. "Maimonides, the Disciple of Alfarabi," *Israel Oriental Studies* 4 (1974), pp. 154–178.

Cohen, Mark R. *Jewish Self-Government in Medieval Egypt: The Origins of the Office of Head of the Jews* (Princeton: Princeton University Press, 1980).

Elazar, Daniel (ed.). *Kinship and Consent: The Jewish Political Tradition and Its Contemporary Uses* (Ramat Gan, Philadelphia, Montreal: Turtledove Publishing, 1981).

Gellman, Jerome. "The Philosophical *Hassagot* of Rabad on Maimonides' *Mishneh Torah*," *The New Scholasticism* 58 (1984), pp. 145–169.

Goitein, S. D. *Letters of Medieval Jewish Traders* (Princeton: Princeton University Press, 1973).

———. *A Mediterranean Society*. 6 volumes. (Berkeley and Los Angeles: University of California Press, 1967–[in progress]).

———. (ed.). *Religion in a Religious Age* (Cambridge, Mass.: Association for Jewish Studies, 1974).

Kogan, Barry S. *Averroes and the Metaphysics of Causation* (Albany: SUNY Press, 1985).

Maimonides. *Crisis and Leadership: Epistles of Maimonides*. Texts translated and notes by Abraham Halkin; discussions by David Hartman. (Philadelphia: Jewish Publication Society, 1985).

———. *The Guide of the Perplexed*. Translated by Shlomo Pines. (Chicago: University of Chicago Press, 1963).

———. "Maimonides' Arabic Treatise on Logic." Edited by Israel Efros. *Proceedings of the American Academy for Jewish Research* 34 (1966).

Pines, Shlomo and Yovel, Yirmiyahu (eds.). *Maimonides and Philosophy:* Papers presented at the Sixth Jerusalem Philosophical Encounter, May 1985. (Dordrecht, Boston: M. Nijhoff, 1986).

Roth, Norman. "Forgery and Abrogation of the Torah: A Theme in Muslim and Christian Polemic in Spain," *Proceedings of the American Academy for Jewish Research* 54 (1987), pp. 203–36.

———. *Maimonides: Essays and Texts* (Madison, Wisc.: The Hispanic Seminary of Medieval Studies, 1986).

Stein, Siegried and Loewe, Raphael (eds.). *Studies in Jewish Religious and Intellectual History Presented to Alexander Altmann on the Occasion of His Seventieth Birthday* (University, Ala.: University of Alabama Press, 1979).

Stillman, Norman A. *The Jews of Arab Lands: A History and Source Book* (Philadelphia: Jewish Publication Society, 1979).

Twersky, Isadore. *Introduction to the Code of Maimonides (Mishneh Torah)* (New Haven, Conn.: Yale University Press, 1980).

———. *A Maimonides Reader* (New York: Behrman House, 1972).

———. (ed.). *Studies in Medieval Jewish History and Literature* (Cambridge, Mass.: Harvard University Press, 1979).

Wolfson, Harry Austryn. *Studies in the History of Philosophy and Religion.* Edited by Isadore Twersky and George H. Williams. 2 volumes. (Cambridge, Mass.: Harvard University Press, 1973).

Index

Abbasid Caliphate, 22
ʿAbd al-Raḥmān III, 6, 9
ʿAbd al-Raḥmān, Sanchul, 9
Ablutions, 30
Abner of Burgos, 140
Abraham, 76, 85, 162, 167, 172
Abraham Ibn Ezra, 10, 105
Abraham ibn Ḥiyya, 13
Abū Manṣūr Samuel b. Hananya, 27
Abū Yaʿqūb Yūsuf, 11, 16, 19
Abū Yūsuf Yaʿqūb, 9
Academies, 6, 28–29, 32
Accident, 43
Achilles, 91
Action, human, 139–140
Active life, 137
Agent, 139, 160, 168
Agnosticism, 82
Akrasia, 54–55
Albertus Magnus, St., 117
Alexander of Aphrodisias, 13, 14, 43, 53, 56–57, 62–66, 69, 76, 84
Alexandria, 11, 23
Alfonso VII, 10
Algebra, 13
ʿAli b. Yūsuf, 15
Almagest, 14, 77
Almohad, 2, 9, 11, 17–20, 22, 24
Almoravid, 15
Altmann, A., 140, 141, 145–47, 149–50
Alyūsana, 9
Analogy, 104
Al-Andalus, 3, 5–6, 11, 15, 19–21, 29
Andalusia, 29
Angels, 67, 68, 118, 155–57, 159, 161
Animals, 45–46, 47, 146–47
Aquinas, St. Thomas, 101–4, 107–10, 112–20, 151–52, 171
Arabia, 23
Arabic, 4–6, 11–13, 154
Arguments, 36, 39, 42–43; cosmological, 69; Kalām, 41, 43; poetic, 39; rhetorical, 39, 41; sophistic, 36, 41, 50, 58
Aristocrat, 92
Aristotle, 10–11, 13–14, 36–38, 42, 45, 47–50, 53, 56, 58, 60, 64–67, 69–79, 82, 84–86, 89–99, 107, 109, 115, 117, 126, 132, 152–54, 157–58, 162–71
Asceticism, 96
Ashʿarites, 45–46, 47, 116
Ashkenazic, 25
Ashtor, E., 7, 24
Assent, 85
Astrologers, 141
Astronomy, 2, 10, 13–14, 59, 80–83, 156, 158–59
Athens, 10
Attributes, 43, 130–32
Augustine, St., 104, 106–7
Averroes, *see* Ibn Rushd
Avicenna, *see* Ibn Sīnā
Ayyubids, 23, 30

Babylon, 6, 10, 24
Baghdad, 6, 22, 28–29
Barcelona, 10, 14
Baron, S., 16
Bazaar, 12
Being, necessary, 152
Bellarmine, St. Robert, 83
Benjamin of Tudela, 23–24
Berber, 5
Bible, 8, 13, 17, 102–4, 106–7, 109, 113, 115
Bildad, 116
Birth, 92, 99
Al-Biṭrūjī, 81
Burhān, 42
Burrell, D., 101, 103, 114, 116
Butterworth, C., 88
Byzantium, 24

Cairo, 22–23, 26, 33
Caliphate, 8, 10
Calligraphy, 12
Canaan, 1

Causality, 156–57, 160
Cause, 136, 145–46, 149, 159–60, 170
Certainty, 51
Ceuta, 14
Chance, 45, 148
Change, 49
Character, 142
Chariot, Account of, 109, 156
Chenu, M.-D., 101, 115
Chisholm, R., 140
Christ, 105
Christianity, 2, 103, 153
Christians, 12
Circumcision, 30
Cisneros, Cardinal, 11
Cognition, 102, 121–22, 126, 128, 136
Compatibilism, 139–40, 144, 147
Compulsion, 140, 141
Conjunction, 125, 127, 131
Consensus, 65, 68, 84–85
Constantinople, 6
Contemplation, 136; contemplative life, 89, 132
Contradiction, 132, 134
Conversion, 8, 16–19
Copernicus, 83
Córdoba, 8–10, 12, 17; caliphate, 6; Jewish population, 9; population, 7
Courts, Muslim, 16
Creation, 39, 41–42, 44, 48–50, 72–73, 76, 84, 87, 112, 139–40, 148, 151, 154, 157, 161–62, 164, 167, 172; Account of, 109, 156, 171; *ab aeterno,* 151, 153, 155, 161, 169, 172; *de novo,* 151–55, 158–59, 161–63, 166, 168, 169–70; *ex nihilo,* 151–52, 162–64, 169, 171
Crimea, 6
Crusades, 17
Crusaders, 22, 24, 27

Dalīl, 42
Damascus, 26
Damietta, 23
Davidson, H., 154, 161, 163, 164–65, 169, 170–71
Delphic Maxim, 93
Demonstration, 36–37, 40–43, 46, 51, 62, 69, 75, 79, 85
Determinism, 139, 144
Dhimmis, 15
Dialectic, 36–38, 40, 42–43, 45, 48, 50–51, 54, 66–67, 74, 76, 85–88
Dioscurides, 6
Discrimination, 15, 23
Divorce, 30
Dove's Neck Ring, 7
Dozy, R., 15

Eccentrics, 77–78, 81, 83
Edom, 96
Education, 11–14
Egypt, 10, 20–23, 28–33, 149–50; Jewish population, 24; Jewish settlements, 23, 25, 33
Eight Chapters on Ethics, 14
Eighteen Benedictions, 31
Elements, 109, 158, 169
Elhanan b. Shemarya, 28
Elihu, 114, 116, 117–19
Eliphaz, 116
Emanation, 47, 123
Endoxa, 54–57, 84–85; *see also* Opinions
Engberg-Pedersen, T., 92
England, 25
Envy, 96
Epicurus, 45–46
Epicycles, 77–78, 81, 83
Epistemology, 112, 121, 128, 130
Esoteric teaching, 141, 144, 147, 150, 171
Eternity, 104; of world, 37, 42, 48–50, 67, 69, 70–76, 84, 112, 151–53, 160, 162, 164–66, 167, 172
Ethics, 84, 98
Euclid, 14
Eudemian Ethics, 38
Eulogio, St., 12
Europe, 25
Evans, J. D. C., 36
Exegesis, 2–3, 104–8, 115
Existence, 43, 153
Exposition on Job, 116
Expulsion (of Jews), 1–2

Faith, 102, 151; confession of, 18
Fakhry, M., 151
Falāsifa, 68, 85–86; *see also* Philosophers
Famine, 24
Fandila de Acci, St., 12
Al-Fārābī, 13, 48, 64, 73–74, 86, 111, 122–28
Fatimids, 22–23, 26–27, 33
Fayḍ, see Emanation
Fayyum, 23
Ferdinand, 2
Ferdinando III, 10
Fez, 17, 20
Fons Vitae, 3, 4
Form of forms, 131–32, 135–36

Forms, 123, 127
Fountain, 160–61
France, 2, 21, 25, 29, 33
Freedom, 46, 114, 139, 141, 144, 147
Free will, 103, 142–44, 146, 148, 150, 154, 163
Friendship, 38
Fustat, 23–24, 26, 28–30

Galen, 73
Galileo, 83
Gaon, 6, 26, 28, 29
Geniza, 23–25, 27, 33
Geometry, 13
Geon, *see Gaon*
Germany, 2, 17, 25
Gersonides, 101
Al-Ghazālī, 13, 15, 170
Gilson, E., 151
Giver of Forms, 47, 124, 127
God, 65, 103, 132, 135–36, 142, 148, 150, 161, 168; actions, 46; arm, 113; attributes, 43, 45; existence, 43–44, 74, 95, 97, 151–53, 155; form of universe, 131; incorporeality, 43–45, 74, 109, 153–55, 164; justice, 46; knowledge of, 14, 98, 130; simplicity, 109; unity, 41–43, 74, 109, 153, 155, 162; will, 45, 48–49; wisdom, 46, 48, 166, 168
Goitein, S. D., 24, 28, 33
Golden Age, 1, 29
Gonzàlez Llubera, I., 5, 20
Gonzalo Maeso, D., 5, 20
Grammar (Hebrew), 4
Granada, 3, 10, 13
Gregory the Great, St., 103, 107
Gui, Bernard, 113
Guide of the Perplexed, 27, 35–36, 40–43, 50, 53–54, 88, 108, 154–55; in Spanish, 20

Ḥakham, 96–97
Ḥasdai Crescas, 140
Ḥasdai Ibn Shapurt, 6–7
Ḥasid, 94, 96–98
Head of the Jews, 25–28, 32, 34
Heart, Law of, 106
Hebrew, 1, 8, 12–13, 106, 160
Hermeneutics, 106, 108, 110, 115
Hishām II, 9
History, 150
Hobbes, T., 140
Holy Roman Emperor, 6
Holy Spirit, 103
Homer, 91
Honor, 91–93, 97–99
Hubris, 118
Hume, D., 140
Humility, 89–91, 93–98

Ibn Abī Uṣaybiʿah, 16
Ibn al-ʿArabī, 13
Ibn al-Khaṭīb, 13
Ibn al-Ṣā'igh, Abū Bakr, 78
Ibn Bājjah, 13–14, 16, 77–78, 81–82, 122, 125, 127–28
Ibn Ḥazm, 7–9, 12
Ibn Hishām, Muḥammad, 9
Ibn Rushd, 9–10, 61, 68, 78, 81, 86–88, 115
Ibn Sīnā, 13, 43, 122, 124–25, 127–28, 130–31, 156
Ibn Tibbon, 42, 79
Ibn Ṭufayl, 13, 16, 78, 81
Ideas, 85
Identity, 123
al-Idrīsī, 8
Ifḥām al-yahūd, 8
Ignorance, 93
Ijāza, 13
Imagination, 50, 58, 125–26, 130, 161
Imitatio Dei, 95, 137
Immortality, 117
India, 10, 23, 25
Insight, 125
Intellect, acquired, 125, 128; Agent, 47, 85, 122–31, 156; human, 80; limitations, 43, 61, 118; potential, 123; separate, 155–56, 159, 161
Intelligence, Active, 122–31
Intelligences, 121–22, 129
Intelligibles, First, 39–40
Intermarriage, 30
Interpretation, 109
Intuition, 124, 129
Iraq, 22, 24
Irwin, T., 91
Isaac b. Samuel ha-Sefaradi, 28
Isabella, 2
Isḥāq b. Ḥunayn, 70
Ishmaelites, 149
Islam, 18–19, 153
Israel, 1
Italy, 6

Jābir Ibn Aflaḥ, 14, 82
Jacob, 159
Jeremiah, 134–35
Jeroboam, 143

Jerome, St., 106
Jerusalem, 28
Jews, in Spain, 1–2
Jiménez de Rada, R., 15
Job, 101–3, 108, 113–20
Joseph, 147, 149, 150
Joseph ben Judah, 35, 43, 58–59, 61, 63, 73, 137
Joseph Ibn ʿAqnin, 14, 18–19
Joseph ibn Ṣaddiq of Arévalo, 9
Joseph Ibn Shimʿon, 14
Judah al-Ḥarizi, 3
Judah ha-Kohen Ibn Sūsan, 20
Judah ha-Levy, 3–4, 152
Judaism, 103
Justice, 46, 115–17

Kalām, 41, 43, 50, 144, 152–53, 165, 167–68, 170–71
Kant, I., 63, 84
Karaites, 24, 30–31
Khazars, 6
Knowledge, 11, 47, 57, 102, 105, 114, 117, 131
Kufic script, 12
Kuhn, T., 83

Lamentations, 17
Language, 104, 106
Latin, 12
Law, Jewish, 2–3, 6, 18, 32, 46–48, 50, 122, 133, 155–57, 162, 164–65, 167, 169, 171–72
Lectio divina, 107
Letter of Consolation, 17
Letter on Astrology, 142
Letter to Yemen, 8
Lexicography, Hebrew, 4
Libertarianism, 139–41, 143, 145–46, 149–50
Lightning, 128–29
Literalism, 105, 112–13
Logic, 2, 35, 53, 58–59, 63–64
Lucena, 9–10
Lunel, 21

Madīnat al-Zāhira, 9
Madrasa, 13
al-Maghrib, 3
al-Mahalla, 23
Maimonides, Abraham, 27, 31–32
Maimonides, David, 25
Maimonides, Moses, 10–11, 14–19; and Aristotle, 37, 39, 53, 56, 69, 71–72, 75–76, 79, 89, 94; and contradiction, 154, 162, 169; and conversion, 16–19; physician, 25; in Egypt, 21–25, 27, 30, 33; as "Egyptian," 20–21; esoteric works, 108; Head of the Jews, 27–29, 34; scholarship on, 111; skepticism, 82, 84; as "Spaniard," 20–21; *Maimonides Latinus*, 155
Mamluks, 23–24
al-Manṣūr, 9
Manzanedo, M. F., 113
Maqāmāt, 4
al-Marrākushī, 11
Martyrdom, 18
Masliah ha-Kohen b. Solomon, 26, 28
Mathematics, 59–60, 62, 63, 75, 78, 80–81, 156
Matter, 48, 62, 123, 125–26, 128, 136, 154, 162, 167, 169
Maymūn, 17, 20
Mean, Doctrine of, 89–90, 94–95
Meaning, 104, 106
Medicine, 13, 14
Members, Law of, 106
Memory, 124
Menéndez, Pelayo, M., 5, 20
Menstruation, 30
Merchants, 24–25
Mercury, 158
Metaphysics, 43, 58, 62–64, 75, 84, 87, 109, 115, 136, 155
Method, 53; Baconian, 54, 56
Midrash, 2, 28
Millás Vallicrosa, J., 5, 10, 20
Miracle, 50, 165
Mishnah, 2, 20, 32, 143
Mishneh Torah, 2, 14, 27, 29, 42, 109, 142–44
Money, 92
Money lending, 25
Moon, 169
Morocco, 19, 21–22
Moses, 3, 21, 48, 76, 85, 98, 128, 142–43, 172
Moses Ibn Ezra, 3–4
Mosque, 10, 12, 31
Motion, 49, 69, 78
Mover, Unmoved, 152
Muḥammad II, 9
Mūsā ibn Maymūn, *see* Maimonides
Muslims, 2, 5, 8, 31
Mutakallimūn, 35, 41–42, 44, 59, 72, 75, 84, 86–88, 151
Muʿtazilites, 45–47, 116
al-Muẓaffar, 9

Nagid, 27, 32
Necessity, 165, 168
Negation, 43
Nethanel (Hibat Allah) ha-Levi b. Moses, 27
New Testament, 106
Nicomachean Ethics, 37, 90, 124
Nile, 21
Noncontradiction, 123
Non-existence, 152
North Africa, 2, 5–6, 20
Nussbaum, M. C., 55–56, 84

Obedience, 117
Objects, intelligible, 126
Occam's Razor, 84
Old Testament, 106
On Sophistical Refutations, 36
Opinions, 37, 39, 40
Order, natural, 45, 148, 149–50
Organon, 36
Orthodoxy, 154
Overflow, 124, 125, 127, 129, 135, 136, 155–61
Owen, G. E. L., 54–56, 84
Owens, J., 151

Pain, 136
Palace, parable of, 51, 64
Palestine, 22, 24
Pantheism, 105
Parable, 114
Paradigm, 83
Partnerships, Jewish-Muslim, 25
Paul, St., 1
Persecution, 2
Perception, 40, 85
Pérez de Guzmán, F., 10
Perfection, 35, 47, 121, 132–35
Peripatetics, 74
Perplexity, 75, 78–80, 111, 137
Persian Empire, 10
Persian Gulf, 22
Phainomena, 54, 55, 56, 68
Pharmacology, 13
Philoponus, John, 14, 170
Philosophers, 37, 109, 129–30, 132, 135, 153, 158, 164, 170, 172
Philosophy, 2, 86, 88
Physics, 43, 62–64, 75–77, 79, 81, 84, 87, 109, 115
Pietism, 32
Piety, 95–96
Pines, S., 42, 53, 63, 72, 76, 82, 84, 128, 140–41, 145–47, 150–51, 155, 169
Pirqey Avot, 19
Place, 55
Plague, 24
Planets, 49
Plato, 13, 14, 48, 69, 111, 154, 161–65
Poetics, 88
Poetry, 4, 12, 14, 17, 86
Politics, 87
Posterior Analytics, 36, 54
Pride, 89–95, 118, 120
Prior Analytics, 54
Privatio, 152, 162–63
Privation, 43
Proof, 39, 41–42, 59, 66
Prophecy, 39, 48, 49–50, 153, 158
Prophets, 118, 126, 128, 130, 133, 142, 148
Prostitutes, 15
Provence, 33
Providence, 39, 45–48, 50, 79, 101, 103, 112–14, 117–20, 130
Psalms, 157
Ptolemy, 14, 77–78, 80–82, 84
Purity, 30–31
Purpose, 104, 170
Pythagoras, 14

Qayrawan, 22
Qibla, 31
al-Qifṭī, 16
Qur'ān, 8, 11–13, 88
Qus, 23

Rabbanite Jews, 24, 30–31
Ra'īs al-yahūd, see Head of the Jews
Reason, 115, 117, 119–20
Red Sea, 22
Reform Judaism, 31
Reid, Thomas, 140
Religion, 88
Repentance, 143
Responsa, 2, 14, 16, 20, 25, 28–30
Responsibility, 90
Revelation, 102, 104, 115, 171
Riera i Sans, J., 5
Romans, 1
Ross, David, 55
Ross, W. D., 36

Saadia Gaon, 105
Sabbath, 30
Ṣābians, 85
Sages, 64, 85, 88, 105, 133, 156, 158
Saladin, 23, 27
Samau'al al-Maghribī, 8

Samuel Ibn Naghrillah, 3, 7–8
Samuelson, N. M., 114
Sar Shalom ha-Levi, 27
Satan, 117–18
Schwarzschild, S., 95–98
Science, 11, 155, 160
Scribe, 130
Seljuk, 26
Septuagint, 102, 106
Seville, 10–11, 15–16, 20
Shemarya b. Elhanan, 28–29
Shem Tob ben Joseph ibn Shem Tob, 47
Shiite, 22–23, 30
Sicily, 24
Sisenado Pacense, St., 12
Smalley, Beryl, 107
Solomon Ibn Gabirol, 3
Song of Songs, 19
Sophism, 86
Soul, 47, 109, 117, 159
Spain, 1–3, 20, 21–23, 29, 32; Jewish community, 6; Muslim community, 6; population, 7
Spheres, celestial, 47, 60, 64, 72, 121, 156–59, 166, 169
Stars, 62, 78
Strauss, L., 111
Sufism, 32
Summa Theologiae, 109, 112, 116
Sunnite, 22–23
Syllogism, 36, 40, 58, 66, 80, 85, 87, 129; poetic, 86; rhetorical, 85; sophistical, 85
Synagogue, 5, 23, 31–32
Syria, 6, 22, 26

Taifas, 3
Talmud, 1–2, 21, 28–29, 64, 105, 157–59
Taqlīd, 69
Tarragona, 10
Taylor, R., 140
Temple, 1
Themistius, 13, 14, 57
Theocentrism, 98
Theology, 108; negative, 130–32
Time, 70, 74, 104
Tocco, Guillaume de, 113
Toledo, 4, 15
Topics, 36–37, 53
Torah, 17–18, 21, 30, 35, 64, 104–5, 108–10, 112, 116, 141, 157, 164
Tradition, 39–40, 85
Treatise on the Art of Logic, 20, 35–36, 39–40, 76, 111
Trigonometry, 13
Truth, 107
Tunisia, 22

Union, 124
Universal, 124–25, 127
University, 12–13

Vacuum, 45
Vandals, 3
Vanity, 90
Venus, 158
Vice, 90, 94, 141, 143
Virtue, 89–91, 93, 96, 99, 133, 141, 143
Visigoths, 2, 6
Vizier, 6
Volition, 145, 157, 170

Wealth, 92, 99
Wisdom, 79, 95, 115–17, 119–20, 133, 135, 137
Wise man, 94–95
Wolfson, H. A., 151–52, 160
Women, 12
World, 166

Yaffe, M. D., 113, 115–17
Yemen, 18
Yeshiva, 6, 24, 26, 28–29, 34

Zechariah, 159
Zophar, 116
Zuta, 27

www.ingramcontent.com/pod-product-compliance
Lightning Source LLC
Chambersburg PA
CBHW031418290426
44110CB00011B/431
9780813230788